Shakespeare's
Art of Orchestration

Shakespeare's Art of Orchestration

STAGE TECHNIQUE AND AUDIENCE RESPONSE

Jean E. Howard

University of Illinois Press
Urbana and Chicago

Publication of this work was supported in part by a grant from the Andrew W. Mellon Foundation.

This book is printed on acid-free paper.

Library of Congress Cataloging in Publication Data

Howard, Jean E. (Jean Elizabeth), 1948-
  Shakespeare's art of orchestration.

  Includes index.
  1. Shakespeare, William, 1564-1616—Technique.
  2. Shakespeare, William, 1564-1616—Dramatic production.
  3. Theater audiences.   I. Title.
  PR2995.H65   1984   822.3'3   84-56
  ISBN 0-252-01116-3

For Jim and Kate

Contents

Acknowledgments

WRITING THIS BOOK has taught me many things, among them, how many debts I owe. I am lucky to have studied with a succession of scholar-teachers who conveyed to me not only their knowledge of Renaissance literature, but also their passion for it: Shirley and Cleon Hatch, Elmer Blistein, Barbara Lewalski, Basil Greenslade, Eugene Waith, G. K. Hunter, the late Richard Sylvester, Bernard Beckerman, and especially Maynard Mack, a man whose learning, kindness, and exacting standards exemplify for me what is best in the humanist traditions of our time.

I am equally fortunate in the colleagues at Syracuse University with whom I have worked in my first years of professional life: Jack Halkett, John Elliott, and Peter Mortenson, all learned in Renaissance matters and generous to a newcomer in their midst; Steven Cohan, John Crowley, Richard Fallis, and Mas'ud Zavarzadeh, colleagues whose conversation and whose work have been a constant stimulus to my own; and especially Felicity Nussbaum, whose judgment and friendship I value very dearly.

Debts to family and friends can hardly be reckoned, but in lieu of better payment, I would like to thank some of those whose help I have steadily felt, especially my parents, who showed me how to work hard and love it, and my husband and daughter, who have shown me how to take pleasure in many other things as well. My sister and brother-in-law, Barbara and Daniel Traister, both Renaissance scholars themselves, have shown unfailing interest in what I was about and have laughed me out of some of my more absurd notions. My brother Woody, Marion O'Connor, Elizabeth Heale, Katherine Sorenson, Mike McTighe, Carolyn Carter, Terri Ebert, and Betsy and Charlie Wallace have been extraordinary friends. I would like to say a special thanks to Barbara Theiner, who at a crucial time gave me very special help and friendship without which this manuscript could not have been completed. I am grateful to them all.

I also wish to thank Syracuse University, which has twice supported my work with summer research grants and with funds to prepare the manuscript for publication; and the NEH, which granted me a stipend to participate in a valuable seminar, conducted by Bernard Beckerman at Columbia University in the summer of 1976, on the teaching of drama. Jean Rice, performing Herculean labors with aplomb, typed this manuscript with scrupulous care. I wish to thank, as well, the editors of *Shakespeare Quarterly* for permission to use in chapter 3 of this book material which appeared in shorter form under the title "Shakespearean Counterpoint: Stage Technique and the Interaction between Play and Audience" in *SQ* 30 (1979): 343–57; the editors of *Studies in English Literature, 1500–1900,* for permission to use, in a much altered form, material published originally as "Figures and Grounds: Shakespeare's Control of Audience Perception and Response" in *SEL* 20 (1980): 185–99; and the editor of *Bucknell Review* for permission to use in chapter 1 several pages from my essay "Shakespeare's Creation of a Fit Audience for *The Tempest*," which first appeared in *Bucknell Review* 25 (1980): 142–53. The part of chapter 5 dealing with *King Lear* I first presented as a talk at the Nazareth Shakespeare Conference in the fall of 1981, and I benefited greatly from the comments of my audience on that occasion. In the summer of 1981 I presented some of my work on silence, now incorporated into chapter 4 of this book, to John Styan's seminar on audience response at the International Shakespeare Congress in Stratford, England. Again, I am grateful to the members of that seminar for their helpful critiques and especially to John Styan, whose pioneering work on Shakespeare's stagecraft has influenced this book in countless ways. To other Shakespeareans, often known to me largely through their articles and books, I owe debts that I have tried to acknowledge in the pages which follow, though Shakespeare scholarship has become so voluminous that I am not sure I have always remembered where I first encountered a particular idea. I hope that my chief debts are recorded and that the folly which remains is properly seen as my own.

CHAPTER 1

The Orchestrated Play

I REMEMBER THE FIRST TIME I saw *Macbeth* performed.[1] I was a college sophomore, had never read the play, and had probably been to only one or two professional theater performances in my life. Fifteen years and three or four stage *Macbeths* later, I can still recall parts of that performance, such as the spectacular moment in the banquet scene when a spotlight suddenly revealed the bloody body of Banquo rising eerily on a kind of elevator from a trap door in the stage floor to assume his silent place at the feast—no imagined ghost in that performance!—or the moment when the sleepwalking Lady Macbeth first appeared, a single candle throwing a wan light over her pale face and plain gown so that she seemed more a restless spirit from the underworld than an earthly queen. When she said, "Hell is murky" (V.i.33),[2] the audience knew from her agitated gestures and haggard appearance that this was a woman who knew what psychic torment was about.

I am recalling this production of *Macbeth* at the distance of fifteen years, not because it was the best *Macbeth* I have seen, though it was a good one, but because it was a seminal experience in my own initiation into the pleasures of theatergoing. I was as close to an innocent spectator as one can get. I had seen no other stage *Macbeths;* I did not even know the plot. But I was overwhelmed by what I saw, heard, and experienced. It was the beginning of my own personal realization that drama is more than a printed text. Drama means performance—sights, sound, movement, the energy created by actors performing for the ears and eyes of a living audience.[3] It was also the beginning of my own awareness that

1

Shakespeare creates scripts overwhelmingly rich in performance potential. Handled at all adeptly, Shakespeare's plays have remained good theater for nearly four centuries. Clearly this is not chance. Not only are the plays thematically and emotionally resonant, but they were also crafted by someone who knew how to use the theatrical medium to best advantage — who knew, for example, how to shock and startle the spectator by unexpectedly introducing into a scene of fellowship and feasting the bloody ghost of a murdered man.

In this book I want to look at some of the ways in which Shakespeare works his theatrical magic. Specifically, I will examine his orchestration, through the playscript, of the aural, visual, and kinetic dimensions of stage production — in other words, his control of the sensory dimensions of the implied performance. Quite simply, I argue that Shakespeare's plays are carefully crafted to control and shape what an audience hears, sees, and experiences moment by moment in the theater and that this verbal and visual orchestration is central to the effectiveness and meaning of every play. Clearly, *all* plays engage the minds and emotions of the audience by a variety of means. Dialogue is important, but so too are gestures, movements, silences, and shifts in tempo and tone by which the continuum of stage action is shaped. The present study examines this shaping process insofar as its dynamics are implied by the playscript itself. My intent is to begin to identify a repertoire of techniques by which Shakespeare implicitly prepared his plays for effective stage presentation.

In using the term *orchestration* to describe Shakespeare's management of aural, visual, and kinetic effects, I do not mean to imply a strict analogy between music and drama. In fact, I usually find such direct comparisons unprofitable because they must often be conducted in terms so general as to be meaningless.[4] Rather, I use the term *orchestration* metaphorically. By it I wish to suggest that drama, like dance and music, is a serial art in which the audience sees and hears things in a predetermined order, with no replays allowed. How the dramatist controls the temporal continuum of impressions flooding in upon the spectator largely determines the nature of the audience's theatrical experience and its cognitive and emotional responses. It is to the purposeful management of this aural, visual, and kinetic continuum that I have affixed the label *orchestration,* and, not surprisingly, it is Shakespeare's plays which seem to me to offer a particularly rich area for an investigation of this aspect of successful dramaturgy.

Before I go further, however, I ought to make explicit some of the assumptions that underlie this study and some of the methodological problems it poses. First, I clearly find congenial the emphasis upon Shakespeare as theatrical craftsman in much criticism written in the last two decades.[5] It has always seemed odd to me that there should be a kind of rivalry between those who primarily study the plays as literature and so focus on issues of language, theme, and character, and those who primarily study the plays as drama and so focus on issues of stage conditions, theater conventions, dramatic structure, and acting problems. Surely in our teaching all of us draw upon the insights of both groups, and neither can lay claim to exclusive possession of the "real" Shakespeare. As Michael Goldman has written: "it is a mistake to speak as if we have a choice between a literary Shakespeare and a theatrical Shakespeare. The choice is rather between some of Shakespeare and more of him."[6] I have found useful much of the recent theater-oriented criticism simply because it provides a way of approaching the plays that supplements earlier or different critical traditions.

In this study, therefore, I assume that Shakespeare created works that he intended to be performed by actual actors, on real stages, with all the potential for disaster, as well as success, those circumstances imply. I further assume that in drafting his plays, Shakespeare realized that in the theater an audience responds, not just to the logic or images of dramatic speech, but to all the elements of a three-dimensional stage event, and that he consciously or intuitively developed strategies and techniques for shaping the three-dimensional event to make the greatest emotional and intellectual impact upon the spectators. I approach his plays, therefore, as works designed with performance in mind—look at them not as a series of texts, but as a collection of playscripts, each of which is a blueprint for production, an encoding of potential energy waiting to be released by all the sights and sounds of live performance and, above all, by the energies of the living actor.[7]

Of course, when looking at the play as a work designed for

performance, one has to be careful to distinguish between *Shakespeare's* orchestration of the stage event and a *director's* performance choices. Clearly many elements of any actual production — much stage business and many aspects of lighting, blocking, and costuming — rightly lie in the director's province.[8] Nonetheless, it is surprising how fully the playscripts themselves indicate both the broad contours and also many of the local details of performance. For example, we know from the dialogue or from the stage directions that Hamlet in Act I wears an inky cloak (*Ham.* I.ii.77), that Toby and his friends watch from "the boxtree" as Malvolio reads the counterfeit letter dropped in his path (*TN* II.v.13), that Lear enters in the last act of his play with Cordelia in his arms (*Lr.*s.d. V.iii.257), that when Brutus and Cassius talk together in Act I of *Julius Caesar,* their conversation is punctuated by offstage clamor from the marketplace (*JC* I.ii.79, 132), and that at the crucial moment of deposition in *Richard II* the anointed king and the usurper both stand with a hand upon England's crown (*R2* IV.i.181–83), a wonderful symbol of the spoiled sanctity of English kingship.[9] When the plays are enacted, each of these details communicates important information or creates a striking emotional effect; but when the play is read, these sounds and actions may never be noted, for their effectiveness depends upon the fact that in the theater the audience does not read a text. It watches a constantly changing visual panorama and hears a constantly changing sequence of sounds and words.

An examination of the playscripts, moreover, reveals quite clearly that Shakespeare not only had an eye for engineering striking visual and aural effects of a local nature, but that he also took thought for the sustained orchestration of these elements throughout whole plays. In *Romeo and Juliet,* for example, from the very first scene in which the public brawl is followed by the solitary, brooding entry of the young Romeo, Shakespeare seems at pains repeatedly to juxtapose scenes involving a crowd with private scenes involving one or both of the lovers. The only time Romeo and Juliet appear together "publicly," unless one counts the gathering at their tomb at the play's end, is during old Capulet's ball. Even there, an audience is made aware of their separation from the other maskers. As Juliet's remarks to the nurse at the end of the scene make clear, Romeo does not dance (*Rom.* I.v.132), but holds himself aloof from the general merriment. Too, when he and Juliet speak together, they must be separate from the dancers so that their words and kisses can go unobserved.[10] And, as many have remarked, the lovers employ the stylized language of the sonnet, a fact that sets them apart linguistically from the others.[11] Elsewhere in the play their separateness from the public world is suggested by the use of the second-tier playing area as it functions as Juliet's bedroom or as the balcony outside her window. This sustained visual separation of the private world of the lovers and the strife-ridden public world of Verona is hardly incidental. It reinforces, on a visual level, the most powerful tension felt in the play.

While my first assumption, therefore, is that Shakespeare's plays were designed for performance, which means that attention was paid to the aural, visual, and kinetic orchestration of stage events, my second assumption has to do primarily with critical methodology. Though it is clear that the plays were meant to find their full realization upon the stage, the critic interested in identifying Shakespeare's theatrical strategies would do well to start with the playscript, and only then turn to actual productions of the plays. There is a crucial difference between examining the plays viewed as blueprints for performance and examining the plays as enacted in *particular* performances. The chief difference lies in the incalculable role played by director, actor, and set and costume designer in putting any drama on the boards. Ideally, all these people will respond carefully to the design of the playscript and work to realize what is implied—potential—in that script; but as Helene Keyssar has recently reminded us, this is not always so:

> In speaking specifically of the strategy of drama, there are two separate but interrelated strategic processes: the strategy of the text as designed by the playwright and the strategy of the performance as commanded by the director, actors, and designers. While it is not always the case, the latter should be dependent upon the former; that is, part of the importance of the notion of strategy to drama is that the director's knowledge of the strategy of the text should be the basic resource for production decisions of every kind.[12]

Since this possible disjunction always exists between the aims of the dramatist as apparent from the text and the aims of the director as apparent from the performance, in this study I will be focusing upon the playscript and upon what we can learn from it concerning the implied orchestration of the theater event.[13]

At the same time, I know that seeing dozens of Shakespeare productions, both good and bad, has helped to shape this book in innumerable ways, sometimes by making very clear the enormous effectiveness of a particular stage strategy, sometimes by demonstrating how badly some performance choices distort the underlying dynamics of the script, but always by helping to make me more sensitive to the three-dimensional nature of drama and the partial nature of purely literary dramatic criticism. Granted the usefulness of seeing stage productions, however, I still believe it is vitally important that when critics talk about the theatrical or performance qualities of Shakespeare's plays, they keep in mind the distinction between evaluating a particular performance, in the manner of a theater critic, and examining the script for its performance potential, a potential which actual performance can realize or which, in many different ways, it can also distort or destroy.

Finally, I assume that in writing plays for performance Shakespeare was partly writing with an eye to the potential responses of the audience; that is, as he orchestrated the play, he was indirectly orchestrating the theatrical experience of the viewer. I argue that in the largest sense drama is one of the rhetorical arts insofar as its aim is to move or engage an audience. And, as with all types of rhetoric, an underlying premise is that audiences are not static entities, but are shaped by the skill of the artist and made malleable to his control. While Shakespeare left us no formal *ars poetica,* internal evidence provided by his plays indicates that he was very aware of the role of the audience in successful theater and of the playwright's obligation to help create a responsive audience.[14] First, Shakespeare repeatedly indicates that audience participation and response are necessary to the success of his art. Rosaline, in *Love's Labor's Lost,* says that "A jest's prosperity lies in the ear / Of him that hears it" (*LLL* V.ii.851–52); and Shakespeare indicates that the same thing is true about his plays: they have life through the responsive spectator. The epilogues that close plays such as *As You*

Like It and *The Tempest* request the applause that will symbolize the completion of the artist's efforts in the answering response of the audience; and throughout *Henry V* the chorus enjoins the spectators to help the playwright, to clothe his pageants with garments supplied by their own imaginations: "For 'tis your thoughts that now must deck our kings" (*H5*, I.Pro.28). The audience's active participation in the drama is thus clearly not confined to a culminating burst of applause, but must occur throughout the play.

But while stressing the necessity of an involved and responsive audience to successful theater, Shakespeare also implies that the fashioning of an engaged and receptive audience is largely the dramatist's responsibility. Of course, there will always be intractable spectators such as Polonius, who, when he hears the visiting player recount the death of Priam and the grief of Hecuba, can only comment upon the actor's "good accent" (*Ham.* II.ii.454–55) or the diction of his speech: "That's good. 'Mobled queen' is good" (II.ii.492). But often, especially by the device of the play-within-the-play, Shakespeare indicates that it is through the dramatist's own ineptitude that he forfeits control over his spectators. The courtly audiences, for example, which watch the pageant of the Nine Worthies in *Love's Labor's Lost* or the "tragedy" of Pyramus and Thisbe in *Midsummer Night's Dream* do not respond as the actors intend. In exasperation, poor Holofernes cries out, "This is not generous, not gentle, not humble" (*LLL* V.ii.621); and he is right. His spectators are too busy making their own jests to receive an offered gift with grace. However, in both plays, the interior audiences face "plays" that do little to encourage more generous responses. In the case of *Pyramus and Thisbe,* Peter Quince's actors are inept, their script is most lamentable, but above all their play fails to fashion an active and involved role for the spectator or to create a coherent theatrical experience. The actors strive for a realism which allows no room for the free play of the spectator's imagination, all the while popping in and out of character to remind the audience that it is only watching a play. Small wonder that the audience remains detached and derisive. The implications of this fiasco are clear: the dramatist is largely responsible for the responsiveness of his audience. It can, to a great extent, only play the role and be the creature the playscript and the actors allow; in this instance, the play and its actors un-intentionally call into being a laughing and overdistanced audience.

On the other hand, Shakespeare also depicts audiences that are almost entirely within the control of the skillful artist. Hamlet, through *The Murder of Gonzago,* causes his great enemy, Claudius, to flee the theater and fall to his knees in prayer. Benedick and Beatrice, made unwitting spectators to "plays" staged by their friends, are led to reexamine their emotions for one another, just as those friends intend. Othello, fooled by Iago into believing he is witness to a conversation about Desdemona, which in truth concerns Bianca, becomes so overwhelmed by jealousy that he cooperates utterly with the evil designs of the producer of this deceptive pageant, interpreting all as Iago has given the cue. Shakespeare thus implies that the manipulation of illusion, the dramatist's stock-in-trade, can give the artist enormous power over the spectator and that this power can be used in a variety of ways. If Don Pedro, through art, increases the spectator's self-knowledge, Iago merely uses his "play" to victimize Othello and to bring forth his worst self.

Shakespeare's plays thus give every evidence that he thought a good deal about audiences: their potential recalcitrance and sug-gestibility, the techniques by which the dramatist wins or forfeits control over them, the potential abuses and benefits of such control. And as a number of critics have suggested, Shakespeare not only discussed and depicted audiences *in* his plays, but he also created scripts that reveal his constant concern with guiding the perceptions and responses of those who watched his own dramas.[15]

In this book I want to combine an interest in stage technique with an interest in audience response because I believe the two are naturally and inevitably linked in Shakespeare's own practice. As Shakespeare orchestrated plays for performance, he was orches-trating indirectly the responses of an imagined audience. Of course, he realized that in real-life situations, uniformity of response will not always occur: witness his depiction of the contrasting responses of Hamlet and Polonius to the actor's account of the fall of Troy. In actual theaters many factors influence reactions to a production: the occasion for the performance, the skill of the actors, the per-sonality structure or the theatrical competence of individual spec-tators. Over many of these factors the dramatist can exercise little control. What *does* lie in his control, in determining response, is the design of the playscript; and what I will investigate in this book is the potential effect upon an audience of the performance strategies encoded in Shakespeare's scripts, in particular, his orchestration of the sensory dimensions of the implied theatrical event.

Clearly I am not proposing a total theory of response, but examining one aspect of this intricate activity. With its focus on the design of the playscript as a key element determining response, my book owes obvious debts to the early response studies of Stanley Fish and to the work of Wolfgang Iser. I am not concerned, as are critics such as Norman Holland, with querying real readers/spectators to determine how their psychology influences their responses to a text/script.[16] However, at this point, the best way to indicate what I am attempting in this book is to turn to the plays for some brief illustrations.

One of the simplest elements in Shakespeare's implicit orchestration of stage events is his use of nonverbal sounds, which, while easily overlooked in reading a play, can be crucial to the effectiveness of the enacted drama.[17] For example, in *Macbeth,* the knocking at the gate in Act II led De Quincey to produce one of the best and earliest examples of what we would now call "affective criticism."[18] One can, of course, write very usefully about the scenes in which the knocking occurs in purely literary terms, that is, in terms of themes, symbolism, or possible dramatic analogues for the moment. Glynne Wickham, for example, feels the event has correspondences to the Harrowing of Hell in certain medieval cycle plays in which a semicomic porter is the keeper of Hell. The knocking at the gate represents the coming of the Christ figure, Macduff, to release the souls of those imprisoned within.[19] This is a useful analogy which, if not used to push the play into a rigid allegorical grid, reminds us of the Christian frame of reference within which the play undoubtedly operates.

But one can also choose to speak, as De Quincey does, of the affective dimensions of the sequence and of its psychological impact upon an audience that has for some time had its attention riveted upon two figures in a darkened castle preparing to commit regicide and then responding to the murder. In this strained, macabre context, the knocks strike upon our eardrums like a thunderclap, break-

ing our horrible, enthralled fascination with the Macbeths and reminding us of a world beyond the castle walls. The experience is
like being wakened from a trance; and the awakening is both frightening — because unexpected — and then reassuring, because it promises us that the circumscribed space of the Macbeths' castle does
not define the whole world. Yet this very experience of the painful
awakening, both startling and reassuring, is as much a part of the
play's meaning, certainly, as is Macduff's possible similarity to Christ,
since in this instant of awakening the audience recognizes the mesmerizing attraction of evil, the overwhelming fascination of minds
intent on committing an act that violates the most important stric-
tures of their society. The knocking is orchestrated to make us
start, like "guilty creatures sitting at a play," showing us how close
has been our identification with the pair before us and yet beginning
to open a distance between them and us.

Later in the same play, another offstage sound, this time the cries
of women that first signal the death of Lady Macbeth, both marks
a major turning point in the action and helps the audience assess
Macbeth's emotional state. The Queen's offstage death occurs right
in the middle of those short, nervous, active scenes that comprise
nearly all of the last act of this very compressed play. Shakespeare
carefully prepares the theatrical context in which the cries of the
dead Queen's attendants are first heard. Fear is in the air; Malcolm
and his men are drawing close; Macbeth, ranting, is holed up in
his castle with his reluctant followers. As V.v opens drums beat for
battle and Macbeth proclaims desperate defiance of his enemies. It
is then that the audience first hears the chilling "night-shriek" of
grieving women.

Unexpected and at first unexplained, these cries interrupt the
preparations for war and silence the bravado with which Macbeth
is trying to mask the collapse of his control over the external world.
It is as if, with those cries, the impregnability of both the castle
and Macbeth's personal defenses crumbles. The shrieks splinter and
shiver the fragile illusion of order that the beleaguered king has
been trying to maintain. Thirty lines later, the woods have "moved"
and Macbeth has rushed from the castle to seek death in the cut-
and-thrust of battle. If, in production, those cries of grieving women

are allowed their full weight, they become the pivot upon which a whole stage sequence turns.

At the same time that the offstage clamor stunningly articulates a turning point in the action and provides the catalyst for the collapse of the castle's defenses, it also evokes a thrill of terror and foreboding in the audience that becomes an index of the extent to which Macbeth's own sensibilities have been deadened. When he hears the cries, he greets them with unnatural calm. With effort he recalls how once he *would* have responded to such a "night-shriek"; but now, having "supped full with horrors, / Direness, familiar to [his] slaughterous thoughts, / Cannot once start [him]" (V.v.13–15). When a servant tells him what the cries mean, he can only respond with the profound world-weariness of "To-morrow, and to-morrow and to-morrow" (19). Though the audience's hair may not literally "rouse and stir / As life were in't" (12–13) when those night shrieks are heard, nonetheless, the surprise and fear they engender in the audience make Macbeth's resignation and deadened emotions the more apparent. The differing responses of audience and character to the same events clarify the monstrous consequences of crime upon his nature.

There are any number of ways in which nonverbal sounds, many of them originating offstage, become important parts of the enacted play. In *Othello* II.i, for example, while those on shore wait to learn which of the Venetian ships has weathered the storm, cannon shots are heard at intervals, along with offstage cries of "A sail, a sail" (II.i.51, 55, 93). The cries and the thunder of guns, contrapuntally intertwined with ongoing stage speech, wind up the dramatic tension for us and for those waiting on the shore. Who has survived the storm? Similarly, in *Julius Caesar,* the shouts of the offstage crowd (I.ii.79, 132) lend urgency to Cassius's conversation with Brutus. Is Caesar being crowned king? The offstage shouts raise this possibility and fix it in our minds even as Cassius is impelling Brutus to scotch the "snake." In both cases, the repeated offstage sounds create tension by dividing the audience's attention between an onstage series of events and offstage sounds, the meaning of which is not entirely clear, but which will surely affect the lives of those directly before us. By contrast, in *Lear,* the sounds of the storm in Act III, objectifying and magnifying the passionate storm of emotions within

11

the old king, help to convey to the audience the enormity of his suffering. In this instance, the nonverbal sounds primarily create neither suspense nor surprise, but intensify the audience's awareness of terrible inner pain.

Like the striking visual effects earlier described, such as Richard and Bolingbroke's hands upon England's crown, the individual uses of nonverbal sounds can considerably heighten the impact of particular stage moments. More complicated, of course, is Shakespeare's orchestration of speech itself or the inclusion of music proper within the play, as in *Othello* IV.iii when Desdemona sings the willow song. This scene provides an excellent example in miniature of the way in which an aural transition—in this case the transition from prose to song—can transform the tempo and emotional coloration of a stage sequence and so decisively affect the experience and responses of an audience.

The impact of the willow song depends partially upon the fact that it follows dreadful scenes of anger, frustration, and high passion. Desdemona has been publicly disgraced, called a whore by her husband, and had all her pleas in Cassio's behalf denied. Now, in her private chamber, she sings a song that reflects her own weary despair and also allows the audience to feel for the first time the full pathos of the poisoning of the Moor's mind. As Desdemona sings, the tale of a maid who died for love conveys the heroine's own feelings of betrayal and loss and foreshadows her death as passion's victim.

But the ballad—old even in Shakespeare's day—captures more than Desdemona's private emotions.[20] It expresses a sorrow at love's cruelty and at the horror of love's passing that is as universal as delight in love's growth and fruition. The ballad is an elegy for the love of Desdemona and Othello as we saw it displayed in the opening scenes of the play and a reminder of the pain that ever and always ensues when brightness falls from the air and things of great worth are destroyed.

During Iago's acutely psychological temptation of Othello, the audience has little time to reflect upon the final meaning and consequences of Othello's growing rage and jealousy. The *process* by which he becomes the antithesis of his former self commands all our attention. Desdemona's distracted song creates a moment of slackened tension in which the ultimate *consequences* of that trans-formation can be assimilated. Desdemona is not yet dead, of course, though that will come and is here ominously foreshadowed; but, more important, bonds of love and trust have been severed in a way that makes life itself meaningless, irrelevant. The song is thus important not only because its words have a direct bearing on Desdemona's situation, but also because it forms part of the complex tonal tapestry of the work and helps to pace the audience's experience of the theatrical event. By having direct recourse to music at this particular point, the dramatist breaks the strong forward rush of dialogue and allows the audience space in which to assimilate what has occurred before being once more caught up in the hasty dramatic sweep of the action.

My aim in this book is to move beyond discussion of isolated dramatic moments, such as Desdemona's willow song or the knocking at the gate in *Macbeth*, to the identification of some of the recurring techniques that underlie Shakespeare's art of orchestration. The five succeeding chapters do just that. Chapter 2 examines Shakespeare's management of the verbal diversity found in his plays, particularly the striking contrasts often effected in successive stage moments through shifts in tempo, tone, or the formality of stage speech. Chapter 3 looks at the technique of counterpoint, the simultaneous juxtaposition of two strands of action and speech, as in an eavesdropping encounter. Chapter 4 turns from language to its opposite, silence, and the role of absolute or relative silences in a play's total stage effectiveness. Chapter 5 examines Shakespeare's orchestration of bodies, of the changing number and the changing configurations of actors upon the stage. Chapter 6 looks at the role of orchestration in determining a play's theatrical structure and the audience's total theatrical experience. The final chapter examines the orchestration of a single play, *Twelfth Night,* in its entirety. My hope is that my analysis will enable others to see how the manipulation of visual, aural, and kinetic effects constitutes an important part of Shakespeare's dramatic art and is one of the chief means by which the playwright makes the audience his creature and establishes a meaningful and engaging theatrical event.

In the following chapters, as I look at specific techniques of orchestration, my analyses may at times seem artificially to fragment

Shakespeare's stagecraft into discrete components, when, in actuality, visual, kinetic, and aural phenomena work in consort and not in isolation from one another. I see no way around this methodological problem without addressing so many issues at once that I do justice to none. In earnest, therefore, of my last chapter, in which I attempt to put all the shards of the argument together in discussing *Twelfth Night*, I would like now to examine, not an entire play, but a sequence of events occurring in *Hamlet* IV.vii and V.i that shows how many elements of the stage event—tempo, kinetic effects, visual happenings, tonal shifts—work together to produce a complex field of meaning and to control the perceptions and responses of the audience. In particular, I wish to look at Gertrude's report of Ophelia's death as it occurs in the context of the preceding conversation between Claudius and Laertes and as her speech, in turn, gives way to the ensuing graveyard scene. From this sequence we can clearly see the complexity of Shakespeare's art of orchestration and its necessary relationship to the audience's understanding of dramatic meaning.

In the theater, the impact of Gertrude's report of Ophelia's death clearly depends upon the movement and tone of the conversation that precedes her entrance. The confrontation between Claudius and Laertes has a strong forward impetus. A letter from Hamlet informs the king that he will return to Elsinore the next day; Claudius uses a Frenchman's reported praise of Laertes's swordsmanship to suggest a plot against Hamlet's life; the plot is refined by Laertes, then by Claudius. Throughout, the rage of the younger man is manipulated and exploited by the older man, until the united energies of both coalesce around the intricate plan to kill the prince.

At the very height of this feverish scheming, during which the audience's attention is riveted upon Claudius's cleverness in bending Laertes's will inexorably to his own, Gertrude enters. Her entrance is a surprise and shock, partly because she is a woman intruding upon the bloody and violent councils of men, partly because of the message she bears: "Your sister's drowned, Laertes" (IV.vii.163). Her sudden entrance and sudden news cut short the complicated plotting of the two men in a way that forces the audience to sense how easily the blows of fortune or of fate can mock man's purposeful intents, just as this same queen, who now interrupts the plans for the duel, interrupts and turns awry its execution in Act V by drinking the poison meant for another.

Perhaps more startling yet is the way in which Gertrude's subsequent words contrast both with the fevered plans of Laertes and Claudius and with her own first, blunt report of Ophelia's death. In describing how the young woman came to drown, Gertrude dwells upon details: the names of the flowers in Ophelia's garland, the exact position of the willow tree, Ophelia's mermaidlike appearance in the water, and a mention of the songs she sang.

> There is a willow grows askant the brook,
> That shows his hoar leaves in the grassy stream.
> Therewith fantastic garlands did she make
> Of crowflowers, nettles, daisies, and long purples,
> That liberal shepherds give a grosser name,
> But our cold maids do dead men's fingers call them.
> There on the pendent boughs her crownet weeds
> Clamb'ring to hang, an envious sliver broke,
> When down her weedy trophies and herself
> Fell in the weeping brook. Her clothes spread wide,
> And mermaid-like awhile they bore her up,
> Which time she chanted snatches of old lauds,
> As one incapable of her own distress,
> Or like a creature native and indued
> Unto that element. But long it could not be
> Till that her garments, heavy with their drink,
> Pulled the poor wretch from her melodious lay
> To muddy death.
>
> (IV.vii.165–82)

The tone here is elegiac and unhurried, and it is not a tone elsewhere associated with Gertrude. However, the speech is less an indication of changes within the queen than an impersonal reverie upon the young woman's death. As such it establishes a meditative mood that is utterly at odds with the feverish excitement and strong forward movement of the preceding dialogue. Plots for revenge are suddenly eclipsed by the fact of death, which ends all acts and all plots.

Repeatedly this play moves between the poles of meditation and action, between the impulse to do and the knowledge that all doing ends in death, that all plots can go awry and lose the name of action. This dialectic is felt, kinetically, in the abrupt transition between the impassioned conversation of Claudius and Laertes and the elegiac and oddly peaceful reverie of Gertrude. The audience's response to this transition must of necessity be complex. It is not merely the painful fact of Ophelia's death that plays upon our emotions, nor the languor of a rhetoric that shrouds the horror of death in pretty phrases. The audience's experience of this moment must also include the sensation of disorientation. The language, tempo, visual focus, and emotional coloration of the action alter radically and swiftly. We grope for certainties and continuity and find, instead, discontinuity and contradiction.

What the play *does* to the audience—and it is a *doing* felt fully only in the theater—is to force the audience to experience the interruption of the purposeful thrust of active life by the interjection of a report that reminds us of all in life not subject to human control and will. Gertrude's speech thwarts utterly the established momentum of stage action that has, to this point, been moving along a carefully controlled trajectory determined by the will and cunning of Claudius. Suddenly, that trajectory is broken and the action eddies about a still point, Ophelia afloat on a stream and then swallowed by the waters. The report of her death becomes a felt comment on the ultimate futility of all plots and on man's tenuous control of circumstance. At the scene's end, Laertes cannot even control his tears. He has "forbid" them, but Nature is stronger than his will. In frustration, his anger displaced by shock and grief, he says, "I have a speech o' fire, that feign would blaze / But that this folly drowns it" (IV.vii.189–90). For the theater audience, the entire Gertrude segment, following in the wake of Claudius's conversation with Laertes, evokes a similar feeling of thwarted purposes, as the pathos inevitably caused by Ophelia's death deepens into a recognition of the fragile nature of all human striving and the puniness of men's wills before the impersonal forces that shape their destinies.

If audience response to Gertrude's message depends upon the complex ways in which her entrance clashes with and contradicts the mood and movement of the immediately preceding conversation, so, too, the slow rhythms and rich lyricism of Gertrude's speech affect responses to what next moves to the foreground of our attention: the action of two clowns digging a grave. A rough narrative continuity threads the two dramatic segments together. A woman has drowned; her grave must be prepared. But there continuity stops. The two men are active—active with their spades and with their wits—and ingenious as are their jests and parodies of legal logic, they can speak homely truth: "If this had not been a gentle-woman, she should have been buried out o' Christian burial" (V.i.21–23). They know how the great world orders its affairs and know, too, that death means worms and skulls and a narrow house of dirt.

It has become a critical truism that the clowns' matter-of-fact approach to death contrasts with and defines, respectively, the lyrical and strangely soothing reveries of Gertrude upon the death of Ophelia and the probing and horrific speculations of Hamlet upon the skull of Yorick and the dissolution of great Alexander. Variously, these characters offer three perspectives upon the inescapable fact of death. Yet only retrospectively, I would argue, do we contrast, dissect, and "rank" their speculations. As we experience the play temporally, the appearance of the clowns acts upon the audience directly and powerfully, first of all as a release from the stasis of the Gertrude segment. I have noticed in attending performances of *Hamlet* that with the appearance of the clowns the audience inevitably shuffles its feet and repositions itself in its seats. These bodily stirrings are not a sign of inattention, but evidence of the power of what has gone before and evidence of our relief that, after all, life goes on, even in the face of death. We have not seen the clowns before, but their anonymity, their shovels, and their humorous prose mark them as casual players in this tragedy, men with a job to do and a sanely detached view of life, death, and the thorny issue of Christian burial for a suicide. Feelings of relief and release are evoked by their presence, even though they give the audience only a reprieve, and not an escape, from more troubling meditations.

Without doubt Shakespeare realized that the flow of dramatic action cannot be held at a single level of intensity continuously. There must be a rich and varied elaboration of moods, visual effects, pauses, and tonal shifts if the living pressures of an intricate audience experience are to be maintained. Thus the clowns allow us a breathing space between Gertrude's report of Ophelia's death and Hamlet's relentless meditation on the skull of Yorick. But the orchestration of the events from Claudius's conversation with Laertes to Hamlet's colloquy with the tongueless skull does more than just provide variety in speech and visual effect; it also catches, kinetically and aurally, the harrowing tensions of this play, the collision of action and stasis, purposeful desire and unforeseen obstacle, the casual optimism of those who, like most of us, just live, and the painful intensity of those who, like Hamlet, struggle to know how to live. In such purposeful management of moment-by-moment stage action, we can see how Shakespeare shapes the audience's theatrical experience by the careful orchestration of successive stage moments.

In the final chapter of this book I will look at the sustained orchestration of an entire play, *Twelfth Night,* to show how, from Orsino's melancholy entrance to Feste's final song, the work is designed for effective stage presentation and the creation of an intricate audience experience. In the meantime, I wish to discuss one by one some of the individual components of Shakespeare's art of orchestration and to draw upon a wide range of plays to illustrate the principles governing their use. To these individual aspects of stagecraft I now wish to turn.

NOTES

1. The production took place at Trinity Square Repertory Theater in Providence, Rhode Island, in the 1967–68 season and was directed by Adrian Hall. Richard Kneeland and Katherine Helmond played Macbeth and Lady Macbeth.

2. Throughout this book all quotations from Shakespeare's plays are taken from William Shakespeare, *The Complete Works,* rev. ed., ed. Alfred Harbage (Baltimore: Penguin Books, 1969).

3. As J. L. Styan has said, "drama is not made of words alone, but of sights and sounds, stillness and motion, noise and silence, relationships and responses. Yet: these relationships and responses are not those between characters, rather those between actor and audience." See J. L. Styan, *Drama, Stage and Audience* (Cambridge: Cambridge University Press, 1975), vii.

4. A notable exception to this generalization is Paula Johnson's useful

book, *Form and Transformation in Music and Poetry of the English Renaissance,* Yale Studies in English, no. 179 (New Haven: Yale University Press, 1972).

5. Pioneers in the study of Shakespeare's stagecraft and in performance-oriented criticism include Bernard Beckerman, *Shakespeare at the Globe 1599–1609* (London: Collier Books, 1962) and *Dynamics of Drama: Theory and Method of Analysis* (New York: Knopf, 1970); John Russell Brown, *Shakespeare's Plays in Performance* (New York: St. Martin's Press, 1967); J. L. Styan, *Shakespeare's Stagecraft* (Cambridge: Cambridge University Press, 1967) and *Drama, Stage and Audience;* Michael Goldman, *Shakespeare and the Energies of Drama* (Princeton: Princeton University Press, 1972) and *The Actor's Freedom: Toward a Theory of Drama* (New York: Viking, 1975); and Alan Dessen, *Elizabethan Drama and the Viewer's Eye* (Chapel Hill: University of North Carolina Press, 1977). This list could be expanded. Increasingly Shakespeare's critics are exploring how his plays operate in the theater, an approach that has led Bernard Beckerman to write, "Far from being supplemental and peripheral as in the past, analysis of Shakespeare through performance is now conceded to be a proper and perhaps central way of approaching Shakespeare" ("Explorations in Shakespeare's Drama," *Shakespeare Quarterly* 29 [1978]: 133–45, at 133).

6. Michael Goldman, "Acting Values and Shakespearean Meaning: Some Suggestions," *Mosaic* 10, no. 3 (1977): 51–58, at 58.

7. Goldman, in *The Actor's Freedom,* provocatively discusses the centrality of the actor to the audience's experience in the theater, particularly its psychological experience. He argues that by publicly assuming a role-playing function, the actor takes risks with a stable sense of identity in ways that both thrill and terrify, excite and repel, an audience. See esp. 3–51.

8. Useful surveys of some of the production choices made in staging Shakespeare through the centuries are provided by George C. D. Odell, *Shakespeare from Betterton to Irving,* 2 vols. (New York: Scribner, 1920); and Arthur Colby Sprague, *Shakespeare and the Actors: The Stage Business in His Plays 1660–1905* (Cambridge: Harvard University Press, 1944).

9. It is always a tricky business to rely on the stage directions printed in modern texts as records of Shakespeare's intentions for a particular bit of stage business. We are not even certain that the stage directions printed in the First Folio or in the early printed quarto versions of the plays are necessarily Shakespeare's own and not, say, those of the manager of the prompt book. In this study I have therefore used the stage directions printed in the Penguin edition of the plays with caution; but I *have* used them, particularly when they confirm an entrance, an exit, a sound, or a

gesture already in some way indicated by the dialogue and when they have behind them the authority of the First Folio or the chosen copy text for the edition. The same caution must pertain in using the act and scene divisions indicated in modern editions, since many of these are additions by later editors. This matter will be more fully discussed in chapter 6 of this book.

10. J. L. Styan, in *Shakespeare's Stagecraft,* discusses possible stagings of the dance scene that would make its visual dynamics clear. See esp. 82–84.

11. See Rosalie Colie, *Shakespeare's Living Art* (Princeton: Princeton University Press, 1974), 135–46.

12. Helene Keyssar, "I Love You. Who Are You? The Strategy of Drama in Recognition Scenes," *PMLA* 92 (1977): 297–306, at 304.

13. John Russell Brown ("The Theatrical Element of Shakespeare Criticism," in *Reinterpretations of Elizabethan Drama,* ed. Norman Rabkin [New York: Columbia University Press, 1969], 177–95) discusses the difficulties of criticism based upon enactment of the plays in "the theater of the mind." Brown insists that the critic concerned with the plays as theater pieces must be familiar with the stage history of the plays and with the theatrical conditions of Shakespeare's day and must, as well, have some direct involvement with the plays in rehearsal and performance. I do not assume, as does Brown, that the critic must literally become actor and director, though total unfamiliarity with the realities of theatrical production will surely cripple the effectiveness of a critic who wishes to discuss the effect upon the audience of the dramatic strategies of the enacted play.

14. For a fuller discussion of Shakespeare's creation of a responsive audience, see Jean Howard, "Shakespeare's Creation of a Fit Audience for *The Tempest,*" in *Shakespeare: Contemporary Critical Approaches, Bucknell Review* 25 (1980): 142–53, in which I am indebted, in particular, to the seminal article by Walter J. Ong, S.J., entitled "The Writer's Audience Is Always a Fiction," *PMLA* 90 (1975): 9–21.

15. Arthur Colby Sprague, for example, discusses Shakespeare's art of exposition, showing how the dramatist prepares his audience for coming events, how he utilizes surprise and how he employs the stage conventions of his time, such as the chorus, the aside, and the soliloquy (*Shakespeare and the Audience: A Study in the Technique of Exposition* [Cambridge: Harvard University Press, 1935]). Maynard Mack concentrates on Shakespeare's ability to move his audience skillfully between the poles of engagement and detachment ("Engagement and Detachment in Shakespeare's Plays," *Essays on Shakespeare and Elizabethan Drama in Honor of Hardin*

Craig, ed. Richard Hosley [Columbia: University of Missouri Press, 1962], 275–96). E. A. J. Honigmann describes Shakespeare's control of the spectator's response to character in *Shakespeare: Seven Tragedies: The Dramatist's Manipulation of Response* (New York: Barnes & Noble, 1976). Alan Dessen focuses on Shakespeare's manipulation of "speaking pictures," the visual configurations on the stage (*Elizabethan Drama and the Viewer's Eye*); and Stephen Booth ("On the Value of *Hamlet,*" in *Reinterpretations of Elizabethan Drama,* ed. Rabkin, 137–76) explores the way the linguistic and theatrical design of *Hamlet* creates a complex experience of indeterminacy for the audience.

16. For Fish's own account of the evolution of his critical theory, see Stanley Fish, *Is There a Text in This Class? The Authority of Interpretive Communities* (Cambridge: Harvard University Press, 1980). I found particularly useful his essay, "Literature in the Reader: Affective Stylistics," first printed in *New Literary History* 2 (1970): 123–62. Wolfgang Iser's position is set forth most fully in *The Act of Reading: A Theory of Aesthetic Response* (Baltimore: Johns Hopkins University Press, 1978). For Norman Holland's more empirical studies of response, see, for example, *Five Readers Reading* (New Haven: Yale University Press, 1975). Recently, a great deal of response criticism has appeared. Two collections of essays that provide useful overviews of this burgeoning field are Susan R. Suleiman and Inge Crosman, eds., *The Reader in the Text: Essays on Audience and Interpretation* (Princeton: Princeton University Press, 1980); and Jane P. Tompkins, ed., *Reader-Response Criticism: From Formalism to Post-Structuralism* (Baltimore: Johns Hopkins University Press, 1980).

17. The most comprehensive work in this area is Frances Ann Shirley, *Shakespeare's Use of Off-Stage Sounds* (Lincoln: University of Nebraska Press, 1963).

18. Thomas De Quincey, "On the Knocking at the Gate in *Macbeth,*" *London Magazine,* October 1823; reprinted in id., *Confessions of an English Opium Eater and Other Writings,* ed. Aileen Ward (New York: New American Library, 1966), 324–29.

19. Glynne Wickham, *Shakespeare's Dramatic Heritage: Collected Studies in Medieval, Tudor and Shakespearean Drama* (London: Routledge & Kegan Paul, 1969), 214–24.

20. Peter Seng has found analogues for this song in late fifteenth-century ballads. At least two separate musical accompaniments were extant in Shakespeare's day. See Peter Seng, *The Vocal Songs in the Plays of Shakespeare: A Critical History* (Cambridge: Harvard University Press, 1967), 191–99.

CHAPTER 2

Cuing the Audience:
The Orchestration of
Speech and Sound

IN THINKING ABOUT how Shakespeare's plays are orchestrated for temporal presentation upon a stage, one confronts first the immense linguistic and tonal variations found in his works. Many other kinds of drama, Racine's tragedies or Ibsen's problem plays, for example, present us with a much greater uniformity of language. Though Phaedra is a queen and Oenone a servant, each speaks in perfect alexandrines. Though Tesman is a dull and plodding academic and Loevborg a creative if erratic visionary, each speaks in middle-class prose. This is not to say that there is no linguistic variety in these plays. Individual characters display idiosyncracies of diction, syntax, and metaphor; but the distinctiveness of any one figure's speech is controlled by the overriding concern for the unified stylistic decorum of the entire play. In Racine, the characters speak in the formal verse appropriate to the high style of neoclassical tragedy; in Ibsen's social problem plays at least, the characters speak in the prose idiom characteristic of realistic theater.

Shakespeare, however, wrote plays differently. Sidney may not have liked the mixing of kings and clowns on the Renaissance stage, but Shakespeare was not a classical purist. In his plays, tapsters, bawds, virgins, kings, and clowns happily commingle and speak with wonderful diversity in prose and verse, colloquially and formally, earnestly and ironically. Bottom's unflappable homespun wit—"Nay, I can gleek, upon occasion" (*MND* III.i.133)—may be a less delicate, less multitoned instrument than his fairy lover's rich lyricism—"The moon, methinks, looks with a wat'ry eye" (183)—but these two dramatic voices reside side by side in the same scene.

What dramatic ends do such juxtapositions serve? Why the immense linguistic and tonal variety of the plays? What principles control and shape its use? A variety of explanations have been offered, such as that by Erich Auerbach, for example, who sees in the variety of styles and voices an expression of the inclusiveness of Shakespeare's world view. Writing in an age of increasing historical consciousness and in an age grown sophisticated in the use of artistic perspective, Shakespeare seems to Auerbach to embody in his art this increased awareness of the multiplicity of human experience, past and present. Auerbach calls the plays "creaturely"—i.e., rooted in the real and the tangible—but also stylized, transcending realism by their heightened reflection of the world at hand.[1] Such a critical view describes what we all in some degree feel to be true of Shakespeare's plays, namely, their ability to weave many perspectives upon reality into an interlocking whole with generous acknowledgment that the Bottoms of this world have value as well as the Titanias.

Other critics have echoed Auerbach's historical/social observations. C. L. Barber, for example, explains the variety of dramatic voices in Shakespeare's "festive comedy" as an artistic reflection of the communal release experienced in Elizabethan holidays. In a society certain of its values and the stability of its social hierarchy, temporary, festive inversion of those values could be tolerated. All classes, from laborers to lords, took part in periodic, Saturnalian celebrations of misrule; and this same social spectrum, Barber argues, found its way onto the Shakespearean stage.[2]

Writers such as Auerbach and Barber help us see that the verbal diversity found in Shakespeare's plays in part reflects the scope of his social vision. Other critics have more particularly emphasized the relationship between Shakespeare's varied dramatic language and his skill at characterization. For example, in dealing with the later tragedies, Maynard Mack has suggested that one of the purposes of the verbal variety found in those plays is to establish by contrast the particular nature of the heroic voice of the tragic protagonist. The depth of the hero's vision is conveyed most vividly by the sustained juxtaposition of his voice and the more prosaic and thinner voices of the world at large. Hence we have repeated oppositions of the language of hero and foil: Romeo and Mercutio, Hamlet and Horatio, Lear and the Fool, Macbeth and Lady Macbeth, Coriolanus and Menenius, Othello and Iago, to name but a few. The plays constantly hold up verbal yardsticks by which we may measure the summons to which the protagonist responds.[3] These contrasts help to define a vision we may justly term heroic and simultaneously reveal the value of the less heroic perspectives forfeited by a mind too demanding to settle for their comfortable certainties. Thus neither can Hamlet assume Horatio's self-possessed stoicism nor Juliet the moral relativism of her nurse, even though the philosophies of Horatio and of Juliet's nurse, of Emilia and of Macduff, offer respectable answers to the problem of accommodating the self to day-to-day existence.

Clearly, however, the juxtaposition of the voices of hero and foil constitutes but a tiny part of Shakespeare's orchestration of stage speech. What I wish to argue is that the verbal diversity of the plays does more than manifest a comprehensive social vision or delineate character, whether the character of the hero or of other figures, though these are important functions. Equally important is the role played by the orchestration of speech and sound in governing the rhythm of the audience's theatrical experience and in shaping its perceptions of and responses to the progressive flow of stage events. What we need to recall is that drama presents an action in progress, the moment-by-moment unfolding of which is meant to produce certain effects upon an audience, not all relating to the revelation of dramatic character.

In performance, the aural shifts and contrasts produced by Shakespeare's commanding range of style and idiom help the hearer to organize and comprehend the meaning of a rapidly unfolding succession of events in ways that go beyond language's necessary links to characterization or to generic decorum. For example, in *Richard II* III.iv gardeners employ a formal—even conceited—verse that reveals little about the character of these particular gardeners or even about the language appropriate to historical tragedy. Instead, their language helps the audience to recognize the emblematic quality of the scene in which they appear and its function as a conventional, if partial, interpretation of surrounding events.[4] Highly formal rhetoric placed in the mouths of inconsequential characters functions as a distancing device. It lessens the intensity of the audience's engagement with stage events and allows a time for reflection, synthesis, "summing up," before the debasement of Richard at Flint Castle, which the audience has just witnessed, is completed in his actual deposition, which is what the audience next sees. As Maynard Mack has shown, such alternation of engagement and detachment is one way in which the rhythm of the audience's theatrical experience is controlled by the skillful dramatist, and in this case the formal rhetoric and static nature of the gardener scene affords the audience the emotional distance to assimilate the cosmic and political significance of a king's fall, rather than being simply caught up in the pathos of Richard's personal tragedy.[5]

My point is that it is often the theater audience's needs that are being served, its experience that is being shaped, through Shakespeare's orchestration of the rich linguistic texture of his plays. It is highly artificial and a little absurd, of course, to sever language's function to express character and social vision or to reveal theme from its function in guiding audience response or creating a particular kind of theatrical experience, but such artificial distinctions may help to call attention to what has been neglected in the study of Shakespeare's stagecraft. In what follows, therefore, I will be looking at some of the ways in which the dramatist controls the audience's perception and responses through the orchestration of language, remembering always that language has tonal, kinetic, and purely aural properties, as well as semantic ones. When, for example, Lear enters with Cordelia in his arms and cries "Howl, howl, howl!" (*Lr.* V.iii.258), the pure sound of this half bestial shriek is what terrifies and rivets the listener, just as on the heath the crack of thunder and the swirling voices of gibbering madman, frightened fool, and raging king create an overall impression of aural cacophony that is as important to the viewer's understanding of what the scene means in psychological and social terms as is the exact language of any of the figures before us.

Similarly, when Petruchio and Kate begin their first private "love encounter," their whizzing one-liners create the impression of intense speed and perfect coordination.

PETRUCHIO   Come, come, you wasp, i' faith you are too angry.
KATE   If I be waspish best beware my sting.
PETRUCHIO   My remedy is then to pluck it out.
KATE   Ay, if the fool could find it where it lies.
PETRUCHIO   Who knows not where a wasp does wear his sting?
            In his tail.
KATE   In his tongue.
PETRUCHIO   Whose tongue?
KATE   Yours, if you talk of tales, and so farewell.
PETRUCHIO   What, with my tongue in your tail?
            Nay, come again, good Kate, I am a gentleman.
                                          (*Shr.* II.i.211–21)

This is a tennis game of wit, a clear displacement of sexual energy into mental give-and-take. The jests are important for their cleverness and for their bawdy subcurrents, but equally important is the kinetic effect of the rapid movement of the dialogue. The audience *feels* an energy and agility in the taut dialectic of this exchange in which words are hurled like shuttlecocks back and forth between two perfectly matched antagonists. This, we sense, is a marriageable pair; this a demonstration of reciprocal vitality we have not elsewhere experienced in the fictional world of Padua.

My intention, however, is not simply to show that Shakespeare knew how to use the sound of speech or the pace of a verbal exchange to further the general expressiveness of his dramatic dialogue, though his ability to do so is part of what singles him out as a master craftsman of the theater. I also wish to argue that his orchestration of speech and sound always has a rhetorical as well as an expressive dimension; that is, the dramatist consistently orchestrates the aural elements of the performed play to "cue the audience," i.e., to control its perceptions and responses and to guide its apprehension of dramatic form and meaning. Repeatedly, all the resources of language (tempo, rhythm, tone, semantic meaning, and figurative device) are brought to bear on moving the audience through a meaningful and coherent theatrical experience. Perhaps the most obvious way to see how such cuing occurs is to look at the role of aural shifts and contrasts in marking for the audience the transition points within the ongoing continuum of stage action.

We all know that Shakespeare's plays are lengthy, complex, and often multiply plotted; and, on the Elizabethan stage at least, they would have been presented with few breaks and without elaborate scene changes. Nonetheless, in performance they do not pass the audience by in an undifferentiated blur. The dramatist finds ways to give closure to discrete dramatic segments, to control the rhythm of rising and falling tension, to underscore the informing thematic polarities of a work, and to signal new movements within the play — to articulate its theatrical "joints" — so that the audience senses a shaping hand controlling the welter of moment-by-moment stage actions. In this shaping process, language, producing aural changes and shifts, is one of the playwright's key instruments, whether, as in *Lear* I.i, shifts from prose to verse to prose underscore for the hearer the crescendo-decrescendo rhythm and unity of a single stage segment; or, as in *Henry IV, Part I,* changes in diction, syntax, and the formality of speech are used throughout the work to help the audience differentiate among the worlds of court, tavern, and rebel camp as the action moves in a controlled round robin among these worlds until all come together, climactically, on the battlefield of Shrewsbury.

In looking at how the orchestration of speech and sound is used by Shakespeare to cue the audience to significant transitions within the temporal progression of a play, I find it useful to compare how such transitions are marked in a strictly poetic narrative. In *Paradise Lost,* for example, the epic narrator can constantly intrude to guide and reorient the reader. When the fall of man is to be described, for example, Milton begins Book IX with a forceful statement of the new action and the new mood to be explored: "I now must change / Those Notes to Tragic" (*PL* IX.5–6).[6]

Drama, of course, lacks a narrator's guiding voice; though in plays such as *Henry V* and *Pericles,* the chorus and Gower do summarize the plot, and their predictable reappearances mark the "joints" of these plays. But such figures are the exception, not the rule. More subtly, in plays such as *Julius Caesar* and *Macbeth,* the reappearance of the crowd and the witches, respectively, at the end of Act III of each play, underscores the basic two-part structure of these works and signals to the audience that now one portion of the action is completed, another about to begin.[7] Aural and visual repetition thus becomes a means of reinforcing the structural hinges of a work. Particularly in the case of the witches, their riddling, rhymed, paradoxical, teasing speech is markedly different from other language in the play. When they reenter, the distinctiveness of their speech, coupled with their fearful and unnatural appearance, sends the viewer's mind back to the opening of the drama and helps to signal a new point of departure for the action.

Shakespeare's plays progress, of course, not only through various stages of plot development, but also through a complex succession of moods and feelings. If significant phases of the action must be signaled, so must significant reorientations of mood. In *Richard II,* for example, Act II, scene ii, opens with a mood of grief and lamentation nearly as impossible to mistake as Milton's overt statement that his notes must now be turned to tragic. The scene follows the long one in which Gaunt dies, Richard appropriates his lands and self-confidently prepares for Ireland, and Northumberland and other lords give the first sign that they are ripe for rebellion. In II.i Richard was cocky and thoughtless, oblivious to impending danger. That scene closed with the vigorous words of the rebel lords preparing to post to Ravenspurgh to meet with Bolingbroke.

> ROSS   To horse, to horse! Urge doubts to them that fear.
> WILLOUGHBY Hold out my horse, and I will first be there.
>   (II.i.299–300)

By contrast, II.ii opens with the queen reflectively speaking to various of Richard's loyal courtiers. The tempo slows; the languid language directs attention toward the inner life of the grieving queen, not toward the outer world of action.

> BUSHY Madam, your majesty is too much sad.
>   You promised, when you parted with the king,
>   To lay aside life-harming heaviness
>   And entertain a cheerful disposition.
> QUEEN To please the king, I did; to please myself,
>   I cannot do it. Yet I know no cause
>   Why I should welcome such a guest as grief
>   Save bidding farewell to so sweet a guest
>   As my sweet Richard. Yet again, methinks,

Some unborn sorrow, ripe in fortune's womb,
Is coming towards me, and my inward soul
With nothing trembles. At something it grieves
More than with parting from my lord the king.
(II.ii.1–13)

Wolfgang Clemen singles this moment out as an example of Shake-speare's "art of preparation."[8] The queen's grief is prelude to the series of reversals and blows Richard is soon to suffer after his apparent control of the action in I.i through II.i. Even in the middle of her lament, Isabel receives word of Bolingbroke's return to Eng-land, news that gives her nameless fears a specific embodiment. The scene thus enacts a telling bit of dramatic irony, as the irrational sadness of Isabel, which all those about her deem groundless, proves to be a harbinger of actual disaster.

Yet Isabel's lamenting mood also serves a more far-reaching pro-leptic function, of which we gradually become aware as we realize that she has sounded the keynote that is to dominate the middle portions of this play from Richard's sorrowing return to England to his deposition. It is he who picks up Isabel's accents of lam-entation and elaborates them endlessly, examining his royal role and his mortal self in a prolonged self-scrutiny that results from his loss both of royal power and of the name of king. Isabel's lament in II.ii anticipates this extended attention to sorrow's pressures upon the human soul. Her speech is a way of reorienting the audience's frame of reference toward the inner life of man and away from the busy world of outward action and public pageantry.

Such reorientations of audience attention, signaling new move-ments in the play's unfolding sequence of actions and moods, can be effected variously, but the point is that Shakespeare never leaves his audience behind. He tends to its needs. He orchestrates the aural and visual texture of the play so that the audience implicitly senses when the play is entering a new phase, even when a chorus or obvious verbal and aural repetition is absent. Consider, for ex-ample, both the economy and the complexity of the transitional moment presented at the beginning of Act III of *Othello*. This act opens with an often ignored conversation between some musicians and a clown. The episode is a raucous and bawdy one. Cassio has hired musicians to play a morning serenade beneath Othello and Desdemona's window, presumably as a means of regaining favor after his drunken behavior of the night before. His attempt to win favor by this means is odd, though, for several reasons. He had not mentioned the plan to Iago the previous night, but had then intended to sue directly to Desdemona for aid, which he eventually does with no mention of the serenade. Further, instead of having a tuneful consort play outside Othello's window, Cassio has brought along musicians who play only the bagpipes or some other harsh wind instrument.[9] Their music is so vile, at least to the clown's ears, that he gives them money to be gone; and as he chases them away, he does so with a series of obscene puns and jests.

What function does this bawdy, noisy, and puzzling episode perform? The first thing to be said is that it adds nothing to the plot of the play. It could be cut, and no information essential to the understanding of the play's events would be lost. Its function, therefore, is more subtle and has to do with Shakespeare's control of the audience's theatrical experience. Clearly, the episode distances the audience from disturbing prior events, with which it provides a striking aural and visual contrast. In the prior scene, Cassio had disgraced himself in a drunken brawl. Othello had been called from his bed to restore order to the disrupted isle, and Iago had capped the scene with a devilish recitation of crimes yet to be committed against the Moor. With his usual frankness and metaphorical vigor, Iago had described how he intended to pour "pestilence" into Othello's ear and turn Desdemona's "virtue into pitch" (II.iii.339, 343). Alone upon stage for most of his recitation of intended evil (Roderigo enters and soon exits near the very end of the scene), Iago forces the audience into an involuntary, but oddly mesmerizing, intimacy with him.

The musician episode releases us from that intimacy with startling rapidity. Suddenly it is day, not night. Instead of listening to one actor reveal his hellish plots directly to us, the stage fills with figures—Cassio, a group of musicians, and a clown—who are busy with one another, not with us. Most significant, Iago's cold, Machiavellian language has been replaced by colloquial, bawdy banter, and by the harsh music of minor characters. Clearly we are in the daytime world of ordinary mortals, and it is a relief. Their bustling activity and crude music instantly evoke the comic and social dimensions of human life, rather than the intense insularity of Iago's sinister monologue.

This transition is highlighted by every aural and visual contrast at Shakespeare's disposal. Its effects upon the audience are multiple and complex. By releasing us so abruptly from Iago's hypnotic spell, the musicians' exchanges perversely reveal how easy it is to be mesmerized by Iago and also how repulsive intimate contact with him can be. It is like enduring the embraces of a snake; and if the audience here escapes Iago's verbal embrace through the good offices of the playwright, Othello is not to be so lucky.[10] At the broadest level, then, the shudder of relief we feel at escaping from Iago into the world of ordinary men ought to deepen our sympathy for and understanding of the man who does not find such release until too late.

In addition, the scene reorients audience attention forward toward a new movement within the play. The night is behind, the day is ahead. Ironically, this comic and noisy interlude raises hopes for the permanent frustration of Iago's power, even as it hints at the futility of such hopes. The episode is proleptic in a more complex way than was true for Isabel's speech of grief and foreboding, largely because while it emphatically distances the audience from disturbing prior events, it establishes its own vague intimations of future discord, leaving the audience with mixed emotions of hope and uneasiness.

This particular transition also has symbolic overtones, but these are subtly suggested by the scene's orchestration, rather than stated overtly. The harsh serenade played beneath Othello's window functions, in part, as an aural objectification of the play's pervasive verbal imagery of harmonious music marred by discord.[11] Iago, watching Desdemona and Othello's joyful reunion on Cyprus, proclaims: "O, you are well tuned now! / But I'll set down the pegs that make this music, / As honest as I am" (II.i.197–99). Later, after Othello has become suspicious of Desdemona, she tells Cassio that her entreaties for him are for the moment useless, "My advocation is not now in tune" (III.iv.123).

As Rosalie Colie has suggested, *Othello* in part explores the proper relationship between love and war, venerian and martial dimensions of human experience.[12] Othello, the warrior, weds Desdemona, the humanized goddess of love. Renaissance mythologists believed that the union of Mars and Venus gave birth to concord or harmony.[13] When properly allied, these two apparently warring impulses enriched and supported one another, leading to wholeness within the human soul. When severed, discord and disharmony were the result. Certainly the union of Othello and Desdemona, opposites in so many ways, produces a love so remarkable that even Iago notes how "in tune" the lovers appear. The ensign's task is the untuning of this and all other harmonies, and we should recall how often Iago is the cause of clamor and noisy chaos in the play's world even before his actual temptation of Othello.[14] It is he who disturbs the peace of sleeping Venice by shouting obscenities outside Brabantio's window in Act I, he who engineers the brawl in Act II and sets ringing the dreadful bell that "frights the isle / From her propriety" (II. iii.165–66), he who later again disturbs the sleep of Cyprus by the attempted murder of Cassio and the actual murder of Roderigo, he who untunes the "daily beauty" of Cassio's life by causing him to lose his "reputation," and he above all who in Act III begins to work directly upon the inner peace of his great general to untune his love for Desdemona.

There is a marked aural dialectic in this play between clamor and calm, cacophony and harmony, which objectifies the psychological dialectic between inner harmony and inner chaos. The harsh music that opens Act III is a minor, but literal, rendering of musical discord. I doubt that any audience hearing this music thinks of its larger symbolic significance, thinks of it, for example, as a sign of Iago's power to disjoin Mars from Venus and so to abort the birth of Concord. The point is precisely that the abstractions we retrospectively use to synthesize and order a work often are adumbrated in performance as concrete elements of our sensory experience, felt or sensed, rather than abstracted into rational paradigms. In *Othello* III.i the sound of the musicians' reedy wind instruments, the source for the clown's bawdy puns, probably simply annoys the audience, as it annoys the clown. The discord grates; it somewhat tempers the relief with which we experience our escape from Iago and turn our attention toward a new day. The aural discord lightly suggests the much greater discord to come as Iago, his preparations accomplished, turns to his primary task of untuning the Moor's love for Desdemona. The interlude involving clown and musicians thus cues the audience to the beginning of this most painful movement of the drama, turning us toward it with an appropriate mixture of hope and uneasiness.

Not all aural shifts in the play so obviously perform proleptic or transitional functions as do Isabel's laments in *Richard II* or the brief appearances of clown and musicians in *Othello*. These incidents reorient the audience, subtly direct its attention toward a new movement in its experience of the play, and help it to sense that a series of stage happenings form a purposeful sequence of moods and experiences. At other times, within or between scenes, abrupt shifts in the rhetorical complexity, formality, diction, tone, or tempo of dramatic speech are used to cue the audience to the defining tensions and dichotomies of a particular dramatic world.

In their extreme form, such marked aural contrasts, which for descriptive purposes I call "changes of key," force the audience to experience in unmediated form clashes of sensibility and perspective that underlie the thematic or ideational polarities informing a given play. Consider, for example, *Antony and Cleopatra*. This is a play often talked about in dialectical terms: Rome v. Egypt, duty v. desire, martial valor v. sensual pleasure, sterility v. fertility, time v. timelessness.[15] Yet in the theater, the playwright does not state these oppositions overtly, neither does an audience perceive them first as intellectual abstractions. Instead, we gradually sense the informing dichotomies of the work through the unusual handling of geographical place and scenic structure—the play contains forty-two scenes, many of them extremely short, and moves back and forth incessantly between Egypt and Rome, with brief excursions to Athens and Parthia—and through the persistent use of marked verbal contrasts. Everyone is familiar, for example, with Enobarbus's famous description of Cleopatra on her barge. It is one of the most gorgeous lyric set pieces in all of Shakespeare. The speech is even more remarkable, however, if we examine it in its immediate dramatic context.

In Act II, scene ii, the two great generals, Antony and Caesar, hold their rather testy meeting after Antony's sudden return to Rome from Egypt. They exchange acrimonious accusations and patch together a reconciliation by deciding that Antony will marry Caesar's sister. When they leave the stage, gossip begins among the minor officers of each camp—Enobarbus, Agrippa, and Maecenas. These characters talk in prose, and the inquiries about life in Egypt are at first posed and answered in bantering tones. Suddenly, however, Shakespeare stretches the boundaries of dramatic decorum by having the bluff Enobarbus relate what amounts to a vision, a dream of mythic proportions about Cleopatra's appearance on the river Cydnus:

> The barge she sat in, like a burnished throne,
> Burned on the water: the poop was beaten gold;
> Purple the sails, and so perfumèd that
> The winds were lovesick with them; the oars were silver,
> Which to the tune of flutes kept stroke, and made
> The water which they beat to follow faster,
> As amorous of their strokes. For her own person,
> It beggared all description: she did lie
> In her pavilion, cloth-of-gold of tissue,
> O'erpicturing that Venus where we see
> The fancy outwork nature. On each side her
> Stood pretty dimpled boys, like smiling Cupids,
> With divers-colored fans, whose wind did seem
> To glow the delicate cheeks which they did cool,
> And what they undid did.

AGRIPPA   O, rare for Antony.
ENOBARBUS   Her gentlewomen, like the Nereides,

> So many mermaids, tended her i' th' eyes,
> And made their bends adornings. At the helm
> A seeming mermaid steers: the silken tackle
> Swell with the touches of those flower-soft hands,
> That yarely frame the office. From the barge
> A strange invisible perfume hits the sense
> Of the adjacent wharfs. The city cast
> Her people out upon her; and Antony,
> Enthroned i' th' market place, did sit alone
> Whistling to th' air; which, but for vacancy,

> Had gone to gaze on Cleopatra too,
> And made a gap in nature.
> (II.ii.192–219)

The language here becomes sensuous, paradoxical, and hyperbolic as Enobarbus describes a woman, half goddess and half witch, who hypnotizes all who come within her orbit. Involuntarily, Enobarbus slips into the present tense midway through his description, the moment of vision collapsing *then* and *now*.[16]

Clearly, this speech is not primarily an index to Enobarbus's lyric temperament. It is, in fact, somewhat out of character for Enobarbus to speak with so little restraint. Rather, amid the expedient atmosphere of Rome, this speech suddenly directs the audience's attention once more to the magical, superhuman dimension of life embodied in this play by the idea of Cleopatra. It helps to keep alive the tension between the values of Rome and the attractions of Egypt. Of course, the Cleopatra we often see, with her petty jealousies and recrimination, her vanity and fickleness, is often just exasperating. Even in Enobarbus's description there are hints that those who pay her homage do so almost against their wills.

Yet for all Cleopatra's mortal flaws, her very existence holds out the possibility that life can be lived transcendently, with a grandeur and excess that dims more prosaic existences. In physics it is axiomatic that every action produces a reaction. Similarly, in the tonal dynamics of this play, it seems as if the wrangling and the waste of human spirit so evident in the generals' opportunistic peace require an answering affirmation of man's expansive imagination. And it is Cleopatra who in this play, whether lying like Venus in the pavilion of her barge or hopping through the streets of Alexandria, most supremely captures the imagination with her magical power to make "defect perfection."

In its dramatic context, Enobarbus's speech enacts a sudden aural shift that projects the audience from the cold, suspicious atmosphere of the generals' meeting to the sensuous lyricism of Cleopatra on her barge. The transition is swift and purposeful. Wedged between the generals' meeting and the ensuing appearance of Octavia, the Cydnus speech in its immediate context heightens the contrast between things Egyptian and things Roman and helps the audience experience the tension Antony must be feeling. It is he, after all, who has been most surely caught in Cleopatra's spell. Although he does not speak the Cydnus passage, it nonetheless functions as a reminder of Cleopatra's power over him. Enobarbus here may be articulating his own admiration for the Egyptian queen, but he is also speaking for that portion of Antony perpetually in thrall to this enchanting woman.

The dramatic segment just considered offers an excellent example of Shakespeare's use of verbal contrast to dramatize for an audience some of the informing dichotomies of this particular work: the difference between fact and myth, business and pleasure, expediency and the irrational pursuit of the sublime. Ironically, however, the many disjunctive elements of the play's stagecraft do not produce a theatrical experience defined solely by a sense of discontinuity. Rather, the sharp aural contrasts and abrupt changes of locale not only define differences, but also lead the audience to experience the paradoxical interdependence of things utterly dissimilar.

Consider, for example, the stage sequence formed by the events of Act IV, scenes viii and ix. The first scene enacts Antony's triumphal return from his second day of battle against Caesar. Unlike the first disastrous battle at sea, the encounter upon land marks a success for Antony, and the tone of the thirty-nine lines of this scene is consequently joyful. Antony enters congratulating his men, and when Cleopatra comes forth to greet him, his delight can hardly be expressed. To Scarus he says:

> Give me thy hand;
> To this great fairy I'll commend thy acts,
> Make her thanks bless thee. — O, thou day o' the world,
> Chain mine armed neck; leap thou, attire and all,
> Through proof of harness to my heart, and there
> Ride on the pants triumphing!
>
> (IV.viii.11–16)

The grandiose image of Cleopatra riding his beating heart as if it were a horse captures the expansiveness of Antony's mood.[17] As Cleopatra answers him in a similar vein, their language forms a hymn of joy. And as the group marches to Alexandria, Antony orders music to sound that will echo their ecstasy.

> Trumpeters,
> With brazen din blast you the city's ear,
> Make mingle with our rattling tabourines,
> That heaven and earth may strike their sounds together,
> Applauding our approach.
>
> (35–39)

It is thus with the blare of trumpets and the rattle of tambourines that this scene reaches its tumultuous conclusion, catching up the audience in its exalting mood of triumph.

But suddenly the prosaic voices of two sentries invite attention:

> If we be not relieved within this hour,
> We must return to th' court of guard. The night
> Is shiny, and they say we shall embattle
> By th' second hour i' th' morn.
>
> (IV.ix.1–4)

Triumphant hyperbole has been replaced by the workaday language of ordinary foot soldiers, the blare of trumpets by the quiet of the night. Yet this contrast is but prelude to a still more striking one. Enobarbus is also on the scene lamenting his treachery to Antony.

> Be witness to me, O thou blessèd moon,
> When men revolted shall upon record
> Bear hateful memory, poor Enobarbus did
> Before thy face repent!
>
> . . . .
>
> O sovereign mistress of true melancholy,
> The poisonous damp of night disponge upon me,
> That life, a very rebel to my will,
> May hang no longer on me. Throw my heart
> Against the flint and hardness of my fault,
> Which, being dried with grief, will break to powder,
> And finish all foul thoughts. O Antony,
> Nobler than my revolt is infamous,
> Forgive me in thine own particular,
> But let the world rank me in register
> A master leaver and a fugitive,
> O Antony! O Antony!
>
> (7–10, 12–23)

This is the language of despair and self-loathing, a recantation of past error and an invocation of death. In one of the play's most powerful images of dissolution, Enobarbus imagines his heart disintegrating from grief and shame. Separated from Antony, he feels separated from life itself. The dried and withered heart becomes an apt emblem of the hollowness of his expedient choice to serve Octavius Caesar. How different from Antony's impulsive thought that Cleopatra could ride the mighty pulses of his heart as she would ride a horse! The triumphal anthem of the preceding scene has changed to a dirge of bitter sadness.

There are a number of "reasons" why these scenes should follow one another. Enobarbus's plight is all the more pathetic because we have just witnessed the triumph in which he might have shared. At the same time, his death brings to mind the shabby sequence of events that precipitated his original desertion of Antony and so causes the audience to remember the "weaker" side of this triumphing general. Yet the effect of this aural and emotional transition is more complex. As an audience we are engaged by the vitality, the energy, and the joy of the triumphal entry into Alexandria. The suddenness with which this vibrant mood is replaced by one of sorrow and despair loosens our hold upon that mood of joy with painful abruptness. We experience loss, a dreadful wrenching of our attention, not just from one set of characters to another, but from immersion in one elemental human emotion to immersion in another.

By distancing us so sharply from Antony's mood of triumph, the stagecraft makes the audience not only recognize, but also experience, the vulnerability of that mood. By this I do not mean simply that Antony's victory can be — and soon is — replaced by military defeat. Rather, the triumphant affirmation of human joy and vitality expressed in his return from war is shown by juxtaposition with Enobarbus's lament to be but a contingent expression of human experience in this dramatic world. Soul-destroying melancholy and despair — symbolized by Enobarbus's image of his dry and withered heart — exist here, too. They enter the play at this particular point through the words of Enobarbus, just as earlier his Cydnus speech brought to the consciousness of the audience the sublimity of Egypt amid the prosaic expediency of Rome.

Such juxtapositions, felt first as aural contrasts, are structured to invite the audience to experience the paradoxical connection between opposites. Both the vulnerability and the glory of Antony and Cleopatra's rich, hyperbolic love are brought home through the sudden transition to an antithetical despair. These emotions do not cancel one another out; in a world of mutability and imperfection, they depend upon one another for their meaning: joy defined by its antithesis, just as the pleasures of Egypt are defined and heightened by the sterner Roman values that threaten them.

The sharp aural contrasts heard so often in this work and forming such a distinctive aspect of its aural orchestration are, therefore, anything but random. They function to make the paradoxes of this dramatic world part of the audience's theatrical experience. Not even Antony and Cleopatra, the play's most capacious souls, can—until death—escape from the world of mutability in which the meaning of joy is comprehended by its very transience and by knowledge of its opposite. "Everything that grows / Holds in perfection but a little moment" (Son.15.1-2). This knowledge becomes ours through the play's complex contrastive orchestration.

Of course, Shakespeare's aural dramaturgy does not depend solely on the kind of abrupt juxtaposition of tone and mood we find so often in a play such as *Antony and Cleopatra*. The absolute contrast between cacophony and quiet, businesslike prose and lyric verse, the expansive rhetoric of triumph and the weary language of despair, may at times simply be insufficiently subtle for Shakespeare's affective designs. Consequently, Shakespeare often orchestrates more delicately modulated aural transitions, and I would like now to discuss one of his characteristic techniques for doing so—a technique notable both for its subtlety and for its role in guiding audience response. I am thinking of what we might call Shakespeare's use of aural "bridges"—dramatic segments designed to disengage the attention of the audience from one dramatic action, marked by a particular use of language, and to prepare that audience to assimilate a quite different auditory experience. Transitional in function, these bridge passages may involve several speeches or a whole scene; but in every instance they wean the ear of the audience from one type of speech and establish a fresh aural ground against which subsequent aural events can be effectively figured. By determining the immediate context in which important aural events are perceived, bridge passages create expectations the dramatist can subsequently confirm, modify, or deny and, in doing so, subtly shape the responses of his audience.

In the opening scene of *Romeo and Juliet,* for example, certain speeches by Benvolio perform such a bridging function. Living up to his name of "well-wisher," Benvolio at first is simply an unwilling party to the stage brawl initiated by the bawdy Capulet servants and their Montague counterparts. By the time he arrives on the stage, swords are already out, and his two brief speeches of reconciliation fall on unresponsive ears. The fight flares despite his efforts, and the stage grows ever more crowded and noisy as the servants and junior members of the Montague and Capulet families are joined by the heads of the two households and finally by the prince himself. While the arrival of Prince Escalus quells the brawl, up to that point the overriding impression created by the scene is one of confusion, haste, and rapidly escalating violence.[18] In the confusion the theater audience probably does not focus on any character too long, including Benvolio.

After the prince leaves, however, attention shifts to Benvolio once more. Montague asks him about the fight; but he seems to recount it as much for the sake of the audience as for the sake of old Montague. His tone is still excited. He is reliving a fierce fight just finished, but the fight is retold without the distraction of the actual sword strokes and the shouts before our eyes and ears. One thing that is heightened, of course, is the role of Tybalt.

> Here were the servants of your adversary
> And yours, close fighting ere I did approach.
> I drew to part them. In the instant came
> The fiery Tybalt, with his sword prepared;
> Which, as he breathed defiance to my ears,
> He swung about his head and cut the winds,
> Who, nothing hurt withal, hissed him in scorn.
> While we were interchanging thrusts and blows,
> Came more and more, and fought on part and part,
> Till the Prince came, who parted either part.
>
> (I.i.104–13)

This account, spirited as it is, puts us at one remove from the fight itself. It serves as an interlude, a decompression chamber, to move us from the swift, confused movement of the opening events to the slow-paced, lyrical section that follows, a section in which all attention will focus upon the figure of the young Montague, Romeo.

Many commentators have noted that from the very beginning of the play Romeo is set apart from the public feuding in Verona. The only struggle that interests him is the warfare of love, though his feelings for Rosaline are worlds apart in intensity and depth from his subsequent feelings for Juliet. The gulf between the world of public feuding and Romeo's world of private love is first suggested by the two-part structure of the opening scene. The crowded stage and noisy confusion of the first half contrast with the subdued tone and much barer stage of the second half.[19]

But the point to which I wish to return is the role of Benvolio in effecting the transition between these two parts. After the speech in which Benvolio retells the fight for Montague's benefit, Lady Montague asks him another question, this time concerning the whereabouts of Romeo. The young man's answer bears little resemblance to his clipped and vibrant speech of a moment before. The key has changed. His language now takes on a new ornateness, assuming in part the leisured measures of verbal scene painting. He begins:

> Madam, an hour before the worshipped sun
> Peered forth the golden window of the East,
> A troubled mind drave me to walk abroad;
> Where, underneath the grove of sycamore
> That westward rooteth from this city side,
> So early walking did I see your son.
>
> (I.i.116–21)

Benvolio's speech moves the audience in stages from the active world of public encounter to the sequestered grove of the melancholy lover. Montague's reply furthers this progression, in lines that are richly metaphorical, as he describes Romeo's attempts to hide himself from the light of the "all-cheering sun."

These speeches are primarily a signal to the audience that the tempo and the direction of the scene have changed. The subject of both is Romeo, and they serve as prologue to *his* entrance and as an index to *his* sensibility, not as an expression of the lyrical temperament of either Benvolio or old Montague. The poetry is directing the audience along a continuum of experience that has at one extreme the cut and thrust of a public brawl and at the other the self-absorbed and self-indulgent paradoxes of Petrarchan love poetry: "O brawling love, O loving hate, / O anything, of nothing first create!" (174–75).

Clearly the scene is designed as a diptych structure. Public feuding is juxtaposed to private love, a group encounter to a dramatic segment involving only one or two figures. Yet the scene is aurally orchestrated to communicate more than this to an audience. Romeo is not just a solitary lover; he is a very special kind of lover. His language is highly self-conscious and relentlessly artificial, and it conveys the impression of someone luxuriating in the tangles of his own emotions.

> Love is a smoke raised with the fume of sighs;
> Being purged, a fire sparkling in lovers' eyes;
> Being vexed, a sea nourished with lovers' tears,
> What is it else? A madness most discreet,
> A choking gall, and a preserving sweet.
>
> (188–92)

The audience *hears* what is contorted, clichéd, and emotionally arid in these verbal pyrotechnics precisely because Romeo's speeches follow the less mannered and ingenious lyricism of Benvolio and Montague. Their language is what slows the tempo of the scene and prepares an aural ground against which Romeo's high-strung speech is conspicuously figured in all its nervous intricacy. Without the aural bridge provided by Benvolio and Montague, the audience would less easily be able to assimilate what is unique and telling in the young man's speech and sensibility.

In *King Lear,* Cordelia's reentry is similarly introduced by means of an aural bridge that again demonstrates the close link between the aural orchestration of the play and the needs of the listening audience. Cordelia disappears from *Lear* in Act I and only reappears in Act IV. After such a long absence from the stage, it is important that her return be managed in a way that allows her exact significance to be perceived. I would argue that IV.iii performs this crucial theatrical function; its primary purpose is to establish a context that helps the audience to realize, when Cordelia actually appears in IV.iv, how far she exceeds—in human warmth and vitality—the stilted praises of her admirers. Of course, IV.iii is a scene not present in the folio version of the text; and recently textual critics have argued that the folio text of the play represents Shakespeare's own careful revision of the 1608 quarto and that modern composite texts, such as the Pelican, are wrong to conflate the 1608 and the 1623 versions of the play. They argue that conflating the two gives us neither Shakespeare's first nor his final intentions, only an editor's fiction.[20]

While recognizing that such arguments about the textual history of *Lear* are plausible, I do not find them conclusive; and until the debate about the revision theory has developed further, I am not ready to give over the use of a composite text of *Lear*.[21] This choice, however, is not based on simple nostalgia. I am not convinced that the shorter folio text, truncated, it has been argued, for greater theatrical effectiveness, must necessarily have been shortened by Shakespeare in a deliberate revision, rather than representing the abridgments of a playhouse promptbook in which the author may or may not have had a hand. Further, while Steven Urkowitz, in particular, argues that changes from the quarto to the folio text reflect Shakespeare's concern for heightening the theatrical effectiveness of his play, I find it impossible to view many of the changes in that light. To take just one example, the folio text of IV.viii, in which Cordelia awakens her father from sleep, cuts all reference to the music that accompanies Lear's return to sanity. That music should accompany these events is not only theatrically effective, it is also typically Shakespearean; and I have trouble believing the cut was made by him or that the play is thereby made more theatrically compelling.

Further, in the scenes presently in question, IV.ii–iv, the deletion of IV.iii seems a debatable theatrical improvement. The direct juxtaposition of IV.ii and IV.iv, as in the folio, speeds up the action and calls attention once more to the contrast between a bad daughter and a good one, since what we see in IV.ii is Goneril's vicious confrontation with her husband upon her return to their castle and in IV.iv Cordelia's selfless concern for her father upon her return to England. But that Cordelia is the antithesis of her sisters we already know. Something more subtle and, I would argue, just as theatrically effective is achieved by prefacing IV.iii with the scene between Kent and a gentleman. While the memory of Goneril's vicious encounter with Albany governs some of our responses to Cordelia's reentry into the play, the intervening episode presents a more immediate aural ground and one that helps the audience perceive Cordelia's significance very precisely.

Obviously, IV.iii serves to reintroduce Cordelia after her long absence from the stage. Kent and the gentleman's discussion of how she behaved when told of her father's mistreatment reorients the audience's attention toward her and toward the love and loyalty she embodies. Yet, paradoxically, even as the gentleman's words bring Cordelia to our consciousness, they distance us from her as well. Describing how she read Kent's letters, the gentleman becomes a maddeningly mannered poet.[22]

> GENT. She took them, read them in my presence,
> And now and then an ample tear trilled down
> Her delicate cheek. It seemed she was a queen
> Over her passion, who, most rebel-like,
> Sought to be king o'er her.
> KENT   O, then it movèd her?
> GENT. Not to a rage. Patience and sorrow strove
> Who should express her goodliest. You have seen
> Sunshine and rain at once—her smiles and tears
> Were like, a better way; those happy smilets
> That played on her ripe lip seemed not to know
> What guests were in her eyes, which parted thence
> As pearls from diamonds dropped. In brief,
> Sorrow would be a rarity most belovèd,
> If all could so become it.
>
>   (11–24)

This description of Cordelia's sorrow and patience is distant and formal, the complex images and similes noticeably contrived. Her tears and smiles, for example, are compared to rain and sunshine mingled together; her passions to rebel subjects who must be quelled. The most baroque image of all—the comparison of Cordelia's eyes to diamonds and her tears to pearls dropping from those diamonds—is both dazzling and cold. Tonally, the passage suggests a worshiper's awed description of a saint. Though we are being given news of the longed-for Cordelia, the gentleman's reverential words distance her frustratingly from the world of ordinary mortals. Most frustrating of all, the two men drift from their discussion of Cordelia to other matters.

With Cordelia's subsequent appearance, relief replaces frustration. Attention to the stage directions indicates that she enters with drums, colors, and a retinue of followers in attendance. The stage is suddenly energized, and the frustrations of the former scene only heighten the excitement of the present moment. Moreover, certain expectations raised about Cordelia by the foregoing scene are, though not completely contradicted, at least modified by her actual arrival. The Cordelia evoked by the gentleman is a saint; the Cordelia before us is a tender and grieving woman, who is actively bent on finding and healing her father. Religious overtones are still present, as when she says: "O, dear father, / It is thy business that I go about" (IV.iv.23–24), but her language has none of the frosty edge of achieved sainthood, all passion spent. Real tears replace the metaphorical pearls of the gentleman's speech, and her words convey living warmth and love.

> No blown ambition doth our arms incite,
> But love, dear love, and our aged father's right.
> Soon may I hear and see him!
>
> (27–29)

The urgency of the last line captures the longing of the flesh-and-blood child for her long absent father. She is both a healing spiritual presence and a loving daughter, and her words and energy deepen and humanize the portrait painted of her in the preceding scene.

The Kent episode serves as an important aural bridge between two more important scenes. In obvious ways it heightens the audience's desire to see Cordelia once again, especially after Goneril's exhibition of bestiality in the preceding stage sequence; and it evokes a strong sense of Cordelia's spiritual purity. Yet the gentleman's formal rhetoric also suggests stasis rather than action, a symbol rather than a person. In effect, the two men weave a romantic artifice of saintliness about Cordelia that is not quite consonant with our subsequent experience of her warmth and vitality but that helps by contrast to set in relief her deep humanity. If Goneril is too frighteningly real to be dismissed as a symbol of bestiality, so, too, Cordelia is too powerful a human force to be dismissed to the ranks of the angels. As the play's action surges forward after the preciosity of the gentleman's description of Cordelia to focus upon her own words and deeds, the audience's expectations are subtly transformed. The saint who has been conjured up rhetorically takes limbs of flesh and translates love into action. The relief and excitement with which we recognize her compassionate energy are rooted in the contrasting stasis and formality of the context established for her appearance. The audience hears what is vital and active in her language precisely because her words are perceived in the context of the formal and static speech of those who praise her.

The role of Benvolio in the opening scene of *Romeo and Juliet* and the roles of Kent and the gentleman in Act IV of *King Lear* provide a good occasion for summing up some of the points this chapter has been making about the relationship between Shakespeare's aural orchestration, his presentation of character, and his control of the audience's theatrical experience. Most obviously, of course, these bridge voices make clear that in Shakespeare's plays dramatic speech does not always strictly adhere to dramatic decorum in the sense of being an accurate reflection of a particular figure's mode of thought or character. By this, of course, I do not mean that Shakespeare's characters often speak in the "unnatural" mode of blank verse or couplets. We would all grant that much of Shakespeare's dramatic speech is highly stylized or rhetorically heightened. What I mean is that characters' words sometimes become less a reflection of their interior beings than the means by which the continuum of theatrical events is shaped for the benefit of the audience listening to and watching what occurs onstage.

Shakespeare seldom uses his dramatic characters didactically, that is, to deliver a message to his audience. But he frequently does use their speeches rhetorically, that is, as a means of directing the responses of an audience. Because Shakespeare delineates character so sharply, we sometimes tend to forget that his dramatic effects depend, not only upon the opposition and juxtaposition of views that, broadly speaking, are extensions of character, but also upon an elaboration of moods, tempos, tonal shifts, and pauses by which are maintained the live pressures of an intricate audience experience. Generally, dramatic speech serves both purposes: it delineates character and discriminates between points of view while automatically contributing to the total rhetorical shape of the scene at hand. But occasionally we lose sight of the character behind the words as the total effect of the dramatized moment supersedes characterization. When I speak, then, of the orchestration of dramatic speech, I mean more than the simple alternation of individual characters speaking their particular idioms; although clearly this is an important element of orchestration. I also mean to include those many instances in which dramatic figures speak in accents that are not idiosyncratically their own but that serve to shape for the audience the significance of the play's unfolding events.

Clearly, Shakespeare's control of the immense linguistic resources at his command is one of the chief means by which his plays achieve meaningful shape for his audience. Shifts from prose to verse, from formal to colloquial speech, or from meditative to active speech, are more than a means to give a sense of social inclusiveness or the individuality of character. They are also ways of controlling the audience's engagement or detachment from the play, creating a specific kind of theatrical experience, controlling the context within which particular events are perceived, and helping the audience to sense the controlling form underlying successive stage events. In the next two chapters I will continue my investigation of Shakespeare's orchestration of speech and of its opposite, silence.

NOTES

1. Erich Auerbach, *Mimesis: The Representation of Reality in Western Literature*, trans. Willard Trask (1946; reprint, Princeton: Princeton University Press, 1953), 312-33.

2. C. L. Barber, *Shakespeare's Festive Comedies: A Study of Dramatic Form and its Relation to Social Custom* (Princeton: Princeton University Press, 1959), esp. 3-15.

3. Maynard Mack, "The Jacobean Shakespeare: Some Observations on the Construction of the Tragedies," in *Jacobean Theatre*, ed. John Russell

Brown and Bernard Harris, Stratford-upon-Avon Studies, no. 1 (New York: St. Martin's Press, 1960), 11–41, esp. 13–24.

4. The garden scene in *Richard II*, along with other emblematic and "detached" episodes in Shakespeare's plays, have been called "mirror scenes" by Hereward T. Price because they reflect in stylized form the larger thematic concerns of the plays of which they are a part. See Hereward T. Price, "Mirror Scenes in Shakespeare," in *John Quincy Adams Memorial Studies*, ed. James G. McManaway, Giles E. Dawson, and Edwin E. Willoughby (Washington: Folger Shakespeare Library, 1948), 101–13.

5. Mack, "Engagement and Detachment in Shakespeare's Plays," 275–96.

6. John Milton, *Complete Poems and Major Prose*, ed. Merritt Y. Hughes (New York: Odyssey Press, 1957), 378.

7. For a discussion of the two-part structure of many plays, see Emrys Jones, *Scenic Form in Shakespeare* (Oxford: Clarendon Press, 1971), 66–88.

8. Wolfgang Clemen, *Shakespeare's Dramatic Art: Collected Essays* (London: Methuen, 1972), 32–34.

9. M. R. Ridley in his notes to this passage in the Arden *Othello*, rev. ed. (London: Methuen, 1959), 90, says that the only other time in Shakespeare that instruments are said to speak or sing "i' the nose" occurs in *The Merchant of Venice*, IV.i.49, in a clear reference to bagpipes. Moreover, in line 19 the clown advises the musicians to "put your pipes in your bag," which may be a play upon the word *bagpipes*. There is no specific indication of what instruments the musicians play except for these hints and the fact that they play "wind instruments" of some sort. F. W. Sternfeld, in *Music in Shakespearean Tragedy* (London: Routledge & Kegan Paul, 1963), 226–30, argues that wind instruments were associated with the lower classes or with the noise of war, while strings were associated with the healing power of music, with the worship of the gods, and with contemplation.

10. For the intimate relationship of a vice-figure to the audience, see Bernard Spivack, *Shakespare and the Allegory of Evil: The History of a Metaphor in Relation to His Major Villains* (New York: Columbia University Press, 1958), 189. A provocative discussion of Iago's power to "abuse the ear" of Othello, so that the hero believes what he hears and not what he sees, is given in John N. Wall, "Shakespeare's Aural Art: The Metaphor of the Ear in *Othello*," *Shakespeare Quarterly* 30 (1979): 358–66.

11. For a full discussion of the emblematic function of this harsh music as it symbolizes both the discord in Cassio, the sender, and in Othello, the receiver, consult Lawrence Ross, "Shakespeare's 'Dull Clown' and Symbolic Music," *Shakespeare Quarterly* 17 (1966): 107–28.

12. Colie, *Shakespeare's Living Art,* esp. 150–52.

13. For a fuller discussion of this idea, see Edgar Wind, "Virtue Rec-

onciled with Pleasure," in *Pagan Mysteries in the Renaissance,* rev. ed. (London: Faber, 1967), 81–96.

14. Robert Heilman notes that *Othello* is a play in which noise and aural cacophony become important symbols of psychic and social turmoil (*Magic in the Web: Action and Language in "Othello"* [Lexington: University of Kentucky Press, 1956], 113–21).

15. My approach to *Antony and Cleopatra* has been influenced in particular by Janet Adelman's fine book, *The Common Liar: An Essay on "Antony and Cleopatra,"* Yale Studies in English, no. 181 (New Haven: Yale University Press, 1973).

16. Francis Berry calls Enobarbus's description an "inset speech," i.e., a narrative speech embedded within dramatic dialogue that describes an event which took place in a time different from the dramatic now. Berry feels that the purpose of this speech is primarily expository; it satisfies an audience's curiosity about how this noblest of love affairs began. (Francis Berry, *The Shakespeare Inset: Word and Picture* [Carbondale: Southern Illinois University Press, 1965], 46–52.) I argue that, while the speech does perform an expository task, its most important function is to change the mood of the stage moment and to direct audience attention from the Roman marriage of Antony to the magical powers associated with Egypt and Cleopatra.

17. Rosalie Colie (*Shakespeare's Living Art,* 168–207) discusses Antony's hyperbolic rhetoric as an example of the "Asiatic style," which for Antony is not merely an inflated and formless mode of speech but a true affirmation of the sublimity of his love. She suggests that in the play both Antony and Cleopatra grow emotionally and morally into the hyperbole of their language and their mythic models. Eugene Waith connects Antony's expansive rhetoric, as well as his great bounty and great rage, with the Renaissance view of Hercules. (Eugene Waith, *The Herculean Hero in Marlowe, Chapman, Shakespeare, and Dryden* [New York: Columbia University Press, 1962], 113–21.)

18. J. L. Styan (*Shakespeare's Stagecraft,* 110) writes that this opening brawl "demonstrates a device for plunging the play, in quasi-realistic terms, into the civic turmoil of the two houses. Some eleven speaking characters are progressively introduced upon the stage, together with an unknown number of others, in order to suggest the unruly streets of Verona."

19. For a discussion of this sequence as a "diptych scene," see Mark Rose, *Shakespearean Design* (Cambridge: Harvard University Press, Belknap Press, 1972), 44–46.

20. The "revision theory" of the textual history of *King Lear* is put forth in some detail in Michael Warren, "Quarto and Folio *King Lear* and

the Interpretation of Albany and Edgar," in *Shakespeare: Pattern of Excelling Nature,* ed. David Bevington and Jay Halio (Newark: University of Delaware Press, 1978), 95–107; and especially in Steven Urkowitz, *Shakespeare's Revision of "King Lear"* (Princeton: Princeton University Press, 1980).

21. Throughout this book the Pelican edition of the play, based primarily on the folio text with lines found solely in the quarto included in brackets, has served as my copytext. My present examination of *Lear* IV.iii is the only discussion of the play in this book that would be substantially altered if I did not use as copytext a conflation of folio and quarto versions. I discuss aspects of the orchestration of *Lear* in both chapters 5 and 6, using the Pelican text; but my assertions about its dramaturgy rest primarily on features of the play shared by both the folio and the 1608 quarto. It should also be clear that the immediate point I wish to make concerning Shakespeare's use of bridge voices does not depend solely on the example of *King Lear* IV.iii; other examples could be marshaled, though this scene provides an especially clear instance of this particular technique of orchestration.

22. B. Ifor Evans (*The Language of Shakespeare's Plays,* 3d ed. [London: Methuen, 1964], 172–73) feels that the language of the gentleman is oddly conceited and immature, a throwback to Shakespeare's earlier dramatic style. He dismisses the scene as insignificant and anachronistic. I am clearly arguing for its importance as a way of preparing the audience to assimilate the meaning of the subsequent aural shift that occurs when Cordelia actually appears.

CHAPTER 3

Shakespearean Counterpoint

IN THE FIRST SCENE of *Love's Labor's Lost,* Costard is hauled
before the king of Navarre for violating the proclamation that no
man within the immediate province of Navarre's court shall consort
with a woman for three years. The officious Spaniard, Don Armado,
having discovered Costard with the fair Jaquenetta, has sent Navarre
a long letter detailing the circumstances of Costard's indiscretion.
As the king reads this epistle aloud, Costard cannot keep quiet:

KING   ". . . . There did I see that low-spirited swain, that base
    minnow of thy mirth—"
COSTARD Me?
KING   "that unlettered small-knowing soul—"
COSTARD Me?
KING   "that shallow vessel—"
COSTARD Still me.
KING   "which, as I remember, hight Costard—"
COSTARD O me!
KING   "sorted and consorted, contrary to thy established pro-
    claimed edict and continent canon, which with—O,
    with—but with this I passion to say wherewith—"
COSTARD With a wench.
KING   "with a child of our grandmother Eve, a female; or,
    for thy more sweet understanding, a woman. . . ."
    (I.i.238–52)

It is difficult to know which is funnier: Armado's turgid prose or
Costard's response to it. Each is essential to the scene's comic effect.
Armado has spilled an ocean of ink to describe a very simple event

and has committed a host of rhetorical blunders in the process. Ludicrously elevated diction, malapropisms, and redundancies stud his letter. But it is Costard's bewilderment before all this verbiage that heightens the comedy and makes clear just how pretentious Armado's rhetoric really is. With each repetition of the monosyllable, *me,* Costard unwittingly punctures the balloon of the pedant's inflated language and reveals his own earthbound sensibility. For the clown, the whole affair involves "me" and a "wench." His mind can soar no higher. By carefully counterpointing Armado's affected prose with Costard's naïve interruptions, the exchange holds these two idioms in continuous opposition, helping the audience to experience the full comic effect of their clash.

This dramatic segment obviously works too well to require elaborate analysis, but I find it interesting as a simple example of one recurring feature of Shakespeare's dramaturgy, namely, the sustained juxtaposition, within a scene, of two separate lines of stage speech that unfold concurrently and prevent the audience from focusing its undivided attention upon either. Often the two lines of stage speech differ markedly in tone, diction, or emotional intensity, thus heightening the audience's impression of their separateness. For descriptive purposes, I call such continuous juxtaposition "dramatic counterpoint"; and in this chapter I wish to look at some of the ways Shakespeare creates and uses contrapuntal effects in his plays.

In music, of course, counterpoint refers to a composition in which two or more melodic lines develop simultaneously, as in the sixteenth-century madrigal.[1] As Calvin Brown and other scholars concerned with parallel techniques in the arts have noted, musical counterpoint cannot be directly imitated in literature.[2] In the strictest sense, counterpoint in drama requires that at least two characters speak simultaneously. When such a situation occurs, utter confusion is the usual result. The *effect* of musical counterpoint, however, can be approximated on the stage by the sustained juxtaposition of two discrete lines of stage speech, such as occurs when a main stage conversation is repeatedly punctuated by a series of asides. My objectives in examining Shakespeare's contrapuntal effects are twofold. First, I want to show the variety of effects made possible by the creative use of a single technique of aural orchestration; second, I wish to continue my demonstration of the close relationship between stage technique and the audience's responses to the dramatic event.

For the theatergoer, a contrapuntal sequence creates a highly complicated theatrical experience. The spectator is forced to tolerate a deliberate division of his attention and to perceive one strand of stage speech in the immediate context of another. In the simplest terms, such a division usually brings to prominence oppositions in outlook, temperament, or values among stage participants and thereby calls into play the audience's powers of judgment and discrimination. More important, contrapuntal stage technique allows the dramatist to control the perspective from which the audience views stage action, inviting us to identify now with one, now with another, stage party or forcing at times our detachment from both. Sometimes, through the deliberate division of the audience's aural and visual attention, sequences of dramatic counterpoint cause the audience to undergo an experience analogous to the experience of psychic fragmentation being dramatized on the stage. The precise effect of contrapuntal exchanges upon the audience depends upon the particular circumstances in which they occur, but in every instance they invite the audience to become active participants in— rather than passive observers of—the dramatic event.

The simplest contrapuntal effects are created by use of that standard Renaissance stage device, the aside. Bernard Berkerman discusses two major types of asides: the "conversational aside," addressed by one figure to another, but not heard by all characters present; and the "solo aside," spoken by one figure in the presence of others, but unheard by them.[3] I am concerned only with the latter type. Especially when repeatedly used to punctuate a stage conversation, the solo aside creates a simple analogy to musical counterpoint. Two lines of stage speech unfold simultaneously, one taking place between certain stage characters and one delivered solely for the ears of the theater audience. The inevitable result is to change the dynamics of the audience's relationship to the central stage dialogue. Even as we listen to an ongoing conversation, we are made privy, through asides, to observations concealed from other stage figures. The bifurcation of our attention creates tension and gives us a special interest in the speaker of the asides. Why, we wonder, does a character thus separate himself from the others;

and what is the relationship between the asides and the main dialogue?

It has become a critical truism that when Shakespeare chose to have both Cordelia and Hamlet speak their first words in their respective plays in asides, he did so to distinguish them quickly in the eyes of the audience and to suggest potential lack of harmony with other figures. Not only do they turn away from the other characters when speaking, but the language they use jars against the surrounding dialogue. Hamlet's punning words, "A little more than kin, and less than kind!" (I.ii.65), stand in stark contrast to the unctuous formality of the dominant court speech. And Cordelia's simple aside, "What shall Cordelia speak? Love, and be silent" (I.i.62), clashes, by its brevity and understatement, with the fulsome hyperbole of her sisters. The disparity between asides and main dialogue alerts the audience to potential conflict and projects our attention toward the future. We wait to see when—and in what way—that potential will be realized.

A continuing series of asides, of course, produces more sustained contrapuntal effects than those just mentioned and is often used to establish a perspective within the play with which the audience can identify. Not only do the speakers of the asides engage our special interest, as do Cordelia and Hamlet, but in many cases they articulate our own responses to the stage action, thus fusing a conspiratorial bond between audience and stage observer. In *Cymbeline,* for example, when the dim-witted Cloten discusses with his retainers his "success" in a sword fight, one lord cleverly uses asides to undermine his master's vanity and another lord's abject flattery.

CLOTEN   . . . . Have I hurt him?
2. LORD [*aside*] No, faith, not so much as his patience.
1. LORD Hurt him? His body's a passable carcass if he be not hurt. It is a throughfare for steel if it be not hurt.
2. LORD [*aside*] His steel was in debt. It went o' th' backside the town.
CLOTEN The villain would not stand me.
2. LORD [*aside*] No, but he fled forward still, toward your face.
                                             (I.ii.5–14)

As the central dialogue unfolds, we simultaneously hear an ironic and covert commentary upon it. By inviting the audience to join the select company of the witty and the insightful, the asides flatter us. Only we—and not the other stage figures—can share and appreciate the observer's wit and discrimination.

While Shakespeare often uses the aside to reveal one figure's judgments about another, audience sympathies are seldom so unambiguously aligned as in the *Cymbeline* episode. In fact, the complexity of contrapuntal stage encounters typically arises from the simultaneous presentation of opposing outlooks, each of them to some degree engaging audience sympathy or respect. Through the counterpointing of voices, the limitations of each perspective are revealed by the simultaneous presentation of the other. Such scenes force the audience to feel, urgently, what Norman Rabkin has called the characteristic "complementarity" of Shakespeare's artistic vision.[4]

To understand how such an ambiguous contrapuntal sequence operates, let us consider a portion of the second act of *The Tempest* in which the good counselor Gonzalo attempts to put the best possible face upon the shipwreck that has cast his master, the king of Naples, upon a lonely island in the middle of the Mediterranean. Their ship apparently destroyed, the king's son seemingly lost at sea, Gonzalo can, like Duke Senior in the Forest of Arden, still find "Sermons in stones, and good in everything" (*AYL* II.i.17). But his praise of the isle, which eventually leads him to talk of the utopian commonwealth he would like to establish on it, does not proceed uninterrupted.

At every point Gonzalo's words are ironically qualified and undermined by the cynical comments of Sebastian, the king's brother, and Antonio, the duke of Milan. The men do not technically speak in asides, because their position assures that they cannot suffer by incurring Gonzalo's wrath. Their running commentary upon the old man's words represents a simple modification of Shakespeare's basic technique of using asides to divide audience attention and to create the impression of two separate lines of stage speech unfolding simultaneously.

GONZALO Here is everything advantageous to life.
ANTONIO True; save means to live.

SEBASTIAN   Of that there's none, or little.
GONZALO   How lush and lusty the grass looks!
             how green!
ANTONIO   The ground indeed is tawny.
SEBASTIAN   With an eye of green in't.
ANTONIO   He misses not much.
SEBASTIAN   No; he doth but mistake the truth totally.
GONZALO   But the rarity of it is—which is indeed almost
             beyond credit—
SEBASTIAN   As many vouched rarities are.
GONZALO   That our garments, being, as they were, drenched
             in the sea, hold, notwithstanding, their freshness
             and gloss, being rather new-dyed than stained with
             salt water.
ANTONIO   If but one of his pockets could speak, would it not
             say he lies?
SEBASTIAN   Ay, or very falsely pocket up his report.

(II.i.49–66)

Gonzalo's optimistic comments are repeatedly counterpointed by Antonio and Sebastian's derogatory jibes, inviting the audience, at least at first, to assume their perspective. They are clever men, and they ask us to see the old counselor as a genial Polonius, verbose and slightly addled, remaking the world in the image of his own desires.[5] But the contrapuntal interjections of Sebastian and Antonio also betray a smug cynicism that complicates the audience's responses to their remarks. Above all, their wit is parasitic: they prey upon Gonzalo's words and mock his good intentions. By laughing with these two men, the audience is to some extent implicated in their cruelty; and that must cause increasing uneasiness. Not only are Antonio and Sebastian mean-spirited; the audience also already knows that Antonio is the usurper of Prospero's dukedom. We realize that we are laughing with villains.

Ultimately, this contrapuntal encounter brings into collision two contradictory perspectives on reality—that of the optimist and that of the cynic—in a way that reveals the limitations of each. While Gonzalo, the eternal optimist, is clearly the more sympathetic character, the deflating interjections of Antonio and Sebastian unmistakably underscore the old counselor's naïveté. At the same time, his benevolence increasingly calls attention to the spiritual poverty of his tormentors. As a result, the audience is prevented from passively adopting the perspective of either stage party. Instead, the spectator must develop a more complicated and comprehensive point of view, one indirectly shaped by the way in which, through its contrapuntal orchestration, the scene progressively defines and undermines the two limited perspectives it brings into such sharp juxtaposition.[6]

If the aside provides one means whereby Shakespeare creates contrapuntal effects in his plays, the voice of an eavesdropper provides a second means.[7] In a conventional eavesdropping situation, one character or group of characters overhears and comments upon the words and actions of a separate figure or group. These comments may be couched in asides to the audience, but more often neither stage party speaks directly to the spectators. Instead, the audience is usually the final onlooker, overhearing both the words of the eavesdropper and the conversation being spied upon. Again, audience attention divides, in terms of both aural and visual focus, between two sets of figures who share the stage but do not speak directly to one another.

To a certain extent, all audiences expect at times to know more about a particular character or situation than do the dramatis personae upon the stage. Such superior knowledge has customarily been the means for creating dramatic irony. Occasionally, however, Shakespeare uses the voice of an eavesdropper to make the audience particularly aware of its privileged perspective and self-conscious about the nature of its role as spectator. As an unexpected voice suddenly disrupts the audience's engagement with a developing line of stage action, a new frame through which to view that action is introduced. Such an occurrence significantly alters the audience's perspective on the central stage action.

Let us consider, as an illustration, *Richard III* I.iii, in which Queen Elizabeth and the nobles of her faction trade bitter accusations with the queen's great enemy, Richard, duke of Gloucester. After Richard's entrance at line 41, the audience is caught up in their verbal warfare. Midway through this "flyting," however, the audience hears a new voice. Old Margaret, the former queen, has come upon the stage and, unperceived by the others, croaks out a venomous commentary upon the quarrel in progress. When Elizabeth says, "Small joy have I in being England's Queen" (109), Margaret icily interjects: "And less'ned be that small, God I beseech him! / Thy honor, state, and seat is due to me" (110–11). When Richard, referring to the queen's low birth, enjoins her to remember "What you have been ere this, and what you are; / Withal, what I have been, and what I am" (131–32), Margaret comments, "A murd'rous villain, and so still thou art" (133). From the old queen's perspective, the archrivals are moral equals: each has risen to power by murder and usurpation; each has played a part in depriving her of throne, husband, and children. Her vituperative comments bring to life the whole history of unsavory deeds in which both Richard and the present queen have been embroiled.[8]

For the theater audience, the dynamics of the scene change utterly with Margaret's arrival. For fifty lines the malevolent interjections of the old queen prevent us from giving undivided attention to the quarrel between Richard and Elizabeth. Instead, Margaret's presence and her devastating language persistently interpose themselves between us and the two figures who a moment earlier had dominated our interest. As her voice, enumerating a list of past crimes, overshadows the present quarrel, the audience gains an ironic perspective upon that quarrel and a distance from it. We have knowledge that Richard and Elizabeth lack; we see an enemy whom they do not perceive. Margaret's presence brings into sharp focus for the audience the ultimate blindness of Elizabeth and Richard. Oblivious to the doom Margaret cries down upon them, they act out their quarrel in the face of her withering scorn, a situation that makes their fight seem a pointless irrelevancy. Nearsighted players in the drama of history, acting in response to present pressures, they are blind to the larger forces that shape their destinies.

Margaret's arrival and the subsequent contrapuntal sequence also call attention to the theatricality of this stage moment. Elizabeth and Richard play out their quarrel oblivious of the unobserved auditor who is, in turn, part of the larger play to which the theater audience is observer. That larger audience alone has the privileged position of omniscience—or does it? The self-conscious artifice of this segment produces multiple ironies. As actors in a play, the figures onstage are controlled by the script of the unseen playwright;

as dramatic characters, they are influenced by historical and providential forces beyond their full comprehension or control. While the audience's vision is certainly more comprehensive than that of any of the stage characters, are the play's viewers really more free than the actors from the playwright's manipulation or more free than the dramatic characters from intangible forces beyond their ken? Such questions are forced upon the audience by the sense the sequence creates of concentric circles of awareness, each broader than the last, but each also implying the possibility of further circles of still greater magnitude. By emphasizing discrepant levels of awareness and control, the contrapuntal orchestration of the scene creates a situation that confirms the audience's superior perspective vis-à-vis the stage characters, while at the same time calling into question the ultimate extent of that audience's autonomy and omniscience. In recognizing the potential limitations of its own vision and independence, the audience experiences—rather than merely observes—the ironies of Richard and Elizabeth's situation.

In *Richard III* I.iii, Margaret's arrival onstage comes as a surprise to the audience. Through the introduction of an unexpected voice, the audience is suddenly forced to perceive itself and the stage action in a new way. Frequently, however, Shakespeare creates eavesdropping scenes that involve some sort of trick played upon one character by another, and the audience is purposely given prior knowledge of that trick. In a comic context, the audience's pleasure springs in part from its expectation that it is about to see a gull hoodwinked, as when Beatrice and Benedick are each made to overhear tales about the other's love in *Much Ado about Nothing*. In such cases the audience expects a division of attention; the presence of the eavesdropper is no surprise. Yet the contrapuntal potential of these scenes allows for a more complicated experience on the part of the audience than the straightforward fulfillment of expectations.

Let us consider, for example, what is probably the quintessential eavesdropping scene in all of Shakespearean comedy: *Twelfth Night* II.v, in which Sir Toby and his compatriots observe Malvolio's reading of the letter they have dropped in his path. Nowhere else in Elizabethan drama, except perhaps for Sir Epicure Mammon's catalog of sensual delights in *The Alchemist,* does a comic gull so fully reveal his insatiable desire for pleasure and power. But while Mammon's rapturous praise of the life he will live when "the stone" is his depends for its comic effect primarily upon the humor of sheer, unchecked hyperbole, the comedy of *Twelfth Night* II.v arises largely from the tensions and oppositions made possible by the scene's contrapuntal orchestration, particularly the way it both confirms and transforms audience expectations.

At the beginning of the episode, we as audience are implicitly coconspirators with Sir Toby and his friends. We know of their plot; we anticipate, with them, the exquisite delight of seeing Malvolio fall prey to a trick that will expose both his gullibility and his presumption. If, in comedy, there is always pleasure in seeing a pompous fool display his folly, there is even greater pleasure in seeing such folly displayed before those whom the fool has tyrannized. In this case Sir Toby and his friends are Malvolio's natural enemies and have had to endure his censure. That we can see the conspirators and hear their comments throughout the scene greatly heightens our enjoyment of the steward's ignominy.[9]

But the scene takes some surprising turns, which multiply the audience's sources of amusement and somewhat alter its original relationship to the group in "the box tree." Before Malvolio even finds the letter, he embarks upon a long monologue in which he fantasizes about his elevation to the position of Olivia's husband, a turn of events that would be especially attractive because of the opportunity it would afford him to condescend to Sir Toby. Malvolio's monologue has a hilarious effect upon Sir Toby. He fumes, he swears, he sputters. But he cannot rush out and punch Malvolio without spoiling his own trick. Suddenly, instead of simply being privy to a gulling, the theater audience finds itself watching the gull unwittingly discomfit his opponents. We are not only laughing *with* Sir Toby; we are laughing *at* him for the way his trick has temporarily backfired. The situation has unexpectedly moved beyond his control and beyond our original expectations; and the more outrageous Malvolio's fantasies become, the angrier Sir Toby grows.

The contrapuntal orchestration of the scene now enables it to flourish into a full-scale clash of idioms. On one side of the stage we hear the steward, uttering a hodgepodge of pompous phrases he assumes to be appropriate for the truly refined man:

And then to have the humor of state; and after
a demure travel of regard, telling them I know
my place, as I would they should do theirs, to
ask for my kinsman Toby —

(II.v.49–52)

or

I extend my hand to him thus, quenching my
familiar smile with an austere regard of control —

(62–63)

On the other side of the stage we hear the salty and decidedly less
stilted language of Sir Toby and his friends: "O for a stone-bow,
to hit him in the eye!" (43); "Fire and brimstone!" (47); "Shall this
fellow live?" (59); "Out, scab!" (70).

The audience can hear, in the tick-tock of the dialogue, the
unresolvable tension between the mirthless, egotistical Puritan and
his pleasure-loving, earthy antagonists. Malvolio is the dour man
on the rise; his voice, the voice of false refinement, is echoed
perfectly in the love letter that has been dropped in his path. His
antagonists speak with outraged voices from "below stairs," where
decorum is slack and life is celebrated by consuming cakes and ale,
dancing jigs, and singing catches at midnight. The verbal counterpoint underscores these oppositions in temperament and outlook,
heightening the comedy of the scene by focusing attention not only
upon Malvolio's expected display of self-love but also upon the
unexpected reactions of his archenemies, sputtering helplessly in
the box tree. Their discomfiture, highlighted by Shakespeare's contrapuntal stage technique, makes the tricksters as well as the steward
fair game for our laughter.

The basic situation just explored — an eavesdropping encounter
that occurs as part of a trick and is contrapuntally orchestrated —
clearly comprises a fixed element in Shakespeare's stage vocabulary.
But to say this is not to say that Shakespeare simply repeats himself.
Each use of the situation involves a purposeful manipulation of the
dynamics of the stage action to create a different experience for
the audience. In the *Twelfth Night* scene, dramatic counterpoint
serves the ends of audience pleasure, creating from a stock situation
a comic experience that exceeds the boundaries of the predictable

and leaves the audience feeling safely superior to all the stage participants.

The audience's experience is very different, however, when a similar situation arises in a tragic, rather than a comic, context. Consider *Othello* IV.i.[10] Of all the dramatic sequences so far examined, this is the one least open to simple interpretative commentary and the one producing the most painfully ambivalent responses in the audience. In this scene Iago makes Othello an observer of a conversation between himself and Cassio. Othello believes the two men speak of Desdemona; in reality, of course, they speak of Bianca. Unlike Malvolio, Othello, the gull in this scene, is the observer of others, not the observed; but Othello is equally unaware that a deception is being practiced upon him. Again, audience expectations have been primed by the trickster. Iago predicts that Othello will interpret "Poor Cassio's smiles, gestures, and light behavior / Quite in the wrong" (102–3); and despite all our hopes to the contrary, he proves correct. The scene confirms the audience's worst fears about Othello's capacity to misjudge and Iago's capacity to deceive.

This scene has led most critics to comment upon Othello's degradation.[11] The tragic protagonist appears as a pitiful eavesdropper, maddened by jealousy and utterly mistaken about the nature of what he sees and hears. Yet the contrapuntal orchestration of the scene mandates a more complex response than disgust at or even pity for the Moor. Othello is not the only character on the stage. Shakespeare conditions our response to Othello's behavior by governing what we simultaneously hear and see on the other side of the platform: the words and acts of Iago and Cassio. The contrasts between the two stage parties are striking. On the one side we see Iago and Cassio, in high mirth, snickering and scoffing about Bianca; and repeatedly Cassio laughs. On the other side we see the anguished face of Othello, who is devastated by their mirth, and hear the passionate exclamations that their behavior wrenches from him.

OTHELLO   Look how he laughs already!
IAGO   I never knew a woman love man so.
CASSIO   Alas, poor rogue! I think, i'faith, she loves me.
OTHELLO   Now he denies it faintly, and laughs it out.

IAGO   Do you hear, Cassio?
OTHELLO   Now he importunes him
            To tell it o'er. Go to! Well said, well said!
IAGO   She gives it out that you shall marry her.
            Do you intend it?
CASSIO   Ha, ha, ha!
OTHELLO   Do you triumph, Roman? Do you triumph?
CASSIO   I marry her? What, a customer?
            Prithee bear some charity to my wit; do not think
            it so unwholesome. Ha, ha, ha!
OTHELLO   So, so, so, so! They laugh that win!

                                        (IV.i.109–22)

The dialectic of this contrapuntal encounter juxtaposes callous-
ness to a perverted form of caring. Cassio's affair with the "monkey"
Bianca is to him an occasion for mirth. His callous jokes about her
indicate that there is a cheap and tawdry sort of love in the world,
which for some can substitute for the love of passionate commitment. By contrast, Othello's whole being is bound up in his love
for Desdemona; and the violence of his interjections signals to the
audience the psychic agony into which her supposed infidelity has
thrown him. The extreme casualness with which Cassio and Iago
speak of the courtesan contrasts strikingly with the urgent and
impassioned interpretation the Moor puts upon each word and
gesture. They laugh; he anguishes. The contrapuntal orchestration
of the scene forces the audience to apprehend one form of degradation in the light of another.[12] With Iago's help, Othello has
debased his love for Desdemona by doubts, fears, and horrible
speculations; but his evident pain springs from the importance that
love has had for him. Cassio's levity, skillfully amplified by Iago,
signals the shallowness of a nature content with compromise, willing
to separate the act of love from spiritual and psychic commitment.
Had Desdemona ever meant to Othello merely what Bianca means
to Cassio, Othello would not have been experiencing the anguish
we witness in this scene; neither would the play transcend bedroom
farce.
    I am not suggesting that the scene invites a sentimental acceptance
of Othello's horrible folly as a preferable alternative to the thin and
callow stance of Cassio. Such an interpretation is as simplistic as

the suggestion that the scene exists solely to highlight Othello's degradation. What I am suggesting is that the complex orchestration of the scene demands a complex and inevitably ambiguous response. Perhaps it is best simply to say that by insistently reminding the audience of the limited range of a Cassio's emotional life, the scene subtly underscores the depth of the protagonist's feelings and heightens our horror at his desecration of his own best emotions. Shakespeare compels the audience to rediscover the paradoxical truth that "Lilies that fester smell far worse than weeds" (Son.94.14); though a world composed of weeds, while immune from the horror of devastating transformations, would hold few hopes for beauty. The scene does more than show the audience a fulfillment of Iago's predictions about Othello's vulnerability to manipulation. It defines the difference between the tortured voice of the tragic protagonist and the voices of men whose range of feeling and imagination is less great, men whose natures are better suited to compromise and to survival.[13] Such an encounter invites, not a simple moral judgment, but a recognition of the gulf that separates the Shakespearean hero from other men and of the vulnerability that accompanies great aspiration.

If *Twelfth Night* demonstrates the comic possibilities of a contrapuntally orchestrated eavesdropping scene and *Othello* presents a tragic variant of the same stage technique, *Troilus and Cressida* offers perhaps the most complex and puzzling instance of this particular mode of scenic orchestration. In V.ii a lovers' dialogue between Cressida and Diomedes is overheard by Troilus and Ulysses, and both of these parties are in turn observed by Thersites. Shakespeare, in effect, is employing the eavesdropping convention several times over. The central dialogue is commented upon by at least three different observers, all of whom evoke, by tone and idiom, contrasting perspectives on what they see.

This complex interplay of voices leaves the audience with no fixed vantage point from which to interpret the action. We cannot sympathize with Troilus's pain in quite the way we do with Othello's in the last scene considered because, while Troilus, like Othello, somewhat misinterprets what he sees, he is not tricked into doing so and because the other simultaneously unfolding commentaries on Cressida's actions help us to realize the inadequacies of Troilus's own responses. At the same time, the scene does not invite comic detachment. The emotional stakes are high, and Thersites, the figure who invites us quickly to dismiss what we see as an inevitable display of human folly and lechery, seems reductive and blind in the context established by the scene's complex orchestration. In many ways, V.ii crystalizes the central moral and aesthetic problem that confronts the audience throughout the work, namely, the problem of determining what perspective to assume in evaluating the play's events.[14] In its careful management of audience response, this scene stands as a masterpiece of Shakespeare's contrapuntal technique.

In V.ii Cressida is the fulcrum of the action, for it is her behavior that the observers primarily interpret, and until she leaves the stage (108), her conversation with Diomedes holds one pole of our attention. What we see is a woman slowly, reluctantly, but ever so surely sliding into a love affair with Diomedes, a man in whom the elements are so crudely mixed that expediency and self-love remain remarkably uncontaminated by chivalry, kindness, or idealism. Cressida's attraction to this man, her teasing and vacillating banter with him, and her half-hearted fidelity to Troilus suggest that her own emotional equipment is none too finely tuned. She *would* not yield to this new lover; yet she *does*, accommodating herself to the new situation in which she finds herself in the Greek camp.

Yet her expediency and coyness are not altogether surprising to an audience that has observed her earlier manipulation of both Pandarus and Troilus and has heard her say, as early as Act I, scene ii, that "Achievement is command; ungained, beseech" (279). What is of more interest than the further revelation of Cressida's character is the response of others to her behavior. Ironically, the more the observers say cruel and dismissive things about Cressida in this scene, the more the audience is likely to extend sympathy to her, a woman incapable of heroic commitment to a vow and simply trying to carve out a path of survival.

It is Troilus's contrapuntal interjections that place the most damning interpretation upon Cressida's actions. For example, when Cressida gives Diomedes the sleeve that had been a love token from Troilus, the rejected lover is barely able to contain his disgust and anger. "O beauty, where is thy faith?" he asks (V.ii.64), thus equating, as he has previously done, Cressida's gorgeous exterior with her presumed inner worth. Here and elsewhere he invites the audience to see in her actions a world-shaking breach of trust. He has cast her in his thoughts as his partner in a world-without-end passion play, and in his eyes she has failed to be worthy. Finding her no goddess, but mortal, flawed, and mutable, he places the blame for his pain upon her and not at all upon his own misjudgment of her capacities or upon the selfish and unreasonable dimensions of his own desire. His idealism cannot bear the shock of disillusionment, and his response to her infidelity is as extreme as had been his initial passion. He will deny the reality of what he sees—"This is not she" (134)—or completely cease to believe in human worth and so begin a nihilistic quest for revenge and death.

What I wish to emphasize, however, is the way the orchestration of the scene prevents the audience from identifying totally with Troilus's point of view. The extremity of the lover's response to what he sees is ironically underscored and defined by the different extremity of Thersites's remarks. In a wonderful example of double counterpoint, as the audience listens to Diomedes and Cressida and absorbs Troilus's commentary, it also hears Thersites. And if Troilus is the disgruntled and disappointed idealist, Thersites is the gleeful cynic who sees his view of the world once more confirmed.[15] Watching Diomedes and Cressida flirt and preen, he exclaims: "How the devil Luxury, with his fat rump and potato finger, tickles these together. Fry, lechery, fry!" (53–54). Thersites expects to see lust and roguery everywhere; so, of course, he does. Far from being a fallen goddess, Cressida is to him nothing but a common whore revealing her true nature and taking her place in the gutter along with everyone else.

The contrapuntal intertwining of these two voices distances the audience from both and reveals the extent to which each man is imposing, not deriving, an interpretation of Cressida. Troilus in his grief is more sympathetic than is Thersites in his wretched joy at another's folly; but the scene helps us to see that idealism undiluted by self-knowledge and realism can be as destructive as a reductive cynicism and, in fact, can quickly turn into such cynicism. Troilus, the idealist, has taken too little heed of human weakness and vacillation. He is no Antony, able to love grandly and generously even after he sees the failings and mutability of the beloved. He has founded his dreams and his values upon his idea of Cressida, and when she proves mutable his world of ideals comes crashing down.

By contrast, Thersites can see nothing but human frailty. While Troilus reaches for impossible perfection, Thersites reduces all human endeavor to "Lechery, lechery; still wars and lechery; nothing else holds fashion" (190–91). Thersites expects nothing of humanity; Troilus perhaps expects too much and knows himself and others too little. It is therefore no surprise when at the end of the scene Troilus, his world of romantic values in shambles, swings about to a perspective not far from Thersites's own and uses a language that echoes the gutter diction of the cankered satirist.

> The bonds of heaven are slipped, dissolved, and loosed;
> And with another knot, five-finger-tied,
> The fractions of her faith, orts of her love,
> The fragments, scraps, the bits, and greasy relics
> Of her o'er-eaten faith, are bound to Diomed.
>
> (152–56)

What Troilus had valued above all else now appears worthless, though the woman about whom he and Thersites speak emerges more clearly to the viewer's eye as neither the fallen goddess nor the worthless whore the men proclaim her, but simply a flirtatious, confused, and weak-willed person struggling with her own weakness and losing the battle.

The complexity of the scene's orchestration, moreover, is further compounded by Ulysses's presence. As Cressida and Diomedes converse, Troilus comments upon their conversation, and Thersites comments upon the behavior of all three. Simultaneously, Ulysses, after one or two denigrating remarks about Cressida, comments almost exclusively about Troilus's behavior and does so in a way that further underscores for the audience the younger man's lack of control and moderation. Repeatedly Ulysses tells Troilus to calm down: "You are movèd, Prince, let us depart" (34); "You have not patience; come" (40); "You shake, my Lord, at something. Will you go?" (48); "You have sworn patience" (59); "May worthy Troilus be half attachèd / With that which here his passion doth express?" (157–58); "O, contain yourself; / Your passion draws ears hither"

(176–77). At other points, he asserts the reality of what he and Troilus have witnessed, as when, for example, Troilus attempts to deny that it has really been Cressida whom he has been observing. Increasingly as the scene shifts focus from Diomedes and Cressida's tryst to Troilus's reactions, Ulysses functions to underscore the dangerously excessive dimensions of those reactions. Troilus's passions once more are outstripping the control of his reason.

The contrapuntal orchestration of this scene is immensely complex and easily destroyed in production. For example, in one production of *Troilus and Cressida* I saw, the careful contrapuntal balance of the scene was destroyed when the actor playing Thersites also doubled as Diomedes.[16] As a result, Thersites's part was cut in V.ii, upsetting the scene's tight structure of contrasting voices. The only comment we heard upon Cressida's behavior came from Troilus, whose words thus took on a primacy they do not have when they are intertwined with the competing comments of Thersites, and when the young man's youthful idealism is constantly juxtaposed to Thersites's blistering cynicism—the seeming antithesis and yet in some ways the mirror image of Troilus's reductive point of view.

As written, the scene, like the whole play, checks and qualifies easy modes of response. Throughout the work there is no heroic gesture left untainted by anticlimax or irony, be it Hector's chivalric combat with Ajax or Ulysses's speech on degree and order; no strain of idealism not infected with some measure of self-love or willful blindness, be it Troilus's defense of Helen's worth or his love for Cressida, or Achilles's response to Patroclus's death. Every element of the play is slightly at odds with the heroic expectations we bring to a tale of the Trojan war; yet the players in this unsettling drama are not simply reduced to the gulls and fools of Juvenalian satire, largely because the figure who would so reduce them is malicious, self-serving, and reductive, and so checks our impulse to adopt his dismissive perspective.[17]

The double eavesdropping scene stands as a notable example of the play's primary strategy of qualifying simple responses out of existence so that a profound disquiet results. We would rest easier with Cressida's conversation with Diomedes if it could simply be seen as the action of a whore or the tragic fall of one of love's votaries. But the contrapuntal orchestration of the scene exposes the self-deception and reductive tendencies of those who would see it starkly in either light. With the commonsensical Ulysses we must realize that what is, is, and that we must find a way to accommodate ourselves to the unheroic, disappointing, but fully human world of opportunism and weak wills.

By inviting the audience to observe an attempt to glamorize Cressida's fall and invest it with significance by seeing it as a tragic betrayal of valuable ideals, while simultaneously inviting the audience to dismiss her fall and empty it of all significance by seeing it as a reflexive demonstration of bestiality, the scene makes it impossible to do either. In the process it also reveals the universal human penchant for altering reality in ways that serve the interests of the observer. The play will not allow the audience to get away with these simplifying operations. The scene, a microcosm of the entire work, testifies to this drama's power to thwart the viewer's understandable, but reductive, desire for easy judgments and complacent responses.

The flexibility characterizing Shakespeare's use of contrapuntal stage technique leads me, in conclusion, to focus upon what is perhaps the most interesting and novel use of this technique: its capacity to objectify psychic divisions within a particular character. Up to this point, I have been examining scenes in which the contrapuntal voices set against one another largely reflect differences in temperament or perspective among discrete characters. Now, however, I wish to look at some cases in which two contrapuntal voices actually are used to reflect the divided consciousness of just one of these characters. In the simplest cases two or more figures talk together on stage while the remarks of an observer contrapuntally punctuate their conversation. These intrusions seem to express not so much the observations of a third party as the unspoken thoughts of a participant in the primary dialogue.[18] In this way, Shakespeare can focus audience attention upon the gap that frequently exists between a character's public speech and his private thoughts and emotions. When the observer thus helps to mirror some portion of the psychic life of another figure, his own status as a fully realized psychological character becomes momentarily unimportant. Instead, the dramatist uses his words, in effect, to articulate the unspoken thoughts of another character and so to underscore the psychic strains underlying surface behavior.

To observe the internal dynamics of such a scene and its impact upon an audience, consider the initial encounter between Isabella and Angelo in *Measure for Measure* II.ii. Isabella has come to beg for the life of her brother, whom Angelo has sentenced to death for getting a woman with child before marriage. The central activity of the scene is persuasion. We wait to see if the young woman can convince the stern and inflexible deputy to be merciful. For most dramatists the conflict between the petitioner and the stern magistrate would be sufficient matter for the scene. But Shakespeare further complicates its dynamics by the presence of two other characters: the provost and the libertine, Lucio. The provost speaks only twice after Isabella enters: he says, "Heaven give thee moving graces" (36), and "Pray heaven she win him" (125). These asides function as choric comments that broaden the context of the debate and suggest that it enacts a struggle between heavenly mercy and legalistic inflexibility.

The asides of Lucio are quite different, however. In the course of 150 lines of dialogue, he speaks in asides to Isabella ten times, each aside a fervent exhortation to her to assault Angelo more vehemently. When Isabella turns to go after her initial plea has been brusquely repulsed, Lucio cries:

> Giv't not o'er so: to him again, entreat him,
> Kneel down before him, hang upon his gown;
> You are too cold. If you should need a pin,
> You could not with more tame a tongue desire it;
> To him, I say.
>
> (43–47)

Isabella again turns to the attack and is again repulsed, only to be once more chastened by Lucio's blunt comment: "You are too cold" (56). Lucio's comments seem to articulate Isabella's own self-criticism. Part of her is reserved and self-contained, awed by the deputy's authority and very willing to acknowledge that her brother's offense is a serious one. This is the Isabella who speaks with a "tame tongue" as she first confronts Angelo. But part of her passionately desires to save her brother's life and to temper the rigors of the law with mercy. This is the Isabella who, with ever-increasing vehemence and eloquence, again and again importunes the stony-hearted Angelo.

Lucio, lurking on the periphery of the scene and speaking only to Isabella, seems to make available to the audience some of Isabella's inner thoughts and emotions and thus makes comprehensible the changing texture of her overt behavior. At first his is the voice of castigation; then, as Isabella warms to her task, his words become spurs of praise, urging her to press with spirit for every advantage, expressing her own growing self-confidence, and revealing the shrewdness that lies behind her reserved exterior: "Ay, touch him, there's the vein" (70); "Ay, well said" (89); "That's well said" (109); "O, to him, to him, wench; he will relent. / He's coming, I perceive't" (124–25).

The counterpoint between Lucio's asides and the dialogue involving Angelo and Isabella heightens the considerable tension already in the scene by lending it an interior dimension and by making the audience a participant in Isabella's psychic struggles. The audience wonders not only, as it would in any persuasion scene, whether one party will successfully prevail upon the other, but also whether Isabella will bring her outward behavior into line with her inner desires. The two questions are clearly related. Her overt success depends upon her responsiveness to that inner voice of exhortation and encouragement. By having Lucio in effect voice Isabella's thoughts, Shakespeare tellingly objectifies Isabella's self-division and permits the audience to glimpse the psychic resources that enable her—finally—to attack Angelo so vigorously.[19] Throughout the scene, moreover, division of the spectator's attention creates tensions within the audience analogous to those we imagine Isabella herself to be feeling. When Isabella prevails, we experience immense relief, for not only has she won a partial victory over Angelo and a victory over herself, but also her success frees us from the pressures created by the sustained division of our aural and visual attention.

In helping the audience to understand the tension between a character's overt behavior and the emotions and thoughts that underlie and structure that behavior, Shakespeare at times further refines his contrapuntal stage technique by having two drastically different "voices" employed in quick succession by one person. In such cases the contrapuntal effect is *not* created by means of two or more stage figures. Rather, in a striking variation of his usual contrapuntal practice, Shakespeare has a single figure simultaneously pursue two lines of speech. Particularly in the tragedies, the protagonist's voice at times splits into two components, and a central stage dialogue between the hero and another character is in essence interrupted by the protagonist himself. With one voice the protagonist expresses his public self; with the other, some ungovernable portion of his inner life not usually displayed to the world.

Consider, for example, Othello's terrible speech when, having struck Desdemona before Lodovico, he calls his wife back to him at Lodovico's request:

OTHELLO   What would you with her, sir?
LODOVICO Who? I, my lord?
OTHELLO Ay! You did wish that I would make her turn.
         Sir, she can turn, and turn, and yet go on
         And turn again; and she can weep, sir, weep;
         And she's obedient; as you say, obedient,
         Very obedient.—Proceed you in your tears.—
         Concerning this, sir,—O well-painted passion!—
         I am commanded home.—Get you away;
         I'll send for you anon.—Sir, I obey the mandate
         And will return to Venice.—Hence, avaunt!
                              [Exit Desdemona.]
         Cassio shall have my place. And, sir, to-night,
         I do entreat that we may sup together.
         You are welcome, sir, to Cyprus—Goats and mon-
         keys!

                                   (IV.i.243–56)

On the one hand, we have the controlled and confident Othello, the military commander and darling of the Venetian Senate. On the other, we have the passionate, enraged Othello who has been tainted by Iago's ideas and language. These two selves at war are imaged aurally by the splitting of the speech, even the lines of the speech, between the two voices of the protagonist.

Consider, too, the feast scene in *Macbeth* (III.iv), in which Macbeth's language fluctuates with terrifying suddenness between the welcoming words of fellowship he offers in his role as "humble host" and the frightened outbursts he utters before the ghost who haunts his table. Or consider the self-division that occurs when Lear talks to the blind Gloucester in Dover's fields. The mad king by turn rages against the corruption that infects the world's body and preaches the lessons of patience and forgiveness. To Gloucester he says, "None does offend, none—I say none! I'll able 'em" (IV.vi.165); "Thou must be patient" (175). But a moment later he fantasizes about shoeing his horses with felt in order to creep up on his sons-in-law to "kill, kill, kill, kill, kill, kill!" (184).

In each case the hero has reached a point at the farthest bound from the self-possession, the vigorous self-assertion, that characterized his first appearance before the audience. The rents, the deep divisions in the unified self, are emphatically dramatized by the splitting of the heroic voice into antithetical components. And the painfulness of such moments is heightened by their public context. The image the protagonist would project to the world is shattered by emotions too compelling to be quelled. The expected progress of ordinary social discourse is interrupted, not by the contrapuntal intrusions of a commentator, but by the obsessive voice of some aspect of the protagonist's inner self that intrudes upon his usual self-possession.

During such moments the audience is faced with the nearly impossible task of assimilating the opposing voices of the psychically divided hero. The bifurcation of audience attention reflects the bifurcation of the protagonist's self and intensifies for the audience the tensions inherent to some degree in all contrapuntal sequences. The splitting of the hero's voice makes all too clear the fragility of psychic stability, the vulnerability of the social image each person daily projects to the world. To some extent we all long for heroes to be strong and self-assured. We like the Othello who commands armies with ease and the Lear who, even in his deepest suffering, can preach the virtues of compassion.

But Shakespeare's heroes do not simply awe us by the image of superhuman nobility they at times project. In their tragic courses they also discover within themselves mankind's terrible potential for irrational and destructive behavior. The evil they experience or commit rouses within each of them frightening and uncontrollable emotions—Lear's rage, Othello's obsessive jealousy, Macbeth's terror—that shatter the ego's hard-won mastery of such passions. We cannot wish such moments away; they are part of the hero's experience of self-discovery and part of our knowledge of him. But the division of the audience's attention between the two voices of the hero — one expressing willed self-control, the other irrational and ungovernable emotions—creates some of the most terrifying moments in the tragedies. The counterpoint of the two voices becomes an aural image of deep psychic division, mirroring our own profound fears of public humiliation and psychic fragmentation.

Shakespeare's contrapuntal stage technique is but one element of the sophisticated dramaturgy that gives his plays their vitality. His varied use of this technique, moreover, reveals his unending attention to his audience, the unnamed participants in each of his dramas. Each instance of dramatic counterpoint sets in opposition two lines of stage speech that are separate and yet presented concurrently so that the audience must tolerate a division of its attention. This division is always purposeful. It is, in part, a means of controlling the audience's perspective upon stage events and thus for controlling its responses to those events—inviting, at times, identification with one stage party; forcing, at other times, ironic detachment; mandating, at still other times, an active quest for a point of view more comprehensive than the limited or partial perspectives articulated on stage.

Contrapuntal sequences tax the audience and stretch its powers of perception and judgment. They often force us to assimilate two sorts of stage happenings at one time: a quarrel and a commentary on that quarrel; a persuasion scene and a simultaneous revelation of the psychic struggles of one of the participants. Frequently, contrapuntal sequences direct the audience's attention to oppositions in outlook, temperament, or value that are impossible to reconcile and that exert competing claims upon our assent and sympathies. Simple judgments become impossible, and a painful ambivalence may be the only appropriate response, as when a tortured Othello humiliatingly voices his rage at the illusory infidelity of Desdemona while watching Cassio and Iago make crude jokes about a courtesan. Most difficult to endure, perhaps, are those instances when the division of the audience's aural and visual attention points to the psychic fragmentation of a character, allowing the spectator to sense the frightening strains that so often underlie public behavior and threaten the stability of the self.

No matter how Shakespeare creates contrapuntal effects—from the use of the aside to the splitting of a character's voice into two warring components—their ultimate purpose is always the same: to make his plays speak more compellingly to the theater audience. It is to guide the audience's perceptions and to stimulate its engagement that Shakespeare so carefully orchestrates his stage events. His contrapuntal technique is but one means by which he makes the experience of his dramas so compelling and, at times, so painful.

NOTES

1. A useful discussion of the development of contrapuntal music in the Renaissance occurs in Donald Jay Grout, *A History of Western Music,* rev. ed. (New York: Norton, 1973), especially chs. 6 and 7, "The Age of the Renaissance: Ockeghem to Josquin," 172–206, and "New Currents in the Sixteenth Century," 207–51. My formal definition of counterpoint is taken from that offered by Grout, 730.

2. Calvin S. Brown, *Music and Literature: A Comparison of the Arts* (Athens: University of Georgia Press, 1948), 39. After stressing that simultaneity is an essential part of musical counterpoint and hence of limited applicability in literature, Brown goes on to suggest that in drama the effect of counterpoint may be approximated by rapid shifts in attention from one stage voice to another. See 39–43.

3. Beckerman, *Shakespeare at the Globe,* 186.

4. Norman Rabkin, *Shakespeare and the Common Understanding* (New York: Free Press, 1967), esp. 1–29. *Complementarity* is the word Rabkin uses to describe Shakespeare's characteristic presentation, in each of the plays, of opposing elements that are mutually exclusive and yet individually compelling. Such a mode of vision denies the viewer a single, coherent, simple reading of reality.

5. Howard Felperin (*Shakespearean Romance* [Princeton: Princeton University Press, 1972], 259) argues that the varying descriptions of the island reflect the state of mind of each speaker.

6. Wolfgang Iser (*The Act of Reading,* esp. 107–34) discusses the way the reader of a fictional text, by virtue of the wandering viewpoint, achieves a perspective more inclusive than that of individual characters within the text, often including the narrator. Despite the generic differences between

drama and the novel, there are similarities between the reading activities Iser describes and the attempts of the theatergoer to assimilate the partial perspectives of separate dramatic characters and to achieve a coherent "reading" of the action more comprehensive than that of any single character.

7. Bernard Beckerman, in *Dynamics of Drama*, 25–26, notes that eavesdropping or concealed observation scenes occur with great frequency in the plays of Shakespeare and his contemporaries and so become a defining form of dramatic activity for the age.

8. For a discussion of Margaret as a semisupernatural figure and voice from the past, see the treatment of *Richard III* in Nicholas Brooke, *Shakespeare's Early Tragedies* (London: Methuen, 1968), 48–79, esp. 68–72.

9. Emrys Jones (*Scenic Form in Shakespeare*, 24–28) discusses the development of comic tension in this scene through the use of dual-stage action.

10. G. K. Hunter first brought to my attention the fact that the eavesdropping device employed in this scene is most typically a comic convention. Rosalie Colie (*Shakespeare's Living Art*, 135–37) outlines in larger terms the comic themes and stock situations that Shakespeare transforms to serve the ends of tragedy both in this play and in *Romeo and Juliet*. See also Susan Snyder, *The Comic Matrix of Shakespeare's Tragedies: Romeo and Juliet, Hamlet, Othello, and King Lear* (Princeton: Princeton University Press, 1979), esp. 56–90.

11. Harley Granville-Barker's remarks on this scene are typical: "Othello is brought to the very depth of indignity. Collapsed at Iago's feet, there was still at least a touch of the tragic in him, much of the pitiful. But to recover from that only to turn eavesdropper, to be craning his neck, straining his ears, dodging his black face back and forth like a figure in a farce—was ever tragic hero treated thus?" Harley Granville-Barker, *Prefaces to Shakespeare*, 2 vols. (Princeton: Princeton University Press, 1946, 1947), 2:54.

12. Alan Dessen (*Elizabethan Drama and the Viewer's Eye*, 118–19) argues that Cassio's jokes and gestures are harmless and that the real focus of the scene is not Othello's degradation, but the "gap between what is truly happening and what Othello thinks is happening." While Othello's misinterpretation of what he sees is surely an important aspect of the scene, I feel that Cassio's levity is far from harmless and that the counterpointing of voices points to an important contrast in outlook and in capacity for emotional engagement.

13. Maynard Mack, in "The Jacobean Shakespeare," 11–41, discusses

Shakespeare's method of defining the hero's voice by juxtaposing it to the voices of various foils.

14. Questions about the play's genre—it has been called a history, a comical satire, a tragedy, a problem play, for example—are one indication of the problems we have in knowing how "to take" what we see and hear in this work. Is this essentially a tragedy in which Troilus's all-consuming love, Hector's chivalry, and Ulysses's studied speeches concerning political and moral order are to be taken as desirable ideals that are betrayed by human frailty; or are those who articulate these ideals so hypocritical, contradictory, blind, or self-serving that the proper response to a Hector, a Troilus, or a Ulysses is Thersites's reductive sneer? Are we to be sympathetically engaged with or satirically detached from the events we watch? The trouble we have in pigeonholing our responses is highlighted in V.ii and, I feel, is part of the play's deliberate strategy of destabilizing audience responses to the traditional matter with which Shakespeare was here dealing. For a discussion of earlier literary treatments of the Troy story upon which Shakespeare could have drawn, see Robert Kimbrough, *Shakespeare's "Troilus and Cressida" and Its Setting* (Cambridge: Harvard University Press, 1964), 25–46.

15. Rosalie Colie (*Shakespeare's Living Art,* 344) discusses Thersites as "the standard rhyparographer, the crier-up of filth, the crier-down of virtue, whose *persona* speaks in paradoxical encomia."

16. This New York Shakespeare Festival production was produced by Joseph Papp and directed by David Schweizer at the Mitzi E. Newhouse Theater in Lincoln Center and ran from November 10, 1973, to January 20, 1974. John Jones and Madeleine Le Roux played the title roles.

17. In discussing the play, Douglas Cole has written: "Figures and events from myth and legend are set forth in a context which distorts whatever values they may have traditionally embodied, revealing instead a far more cynical network of base or deluded behavior. This context and the method which establishes it may be called 'anti-mythic.' Shakespeare works his materials against the heroic or romantic grain, but always allows the grain to show through, thereby maintaining a constant and perplexing contrast between idealized conceptions of love and war and their roots in baser and more absurd motivation. The effect of this contrast is more profoundly disturbing than the conventional satiric effect of debunking or ridiculing figures ordinarily perceived as admirable or heroic. Shakespeare's artistic choices reveal a far more radical critique of human pretentiousness, a critique ultimately leveled at man's characteristic habit of myth-making itself." See Douglas Cole, "Myth and Anti-Myth: The Case of *Troilus and Cressida,*" *Shakespeare Quarterly* 31 (1980): 76–84, at 76–77.

18. Maynard Mack ("The Jacobean Shakespeare," 26) calls such speeches—in which one character seems to voice some portion of the psychic life of another—umbrella speeches, "since more than one consciousness may shelter under them."

19. J. L. Styan (*Shakespeare's Stagecraft*, 86) says of this scene that Lucio and the provost represent respectively "the forces of anarchy and the law." He remarks on the sexual overtones of Lucio's speeches and seems to suggest that Lucio's advice is suspect because he is a libertine. I would argue that what Lucio brings out in Isabella is a warmth that *is* in part sexual in nature and that *does* make her attractive to the lustful Angelo. But this warmth is as much a part of her as is her rigidity, and it must surface if there is to be any possibility of her growing beyond her life-denying entombment in the nunnery and her lack of charity in responding to human weakness.

CHAPTER 4

Speaking Silences
on the Shakespearean Stage

W HEN IAGO BEGINS in earnest to make Othello suspicious of Desdemona's fidelity, his most potent weapons are the veiled innuendo and silence. Seeing Cassio leave Desdemona, the ensign mutters, "Ha! I like not that" (*Oth.* III.iii.35); but when Othello asks him what he has just said, Iago sidesteps a direct reply: "Nothing, my lord; or if—I know not what" (36). A moment later, however, he again indirectly smears Cassio by saying that it cannot be Cassio who "steal[s] away so guilty-like" (39) at Othello's approach. After the general has spoken with his wife, Iago picks up the thread of muted insinuations; but again he backs away from the direct accusation. In seeming innocence he asks, "Did Michael Cassio, when you wooed my lady, / Know of your love?" (94–95); but when Othello asks why he puts the question, Iago murmurs only that it was "for a satisfaction of my thought" (97). Having thus piqued Othello's curiosity, Iago grows progressively less loquacious, dodging Othello's questions and echoing his words; and as a result the Moor becomes increasingly agitated, finally begging Iago to "Show me thy thought" (116).

The ensign's manipulative strategy is a simple, but extremely effective one. By remaining silent about the exact nature of his suspicions, he invites Othello to fill the void with his imagination and to supply for himself what Iago withholds. The ambiguity of the situation creates unbearable tension. In trying to fathom what is in Iago's thought, Othello's free-floating anxiety can draw forth any number of hideous monsters from his own imagination. Iago cultivates Othello's uncertainty in part, of course, for his own self-protection. Before Iago ever makes an explicit accusation, Othello has, in essence, already imagined all possible accusations and so in part removed from Iago the stigma of pointing a finger. But probably of most importance is Iago's recognition that at times silence is far more suggestive than words. By refusing to answer his general's questions, Iago allows the Moor to thrash about in his own horrible speculations until Othello is so overwrought that his reason is laid asleep and his passions are ripe for more explicit manipulation.

Shakespeare as a dramatist, like Iago his creation, is very much in the business of engaging the attention and guiding the responses of an audience. His art, as we have seen in the preceding chapters, depends heavily upon the resources of language. Yet again, like Iago, Shakespeare at times finds silence a more appropriate tool than words. His playscripts are full of moments when, even though the stage may be full of characters, all dialogue stops. In what follows, I will not be examining Shakespeare's narrative omissions: the things he never tells or delays in telling the audience about his characters and their actions.[1] Rather, I will be looking at the function of literal stage silences, deliberate "holes" in the flow of stage speech. When the plays are read, these aural lacunae may go unnoticed, but in performance they become a vital element in the total orchestration of stage events. My purpose here is to focus upon these silences, paying special attention to their role in engaging the imaginative participation of the theater audience and in structuring its responses.

Of course, on any stage, silence often serves the simple but important function of marking the closure of a dramatic action. In these cases, silence helps to make the rhythm of stage action perceptible to the audience and to allow assimilation of one dramatic segment before another begins. For example, since the eighteenth century, editors have regularly divided the plays of Shakespeare into "scenes" on the basis of each total clearing of the stage. Primarily breaks in the visual continuity of stage action, these scene divisions may also mark breaks in aural continuity between scenes. Unfortunately, these pauses are not marked for specific duration, as in music, and there is no certain way of knowing how long a time, if any, intervened between such scenes in an Elizabethan public theater.[2] Nonetheless, the internal orchestration of *certain* scenes, at least, seems to mandate that, in order to effect a necessary sense of completion or closure, the emptying of the stage at scene's end be accompanied by a marked moment of stage silence.

A striking instance is afforded by the first scene of *Lear,* a scene with a pronounced aural and visual rhythm and preoccupied, in part, with the relative value of speech and silence.[3] Beginning with the low-key private conversation of Kent, Gloucester, and Edmund, the scene swiftly builds to two emotional climaxes, each underscored by certain aural and visual events. First, the stage begins to fill (33) as Lear, his daughters, and his retainers join the three figures already present. Second, the prose of the opening lines gives way to the ceremonious verse of Lear's proclamation of the love test and finally to his thunderous denunciation of his youngest child. This crisis, precipitated by Cordelia's refusal to speak of her love—a meaningful silence that is misinterpreted by Lear—is only "resolved" with Cordelia's disinheritance and Kent's banishment and departure from the stage. But at once a second crisis grows to a head as Gloucester enters with France and Burgundy. Only after Lear's rage has once more flashed forth and France has chosen the disinherited daughter does the stage gradually empty and the language subside once more into prose as Regan and Goneril plot together. The highly charged public center of the scene is thus framed by two private, prose conversations.

In every conceivable sense, the scene follows a crescendo/decrescendo pattern as the stage fills and empties, tension rises and subsides, and language moves from prose to poetry to prose.[4] In this case a sustained silence following the exit of Goneril and Regan seems a logical fulfillment of the rising and falling rhythm of the entire scene. However, it not only signals the completion of one dramatic segment, but also bespeaks the finality of Lear's decisions. After the protestations, the curses, and the impassioned rhetoric of the scene, nothing remains at the end but a bare stage and silence. Because of his egotism and the fulsome flattery of his older daughters, Lear was not able, earlier, to interpret aright the near silence and the plain style of his youngest child.[5] To the theater audience the silence at the scene's end is inevitably a reproach to the rash king. It signals, not Cordelia's loving reticence, but the emptiness left when Lear's passion has run its course and altered irrevocably the emotional landscape of the play. Between other scenes the silent pause accompanying the cleared stage may carry less emphasis, but in this instance it imparts a necessary sense of finality to the total movement of the segment.

Silence, then, can help to impart a sense of closure to specific dramatic segments, but it also serves other functions as well. In writing about silences in music, Rudolph Arnheim distinguishes between "live" and "dead" silences. Dead silences are those—such as occur between the movements of a symphony—which mark the formal divisions of the piece and occur when sound *is not* expected. More interesting are those live silences which have the power to create suspense and to produce strong reactions precisely because they occur when sound *is* expected and thus are experienced as interruptions in the forward movement of the musical structure.[6] In drama the same distinctions exist. The implicit silences that occur between dramatic segments, as between *Lear* I.i and I.ii, produce quite different effects from those aural lacunae that occur *within* scenes where verbal continuity *is* expected. While I do not entirely like Arnheim's term *dead silence* because it implies that somehow the silences which mark the closure of structural segments are not purposeful and functional, it is nonetheless true that more startling effects result when silences unexpectedly occur in the midst of ongoing dialogue.

Perhaps unexpected silences most commonly create tension, suspense, or uncertainty in the listener. As part of a theater audience, each of us quickly comes to expect that the back and forth flow of dialogue will continue until the play's end in an uninterrupted flow of words, words, and more words. Consequently, when this expectation is violated and a figure refuses to speak, to play the "dialogue game," we are startled and may, as well, feel frustrated, curious, or threatened. For example, the disconcerting effects frequently produced by ghosts and apparitions in Shakespeare's plays stem, in large part, from their maddening tendency to hold their ghostly tongues. While the phrase *ghostly silence* is a cliché, it aptly describes the eerie quiet with which these apparitions often meet the most urgent entreaties of a questioner. Macbeth, for example, can wrest no word from the gory visage of Banquo when it appears unbidden at his feast in III.iv. Because this silence is so unnerving, Macbeth himself pours forth a torrent of self-accusation and denials, his conscience leading him to supply what he assumes to be the import of the ghost's unrelenting silence.

While in this case the audience already knows Banquo's fate and focuses primarily upon Macbeth's responses to the apparition's silence, in Act I of *Hamlet* the theater audience shares much of the frustration of Horatio and his companions when faced with the taciturn ghost of old Hamlet. In a vain attempt to elicit speech from the ghost, Horatio intones a mesmerizing incantation:

> If thou hast any sound or use of voice,
> Speak to me.
> If there be any good thing to be done
> That may to thee do ease and grace to me,
> Speak to me.
> If thou art privy to thy country's fate,
> Which happily foreknowing may avoid,
> O, speak!
> Or if thou hast uphoarded in thy life
> Extorted treasure in the womb of earth,
> For which, they say, you spirits oft walk in death,
> > *The cock crows.*
> Speak of it. Stay and speak. Stop it, Marcellus.
> > (I.i.128–39)

Only in performance, I think, can the eeriness of this sequence be fully felt, for only in performance, after each injunction to speak, does the silence of the ghost fall with unmistakable finality upon the ear of each listener. Along with the onstage characters, the theater audience feels the frustration of wishing for a response and failing to get one.

This one-sided exchange adds immeasurably to the mysteriousness of the midnight world upon the ramparts of Elsinore.[7] Why won't this ghost speak? Why is it abroad? Who or what can unseal its lips? Its silence becomes a spur to the worst fantasies of the audience. Knowing neither why the ghost has issued forth, nor from what unfathomable region it has come, we, like Horatio, are left in a state of tension and confusion. Of course, these feelings of frustration, uncertainty, and apprehension are carefully elicited; and their purpose is both to introduce us to the disconcerting elements of Hamlet's world and to enable us later to identify with his bafflement and hesitations in such a world. The calculated use of silence thus becomes a means of creating a very particular audience experience, one in which the unexpected and ambiguous nature of a figure's refusal to speak creates anxiety and tension in the listener.

At times, of course, the reactions of the theater audience to a stage silence will differ from the reaction of figures *on* the stage. For example, at the very close of *Lear*, after the old king's entry with the body of Cordelia, there comes the poignant moment when Lear carries on a pitiful "dialogue" with his dead daughter. He speaks to her, but, of course, no reply can ever again come from her lips. In performance, definite silences must punctuate Lear's speech, probably in the fashion I have indicated below:

> A plague upon you murderers, traitors all;
> I might have saved her; now she's gone for ever.
> Cordelia, Cordelia, stay a little. [*Silence.*] Ha,
> What is't thou say'st? [*Silence.*] Her voice was ever soft,
> Gentle and low—an excellent thing in woman.
> I kill'd the slave that was a-hanging thee. [*Silence.*]
> (V.iii.270–75)

To the theater audience, these silences are agonizing because they signal the final rupture between father and daughter. She can never speak to him again, and for us there is infinite pathos in their one-sided conversation. For Lear, however, the desire to have Cordelia reply is so strong that he actually fantasizes her voice. Her silence is too final, too threatening, for him to bear, so he denies its existence. This is an extreme example of the power of silence to trigger strong, even irrational, responses in a listener whose intense desire for a reply is repeatedly frustrated.

The theater audience, while experiencing the horror of Cordelia's death, does not, of course, participate in Lear's final delusion that Cordelia speaks and stirs. We have to accept what the king tries to deny: that silence can at times represent nonbeing and so the end of all communication. But for Lear, the exchange of loving words with his daughter has become a symbol of their hard-won mutual joy. After his reconciliation with her and their capture by Edmund, he speaks of a blissful eternity of deeds and words that will express their reciprocal, all-sufficient affection.

> When thou dost ask me blessing, I'll kneel down
> And ask of thee forgiveness. So we'll live,
> And pray, and sing, and tell old tales, and laugh
> At gilded butterflies, and hear poor rogues
> Talk of court news; and we'll talk with them too—
> Who loses and who wins; who's in, who's out—
> And take upon's the mystery of things
> As if we were God's spies; and we'll wear out,
> In a walled prison, packs and sects of great ones
> That ebb and flow by th' moon.
>
> (10–19)

In this vision, language becomes the preeminent means of reaching out to another, of sharing and affirming love. When Lear speaks to Cordelia's corpse, her silence shatters all illusions that such mutuality can be enjoyed forever. It is not surprising that, on a conscious level, Lear cannot accept the true implications of her speechlessness. He dies in heroic/pathetic protest against the fact of her death. For the theater audience, the silences of Cordelia define the limits of human will and desire. Lear cannot, despite his desire, will eternal life for himself or his daughter. Her silences climax his personal tragedy, while they symbolize the final obstacle before which heroic aspiration must always bow: the simple fact of human mortality.

The silence of an unanswering voice, then, can be immensely frustrating to listeners both on the stage and in the theater audience. To anticipate speech and to have that expectation denied can be mildly annoying or profoundly painful, but such silences are certainly living components of the drama's orchestration. They call attention to themselves; they produce responses in a listener as surely as would a complicated soliloquy. Moreover, living silences can clearly do more than create suspense or evoke frustration. In certain contexts, particularly when a speaker lapses into silence and seems *unable* to speak, stage silences can suggest inexpressibly strong emotions. I think, for example, of moments such as Coriolanus's silent capitulation to his mother (*Cor.* V.iii.182), Titus's stunned silence before he breaks into hysterical laughter in the face of the astounding cruelty of Saturninus (*Tit.* III.i.264), or Macduff's wordless grief as he pulls his hat down over his eyes in solitary anguish at Macbeth's slaughter of his family (*Mac.* IV.iii.208–10). In each of these cases, Shakespeare makes use of what I call "the Timanthes principle," by which the conveying of intense passion is accomplished, not by portraying that passion indirectly, but by leaving its implicit realization to the imagination of the audience, which thereby becomes part of the creative process.

The notion of the Timanthes principle comes from E. H. Gombrich's discussion of the power of an incomplete image or form to evoke an imaginative response in an audience by requiring that audience to supply mentally what the artist has left unfinished. For illustration, Gombrich tells of a famous classical painting described by Pliny.

> We hear that Timanthes painted the sacrifice of Iphigenia and expressed the grief of those around her in such a masterly way that when he came to represent her father Agamemnon, he had to suggest the climax of sorrow by representing him with his cloak drawn over his face, an enclosed world within the picture's world, which excited the admiration of the classical orators.[8]

In this picture, the draped face of Agamemnon clearly sets him apart from the other figures around him, but his emotions beneath that cloak could largely be inferred by the context established by the grieving faces around him.

Similarly, Shakespeare in his plays at times carefully prepares a context in which the expressive import of a silence can be inferred in a reasonably clear manner by the listener, though the moment is enriched by the latitude left for completing the artist's unfinished form in slightly differing ways. For example, throughout *Coriolanus* V.iii, the hero is besieged by impassioned entreaties from Volumnia, and quieter ones from Virgilia, to spare Rome from Volscian attack. This is clearly a climactic scene: all other ambassadors to Coriolanus have been turned back; an attack on Rome seems imminent. Volumnia is the only one who can possibly sway her seemingly adamantine son, and her pleas grow increasingly emotional, even as Coriolanus grows more and more quiet. That he suffers is clear, torn between affection (24), nature (25), instinct (35), tenderness (129) on the one hand, and his all-important vow of honor (20) on the other. The climax of his interior struggle, however, is not marked by an emotional outpouring of his feelings, but, in the first instance, by a moment of silence. Following Volumnia's long speech (131–82), the stage directions read: "[*Coriolanus*] *holds her by the hand, silent.*"

As theater, the transition from words to silence is stunning. The cumulative emotional energy of the entire scene reaches a climax in this moment of silent immobility. Particularly important, however, is the extent to which the playscript here requires the audience to complete the moment and to invest it with significance. For the proud, emotionally awkward Coriolanus, assenting to Volumnia's request is an act of such enormity that it beggars speech. He articulates neither what he feels nor why he has decided to assent to her desires.

This silence of Coriolanus, like the cloak drawn over Agamemnon's face by Timanthes, is a device for suggesting the existence of emotions too painful, too profound, too unfamiliar for direct expression or depiction. It is, however, also an invitation to the audience, a request that it fill the void with its own imagination. Resignation, weariness, shame, love, a sinking feeling of irreparable loss—some or all of these emotions can be suggested by the face of a skillful actor, but it is the audience alone that can invest the moment with its full emotional resonance. The same is true for the moment when Titus falls silent just before his hideous laughter, or when Macduff pulls his hat down over his face and refuses to speak. In each case, silence becomes part of Shakespeare's expressive vocabulary, indicating, in certain carefully prepared contexts, the point at which speech fails adequately to convey the extremes of human feeling. Such moments plumb the audience's own emotional resources, for they ask us to supply, from an intuitive understanding of what the speechless figure must be experiencing, our own silent completion of the stage moment.

So far I have primarily been discussing various types of "live silences," those which occur unexpectedly within the context of ongoing dialogue and serve as a substitute or replacement for speech. Usually, it is precisely the expectation that speech will follow speech which gives to these silences their power to induce tension, frustration, and projection on the part of the listener or to jolt the audience into an awareness that some things may be beyond the power of speech to express. But there is yet another way in which Shakespeare sometimes uses silence, and that is as an accompaniment to stage action that is deliberately meant to be carried on without words, as in dumb shows or less elaborate bits of wordless stage business. Often, the acts performed in mime are brief and their purpose clear. For example, before the decisive battle of Actium in *Antony and Cleopatra,* two extremely brief scenes occur. In the first (III.viii), Caesar, his army, and his general Taurus come on stage. Caesar gives Taurus directions not to engage in a land battle, and they exit. In the next scene (III.ix), Antony and Enobarbus enter, and Antony tells Enobarbus where to place his land troops. After they exit, the stage directions read:

> *Canidius marcheth with his land army one way over the stage, and Taurus, the lieutenant of Caesar, the other way. After their going in is heard the noise of a sea-fight. Alarum. Enter Enobarbus.*
> (s.d. before III.x)

The procession of the two armies is an obvious means of bridging the gap between the preparations for battle and its issue; and, as a bridging device, the procession is stylized and set off from the surrounding action both by its perfect visual symmetry and by its wordlessness.

Certainly functional as a transition, this piece of stage business is also theatrically effective in creating both suspense and irony. The procession underscores that an extremely important battle is in the offing, but it postpones the actual moment of confrontation. Events are engineered to produce maximum tension. First comes the silent, ominous passage of the two armies; then, creating an effective aural contrast, the bare stage fills with the deafening but undecipherable clamor of a sea fight. From these sounds, the audience knows the decisive battle is occurring, but not who is winning or losing. Only when Enobarbus enters with the astounding news of Antony's flight does the suspense suddenly slacken, as the outcome of the battle becomes all too clear.

Together, the silent procession and the offstage cries economically create tension and prepare a context in which the news of Antony's behavior will come as the greatest possible disappointment. In addition, the passage of the two stage armies creates a visual irony. The headstrong Antony has already declared his intention to fight by sea, even though he is stronger on land. Thus the passing of the two land armies on the stage and yet never engaging in battle, becomes a visual emblem of Antony's lost opportunity.[9] Occasion presented to him her forelock, but he turned aside. As dialogue resumes, the transitional episode past, we recognize just how completely all advantage seems now to have slipped through Antony's fingers.

In this case the silence surrounding the mimelike progress of the armies serves simply as one means of setting this event apart from surrounding action. It helps create an effective theatrical bridge between what precedes and what follows Actium. But there are other cases, especially when Shakespeare employs dumb show and pantomime, when he goes much further in deliberately stripping a segment of stage action of verbal properties. In *Hamlet*, for example, a dumb show precedes *The Murder of Gonzago*; and in *Pericles* dumb shows regularly occur as part of Gower's presentation of the upcoming events in each act. While a good deal has been written about these dumb shows, particularly the one in *Hamlet*, I think it is fair to say that most such criticism deals with the deliberately anachronistic aura surrounding such shows and with their proleptic or emblematic functions.[10] What concerns me, however, is their immediate effect, within the temporal sequence of the play, upon the theater audience.

While watching a production of *Hamlet* recently, it first struck me just how eerie most dumb shows seem when they occur in the context of a more "naturalistic" play. When a play establishes "talking action" as the norm, sustained wordless action must to some extent be frustrating, because it removes one of the props by which we interpret and make sense of what we see on the stage. Dover Wilson spent a good bit of time trying to figure out why Claudius didn't rush from the theater when he saw the dumb show, since it depicts essentially the same events as *The Murder of Gonzago*.[11] One perfectly obvious answer is, of course, that Claudius didn't fully understand what he was seeing; at least, its import was not so obvious that it could be applied as a direct parallel to his own former actions. I would argue that, like Claudius, most audiences watching the dumb shows in *Hamlet* and, especially, *Pericles* do not understand with any precision exactly what they see. Without old Gower's gloss, the particulars of the mimed events in the later play would be largely inexplicable. Moreover, in my experience, the audience *feels* slightly more uncertain of what is going on than the facts warrant, precisely because of the contrast between the play proper and the wordless—and hence more mystifying—dumb show.

What I am suggesting is that, largely because of the unnatural absence of words, dumb shows make human action seem strange and unfamiliar, and therefore eerie. No one who has ever seen Pericles, in dumb show, assume sackcloth and lament before the tomb of Marina or the player queen make "passionate action" over her dead king can doubt that, when played feelingly, mimed actions can be very moving. At the same time, by their high degree of stylization and their wordlessness, dumb shows offer a representation of life in which people appear very much like puppets. They go through actions and gestures, sometimes obviously passionate in import; but they lack the humanizing gift of speech. Nuance, motive, explanations are all missing, because language is missing. On the stage, side by side with more naturalistic action, wordless pantomimes seem primitive both in dramaturgy and in feeling—action reduced to passionate gesture, minus the rationalizations and mediation of speech. Especially in *Pericles,* when the dumb shows seemingly exist to guide and reassure the audience, they actually produce the opposite effect. They make clear just how arbitrary and incomprehensible the major events of the drama appear when reduced to what the eye alone can apprehend. We wish for the explanation speech alone can provide; and in so doing, we become aware both of our terror at the possibility of meaninglessness and of the role language plays in the "making sense" process.

But if there is relief when the dumb show ends and the words of Gower and then the play proper recommence, the eerie and disturbing sensations generated by the dumb shows color how we view the action proper. Sensitized to our desire for words and explanations, we become aware that language can describe what happens to Pericles but can hardly explain it. Through the wish-fulfilling paradigm of romance, Pericles is finally reunited with his daughter and wife, but the impression remains of passionate action without purpose or justification. Like his simulacrum in the dumb shows, Pericles laments, journeys, suffers; but neither Gower nor Pericles himself can quite explain why these things occur and neither can we. After all, even Gower, the reassuring narrator, is merely retelling an ancient story that is essentially out of his control. He is its conduit, not its creator; and the story seems to have acquired a self-sustaining autonomy of its own.

The audience watching the dumb shows comes, I feel, very close to experiencing the central tension of the play. It watches figures whose wordless behavior seems strange, artificial, and not altogether comprehensible. These figures behave like puppets twitched by an unseen hand whose purposes are not completely clear. Frustrated, we wish for the words to start again so these figures will become more like "us," so they will assume more autonomy in our eyes, and so their actions will make more sense. Yet, by making us aware of our need for clarity, control, and reassurance, the play raises the possibility that language is merely a tool with which we hide ourselves from unpleasant realities.[12]

In the total orchestration of a play, dumb shows use silence to set off mimed action from the more "realistic" drama around it. In almost every instance, these sustained pieces of action without words make the audience self-conscious about its dependency upon language for interpreting events and demystifying action. Silence, in other words, becomes a means of heightening sensitivity to language and its uses. I think this is true even in *Hamlet,* where the audience supposedly already knows, from the ghost's story, something of what it is to expect from the interior play and its dumb show. Ophelia, certainly, can make nothing of the pantomime, since she has to ask if it relates the argument of the play; and I believe that the other courtiers and even Claudius cannot make much more sense of it. The theater audience, however, has been primed to expect something like the murder of old Hamlet, so I doubt that the dumb show is as incomprehensible to it as the shows in *Pericles,* though it probably seems every bit as far from familiar "reality."

Nigel Alexander has suggested that the dumb show presents the closest thing we can get to a neutral version of the seminal events that lie behind the action of the play.[13] These events are enacted without explanation, evaluation, or interpretation. Yet I think it is important to remember that, for the dumb show in *Hamlet* to make sense, the audience must see it *through* the verbal interpretation of events given earlier by the ghost. Without that help, we, like the stage audience, would probably be mystified. When words are added, even the old fashioned rhetoric of the interior play, the whole story begins to make sense for the first time to the onstage audience, and eventually Claudius rushes from the theater in anger and fear. For the theater audience, however, the striking thing is that, with the addition of words, the previously narrated events in the orchard begin to make sense in a slightly new way; that is, it becomes clear that it is possible to interpret events in various ways or at least to emphasize different elements in these primary events and so to produce different effects. For example, on the one hand the part of *The Murder of Gonzago* we see has less to do with murder than with the question of whether or not a widow should remarry. The Hamlets, father and son, clearly deem such an action one of bestial oblivion, while the player king considers it natural. Though the issue is not a simple one in Gertrude's case, clearly there is more than one way to view certain aspects of her behavior; and adopting one or the other perspective will color considerably one's view of her. On the other hand, the language of the nephew Lucianus reveals a nature even more melodramatically and absolutely evil than one could have imagined from the ghost's account or from the overt behavior of Claudius himself. How true is this mimesis? The damnable thing is, of course, that neither we nor Hamlet can ever recapture those past events directly. We rely upon secondhand reports and interpretations, and it is difficult to know when a dram of poison is being poured in our ears.[14] Speech reassures us, yet it can betray those who trust it too implicitly. In *Hamlet,* as in *Pericles,* the movement from wordless dumb show to normal talking drama is just one way of making the audience self-conscious about its almost automatic reliance upon language to make sense of what it sees, both on the stage and in the world beyond the theater walls.

Finally, in determining what role silence plays in Shakespeare's works, we need not limit ourselves solely to the moments when a clearly indicated quiet falls over the stage or when actions are performed in dumb show. Shakespeare also makes important use of *relative* silence in the aural orchestration of scenes. By this I mean that in the ebb and flow of dialogue, some voice or voices may be heard with unexpected or unusual infrequency. We are aware of these relative silences for a number of reasons, all having to do with the frustration of expectations that have been aroused and not fulfilled. Sometimes, for example, the visual prominence of certain characters or their importance to the developing action of a scene will create the expectation that they will speak. In these cases, their silence or near silence alerts the audience to something unusual. For example, the lords in attendance at Macbeth's feast in III.iv are important figures. The banquet is for their entertainment, and it is their friendship and loyalty Macbeth wishes to cement. However, for most of the time they are onstage, they say almost nothing— rather, they are given few chances to speak. Ushered onstage by Macbeth (1–13), they then remain silent background figures, while Macbeth speaks to the blood-smeared messenger at the door (14–32). Then their host briefly turns his attention to them; but with the ghost's first appearance (37), Macbeth once more becomes distracted and focuses only fleetingly upon his guests until they leave (121).

At this monstrous feast, the expected colloquy between the host and his guests is displaced by Macbeth's macabre dialogue with the murderers and his one-sided conversation with the ghost. The broken dialogue of host and guests, king and subjects, symbolizes the disruption by this man of deep societal and political bonds. He can no longer feast with other men.[15] The lords become, not participants in a dialogue with their host, but horrified onlookers to his disarray and terror. Lady Macbeth's futile instructions as to how they should act give some idea of their actual onstage behavior. She says:

> Sit, worthy friends. My lord is often thus,
> And hath been from his youth. Pray you keep seat.
> The fit is momentary; upon a thought
> He will again be well. If much you note him,
> You shall offend him and extend his passion.
> Feed, and regard him not.
>
> (53–58)

Her words indicate that the lords have risen and are gaping at their host in amazement. From their bodily reactions and from their near silence at this comradely banquet, we see how completely Macbeth has upset the natural relations of the world around him and severed the natural dialogue between king and thanes.

In a slightly different way, the figure of Bolingbroke in much of *Richard II* speaks with a brevity and infrequency that is noticeable amid the extreme loquaciousness of most of those around him, Richard in particular. We first notice Bolingbroke's laconicism upon his return from exile. Northumberland is one of the first to greet him, and he does so with fulsome flatteries, which Bolingbroke meets with noticeable reserve.

> BOLING. How far is it, my lord, to Berkeley now?
> NORTH. Believe me, noble lord,
>   I am a stranger here in Gloucestershire.
>   These high wild hills and rough uneven ways
>   Draws out our miles and makes them wearisome;
>   And yet your fair discourse hath been as sugar,
>   Making the hard way sweet and delectable.
>   But I bethink me what a weary way
>   From Ravenspurgh to Cotswold will be found
>   In Ross and Willoughby, wanting your company,
>   Which, I protest, hath very much beguiled
>   The tediousness and process of my travel;
>   But theirs is sweet'ned with the hope to have
>   The present benefit which I possess;
>   And hope to joy is little less in joy
>   Than hope enjoyed. By this the weary lords
>   Shall make their way seem short, as mine hath done
>   By sight of what I have, your noble company.
> BOLING. Of much less value is my company
>   Than your good words. But who comes here?
>
> (II.iii.1–20)

Of Bolingbroke's sugared discourse we hear nothing. There may, in fact, be some irony in Bolingbroke's praise of Northumberland's "good words," since he himself continues to abstain from speeches of more than one or two lines until at the end of the scene he justifies his return from exile to his uncle York.

This scene is the first of several in which Bolingbroke remains a relatively silent figure despite his importance in the action. When he meets Richard at Flint Castle (III.iii) and again at Richard's deposition (IV.i), Bolingbroke says almost nothing—Richard even calls him "silent King" (IV.i.290)—while Richard speaks at length and with great eloquence. It is commonplace to say that Bolingbroke, the man of action, bests Richard, the man of mere words, the poet. Yet the issue is not so clearly one of personalities. In the opening moments of the play Bolingbroke is certainly not a silent figure. He and Mowbray are equally outspoken in their mutual accusations, and because of the formal nature of challenge and counterchallenge, they end up sounding pretty much like Tweedledum and Tweedledee. But their verbosity, like Richard's, helps to establish the fact that the court is a wordy place, where words are thought by some at least to have absolute power. Guilt is established by formal accusations and formal trial by combat; and what the king speaks determines the fate of whomever he chooses to judge. After Richard banishes Mowbray and Bolingbroke, he suddenly decides to lessen Bolingbroke's exile from ten years to six. Bolingbroke remarks:

> How long a time lies in one little word!
> Four lagging winters and four wanton springs
> End in a word, such is the breath of kings.
>   (I.iii.213–15)

Words, at least in the mouth of a king, are seemingly powerful things. We experience surprise then, when upon Bolingbroke's next appearance he is made to speak a language notable for its simplicity and brevity. The excessive flattery of Northumberland and his friends only makes us sense more profoundly the relative silence of the returned exile.

Are we to assume Bolingbroke has changed? Perhaps. But rather than focus solely on Bolingbroke's psychology, we might also consider how the figure of Bolingbroke is used at various points in the play to reveal a larger dramatic meaning; in particular, how Shakespeare employs him to chart the crumbling of an old order and the establishment of a new one.[16] In the opening moments of the play the atmosphere of Richard's court, its medieval formality and preoccupation with traditional forms of behavior, presses in upon us.

Bolingbroke and Mowbray's rhetoric forms part of an elaborately formal quarrel. Attention centers, not upon the differences between the two disputants, but upon the elaborate verbal and social mechanisms used to mediate their quarrel. Then the long second portion of the play, stretching from Bolingbroke's return to his coronation, pits his relative silence in opposition to Richard's continuing addiction to words and traditional formulae.[17]

Having used Bolingbroke to help create a particular world in the opening scenes of the play, Shakespeare then uses Bolingbroke to embody a challenge to that world. We can personalize that challenge by describing it in a number of ways: the man of action versus the contemplative, the Machiavellian versus the ruler by divine right, the opportunist versus the poet. Depending upon the supporting details we choose, any of these formulations may help to explain the play's central agon. Yet Bolingbroke remains deliberately enigmatic as a figure. His near silence is less the means of characterizing him than of establishing him as counterforce to Richard. What is *primary* is the stage effect created by the opposition of manner between the two men in this middle portion of the play. We may then read back out of this opposition a variety of meanings or explanations.

I wish to emphasize that, as with so many other dramaturgical devices in Shakespeare's plays, the unexpected near silence of a particular character may create an important local effect, but may not necessarily contribute to consistency of characterization. The silence or near silence is a way of calling attention to a potentially important stage moment. Why this silence? But before interpretation comes the simple perception of something unusual and striking occurring onstage. To attempt to explain the purpose of all such silences by recourse to character analysis is futile.

For example, we are accustomed to think of Horatio as the nearly silent companion to Hamlet, especially because in crucial scenes, such as that in the graveyard, his replies are typically brief—"E'en so, my lord" (*Ham.* V.i.189). As a foil to Hamlet, Horatio sets off Hamlet's mercurial and speculative temperament by his own phlegmatic stoicism, and Hamlet's loquacity by his own meagerness of words. At least that is so in many major scenes of the play—in particular, the graveyard scene and the scene that precedes the play within the play. But a quite different Horatio is on display when the play opens upon the battlements at Elsinore. Then he is loquacious, describing recent events in Denmark, painting in vivid detail the horrible portents in Rome before Caesar's death, and even, with Marcellus, introducing a note of hushed lyricism, after the ghost has departed, by his description of the cock, "trumpet to the morn" (I.i.150). The alternating impulses of terror and wonder that catch at us in this opening scene depend largely upon the expressiveness of the poetry spoken by Horatio. Yet, later this same figure becomes the taciturn foil to the wordy prince.

This inconsistency is certainly not a great one. In fact, in reading or seeing the play we would probably not remark upon it, simply because each dramatic moment absorbs our attention to a degree that precludes detailed retrospection. A character may play one role in the dynamic of a given scene and a different role in the dynamic of another. The demands of the given moment are of primary importance.[18] Of course, we must remember that at all times Horatio is a supportive figure, not the dramatic center of interest. He never reveals to us, as does Hamlet, his intimate feelings and thoughts. Though his character in its broad outlines retains a loose unity, Horatio's primary function is to help us understand Prince Hamlet and the changing ambiance of various stage moments, not to be himself the dramatic center of interest. We demand a less unified and consistent portrait of him than of those characters with whom we are more intimately engaged.

In conclusion, the silences and the near silences of Shakespeare's plays serve important purposes. Performance, of course, is a prerequisite for their effectiveness. To serve an expressive function or to foreground some potentially important circumstance, a silence must to some degree be noticed. It must call attention to itself to become, amid the ebb and flow of speech, an active element in the dramatist's communication with the audience. And it is precisely because silence runs counter to our predominant expectation that speech will follow speech that it can produce powerful effects if skillfully used. Silence can frustrate, tantalize, and spur the imaginative participation of the audience. It can make us aware of how much we rely on language to rationalize experience and demystify it through explanations. In every sense, silence is a living component of Shakespeare's orchestration of stage events and of our responses.

NOTES

1. Alwin Thaler, in *Shakespere's Silences* (Cambridge: Harvard University Press, 1929), 3–63, largely deals with such narrative omissions and with verbal reticence as a means of characterization. For a focus closer to my own, see the brief discussion by J. L. Styan, in *Shakespeare's Stagecraft,* 105–8 and 189–92, concerning actual silences that occur in the midst of dialogue.

2. Harley Granville-Barker, for example, believed that Shakespeare's plays were meant to be performed continuously with few or no breaks between our present acts and scenes. He de-emphasized whatever pauses may have occurred with the clearing of the stage by suggesting that new characters frequently would enter before figures from the preceding scene had completed their exits. Granville-Barker's ideas on Shakespearean production are most fully presented in his *Prefaces to Shakespeare.* A useful synopsis is provided by his article, "Shakespeare's Dramatic Art," in *A Companion Guide to Shakespeare Studies,* ed. Harley Granville-Barker and G. B. Harrison (1934; reprint, New York: Anchor Books, 1960), 44–87. Bernard Beckerman (*Shakespeare at the Globe,* 176–77), however, points out that such overlapping between scenes can by no means be accepted as a certainty. He feels that the need to change some stage properties even on the Elizabethan stage and the effect of closure imparted by the rhymed couplets at the end of many scenes may have encouraged the insertion of slight pauses between them.

3. For an excellent discussion of what silences mean in *King Lear,* see Jill Levenson, "What the Silence Said: Still Points in *King Lear,*" in *Shakespeare 1971: Proceedings of the World Shakespeare Congress,* ed. Clifford Leech and J. M. R. Margeson (Toronto: University of Toronto Press, 1972), 215–29.

4. Granville-Barker's comments on *Lear* first drew my attention to the fact that Goneril and Regan's shift into prose loosens the tension from the foregoing dramatic climax and parallels the low-key opening moments of the scene (*Prefaces to Shakespeare,* 1:272).

5. For its discussion of court language and various counterlanguages in *King Lear,* I found extremely valuable Sheldon Zitner's "*King Lear* and Its Language," in *Some Facets of "King Lear": Essays in Prismatic Criticism,*

ed. Rosalie Colie and F. T. Flahiff (Toronto: University of Toronto Press, 1974), 3–22.

6. Rudolph Arnheim says, in *Art and Visual Perception: A Psychology of the Creative Eye. The New Version* (Berkeley: University of California Press, 1974), 382, "when the structure of a piece is interrupted by silence, the heartbeat of the music seems to have stopped and the immobility of what should be motion creates suspense."

7. For a classic discussion of the "world" of this play, see Maynard Mack, "The World of *Hamlet*," *Yale Review* 41 (1951–52): 502–23.

8. E. H. Gombrich, *Art and Illusion: A Study in the Psychology of Pictorial Representation,* rev. ed., Bollingen series, no. 35 (Princeton: Princeton University Press, 1961), 139–40.

9. This particular stage sequence offers an excellent example of what Maurice Charney has called Shakespeare's "presentational imagery," the "significant language of gesture and stage properties which communicates meaning to us" in nonverbal ways (*Shakespeare's Roman Plays: The Function of Imagery in the Drama* [Cambridge: Harvard University Press, 1961], 8). More recently, Alan Dessen has convincingly argued that Elizabethan drama made important and constant use of the visual elements of performance to guide the viewer's eye to the comprehension of dramatic meaning (*Elizabethan Drama and the Viewer's Eye,* esp. 3–31). I will have more to say about the orchestration of visual effects in the next chapter. Here I am concerned not only with the visual information conveyed by this mimelike sequence, but also with the importance of the silence in calling attention to and setting off this "speaking picture" from surrounding events.

10. The best introduction to the role of dumb shows in Elizabethan theater is provided by Dieter Mehl in *The Elizabethan Dumb Show: The History of a Dramatic Convention* (London: Methuen, 1965), first published as *Die Pantomime im Drama der Shakespearezeit* (Heidelberg: Quelle & Meyer, 1964). Lee Sheridan Cox, in *Figurative Design in "Hamlet": The Significance of the Dumb Show* (Columbus: Ohio State University Press, 1973), 3–15, usefully summarizes some of the critical problems posed by the dumb show in *Hamlet* and various solutions that have been offered to those problems. Cox himself argues that the mime has symbolic functions, and he links the dumb show to empty, meaningless action of the sort opposed throughout the play to the "action that gives substance to a performance on the world stage" (31). My focus differs from Cox's in that he is concerned with the place of the show in the symbolic design of the entire play; I am concerned with the immediate effect of wordless action on viewers accustomed to the conjunction of acts and words.

11. Dover Wilson (*What Happens in "Hamlet,"* 3d ed. [Cambridge: Cambridge University Press, 1951], 144–63) concludes that the dumb show was added by the players, to Hamlet's annoyance, and was not seen by Claudius, who was busy talking to others onstage. Wilson assumes that if the king *had* seen the show, it would have been clear and explicable. It is that assumption which I wish to question.

12. Approaching the play from a quite different perspective, Phyllis Gorfain, in "Puzzle and Artifice: The Riddle as Metapoetry in *Pericles,*" *Shakespeare Survey* 29 (1976): 11–20, sees *Pericles* as a work in which riddles point to the "necessary but arbitrary ways we organize experience" (12) and emphasizes the role of language in creating reassuring fictions of order.

13. Nigel Alexander, *Poison, Play, and Duel: A Study in "Hamlet"* (Lincoln: University of Nebraska Press, 1971), 107–8.

14. In a provocative discussion of *Hamlet,* Howard Felperin suggests that the prince himself is prone to use language to interpret a complex and mysterious reality in terms of the simple and distortive paradigms of a morality play, particularly in the confrontation with his mother in her closet. See Howard Felperin, *Shakespearean Representation: Mimesis and Modernity in Elizabethan Tragedy* (Princeton: Princeton University Press, 1977), 44–67. I am arguing that the transition from the dumb show to *The Murder of Gonzago* proper is one of the means by which Shakespeare makes his audience conscious of the ways in which language as a sense-making tool can distort, simplify, or transform the events it purports neutrally to describe.

15. Rose, *Shakespearean Design,* 160–61.

16. Maynard Mack, Jr., *Killing the King: Three Studies in Shakespeare's Tragic Structure,* Yale Studies in English, no. 180 (New Haven: Yale University Press, 1973), 15–74.

17. For an excellent discussion of Richard's tendency to use language to "construct elaborate mazes of ideas or to play off the senses of words against each other, and to immobilize active thought," see James Winny, *The Player King: A Theme of Shakespeare's Histories* (London: Chatto & Windus, 1968), 62.

18. As Dessen says in *Elizabethan Drama,* p. 163, "we cannot flatly assume that every event in an Elizabethan play is part of a psychological progression, an unfolding of character as in a novel by Henry James. As noted in the previous chapter, minor figures (like Philario or Priam) or even major figures (like Cleopatra or Hector) can for a moment cease to be important as individuals but instead can participate in some larger, shared effect achieved by an entire scene or grouping."

CHAPTER 5

Bodies and Movement:
The Orchestration of the
Visual Spectacle

U P TO THIS POINT I have focused primarily on Shakespeare's aural art: his complex manipulation of speech and silence during the implied theatrical event. But, of course, the ear is not the only organ through which the audience assimilates a performed play. Drama is also addressed to the viewer's eye, and it is to the visual orchestration of Shakespeare's plays that I now wish to turn, though not without a caveat. The distinction between visual and aural effects, while clear in theory, often becomes blurred in performance. In contrapuntal stage sequences, for example, the audience hears two discrete lines of stage speech unfolding simultaneously; but the division of audience attention is frequently reinforced at the visual level, as well. Thus, in eavesdropping scenes, the eye of the viewer must move repeatedly back and forth between two quite separate stage parties.

As this case suggests, it is often difficult to disentangle what a complex theatrical effect owes to Shakespeare's management of the aural aspects of performance, from what it owes to his orchestration of the visual spectacle. While there are some dramatic events, such as pantomimes, in which visual action clearly takes precedence over speech, such moments are infrequent; moreover, as we saw in the last chapter, they often gain their power to move us from the very fact that we perceive the absence of language in them to be unnatural or unexpected. Certainly, too, there are crowd scenes, processions,

101

and stage rituals of pomp and circumstance in which a number of actors appear but do not speak. As Prufrock says, they help to "swell a progress"; their bodies are used to create a certain visual spectacle, but they remain silent. Usually, however, when characters come on stage, they speak. They gratify both the ear and the eye of the spectator; and the orchestration of voices and bodies, the aural and the visual, proceeds simultaneously.

In this chapter I am going to be examining some of the elements of Shakespeare's meaningful choreography of stage spectacle, but as I do so I will have frequent occasion to mention how visual strategies are reinforced by Shakespeare's handling of the aural and kinetic dimensions of performance. Here, as elsewhere, I am less concerned with establishing an exhaustive catalog of techniques and effects than with demonstrating the integral and controlled relationship between Shakespeare's management of performance elements and the creation of a meaningful and intelligible theatrical experience for the audience.

When we think about the way in which Shakespeare handles the visual elements of performance, we think, first, perhaps, of those many moments—every student of Shakespeare can name dozens of them—when dramatic meaning is crystallized by a striking visual tableau of "speaking picture." I think, for example, of the moment when the statue of Hermione moves (*WT* V.iii.103), the "faith" of the audience giving life to the immobile work of art; or of the descent of King Richard from the walls of Flint Castle to the base court (*R2* III.iii.178–83), that simple action capturing at once the abasement of a proud man and the fall of a medieval idea of kingship. Mark Rose has argued forcefully that Elizabethan audiences would have been fully attuned to the thematic significance of such speaking pictures, and other scholars have shown how individual visual tableaux carry an increased weight of significance because of their roots in the emblem tradition or their origins in earlier dramatic works, such as morality plays or Tudor interludes.[1]

Important as are these individual visual tableaux, especially when resonance accrues to them from a prior stage history, the orchestration of the visual elements of performance involves much more than the creation of discrete speaking pictures to be read for their thematic or emblematic content. One actor appears, then another, then a group. Visual symmetry may be momentarily established between two stage parties only to be shattered by the arrival of a messenger or a third party. An ordered and ceremonial buildup of characters on the stage may be followed by a succession of short, choppy scenes in which actors barely command attention before they are gone. To talk meaningfully of Shakespeare's visual orchestration one must come to terms with the fluid qualities of his visual stagecraft, not just his creation of a few powerful, but isolated, stage tableaux.[2] In part, as Shakespeare varies the number of figures onstage, as he slows or quickens the pace of the visual action, as he aligns and realigns his actors in various stage groups and configurations, inevitably he highlights—through visual repetition, contrast, or climax—points of significance for his audience. One of my objectives in this chapter is to explore in some detail just how changes in the visual spectacle perform this function of directing audience attention to important events, motifs, or lines of action. At the same time I will be arguing that Shakespeare's management of the unfolding visual spectacle aims, in part, at creating kinetic effects that are of themselves an important aspect of dramatic meaning; that is, the very pace of the events we watch and changes in the tempo of the visual spectacle are meaningful; and their manipulation is an important instrument in guiding audience response.

Consider, for example, the complex effects created by both the design and the pace of visual events in *Othello* I.iii, the scene in the Venetian council chamber. This is one of many scenes in Shakespeare that are structured, visually, in terms of a definite climactic pattern. Typically in such scenes one or two characters enter, then several more, then others, until finally the stage is full of figures, some of whom may have no lines to speak. Gradually, then, these same figures leave, until only one or two are left, the rhythm by which the stage fills and empties contributing to the viewer's sense of climax and resolution within the scene's action. Clearly such visual structures emphasize or foreground the last figure(s) to enter.

This is true when Desdemona appears in the Venetian council chamber. Before her arrival, the scene brings before the audience a succession of characters: first the duke and senators, then a sailor, then a messenger, then Brabantio, Othello, Cassio, Iago, Roderigo, some officers, and finally Desdemona, whom Iago has been sent to fetch. Her climactic entrance, long delayed, stresses her importance. She is a woman entering the territory of men, but by her dignity and forceful speech she sets right their disputes and fortifies the position of her chosen husband. Only after she has had her full say does the scene unwind with the successive departures of the duke and his senators, then Othello and Desdemona, and finally Iago and Roderigo.

At the same time that this climactic visual structure highlights Desdemona's centrality, the slow-paced and orderly succession of entrances and exits conveys to the viewer a general sense of order, hierarchy, and control. *Othello* begins with darkness, confusion, and obscenities.[3] Characters break the peace of sleeping Venice with shouts and lewd insinuations and seek each other by the flickering light of torches. By contrast, the council chamber is a place of light and order. Uncertainty is present there (where, for example, are the Turks really headed?) and acrimony (Brabantio's anger at Othello and Iago's malice), but the scene as a whole suggests that within the confines of this chamber, uncertainty, turmoil, and anger can be controlled and contained. Shakespeare's handling of the visual elements of the scene contributes to this impression by giving to the visual action a clear and orderly climactic structure and by placing it within the lighted council hall. This is quite different from the chaotic and half-seen comings and goings of I.i and I.ii.

Not all scenes, however, that employ a climactic visual organization affect the audience as does *Othello* I.iii. The opening segment of *Romeo and Juliet,* for example, in which a servants' quarrel blossoms into a full-fledged sword fight, brings a succession of ever more important characters onto the stage. But by the way it is orchestrated, the segment suggests haste, violence, and tension, rather than order and control. The reason is obvious. Everything happens much more quickly in this dramatic segment than in the council chamber scene in *Othello.* Characters enter hard on the heels of one another, many speeches are only one or two lines long, and they are increasingly spat out as swords are flashing about. The result is a visual spectacle of constant, rapid motion, until the climactic entrance of Prince Escalus quells the brawl.

By contrast, in *Othello* I.iii, the whole pace of the scene is slower; speeches are longer; and Desdemona does not enter until line 170, while Prince Escalus enters at line 78 of his scene. Moreover, a different context has been established for viewing the two scenes. *Othello* opens with scenes of darkness and confusion; so the council chamber events appear, in contrast, more orderly than what precedes them. The audience viewing *Romeo and Juliet* I.i has only heard the generalized statement of the chorus about the play's plot and themes. Suddenly that audience is introduced to a rapid succession of unfamiliar characters, distinguished, probably, by their liveries into two opposing factions, but waving swords and shouting threats in a way that suggests confusion and a dangerous breakdown of order.

I highlight these obvious differences as a reminder that in the theater the pace of visual events is as important as their order or overarching design. Dramatic art differs from pictorial art in part by the very fact that on the stage the "pictures" move; and the rapidity of these movements, the way in which the dramatist varies their tempo and pace, is an important aspect of his orchestration of the stage spectacle. Thoughout this chapter, therefore, I will focus less on isolated visual tableaux—dramatic moments lifted from context and examined for their emblematic or thematic significance—than on Shakespeare's purposeful management of an ever-changing visual continuum in which both the nature and the pace of what we see undergo repeated alteration.

In manipulating the changing visual spectacle to guide audience perception and response, Shakespeare often organizes successive stage moments to create strong visual contrasts between one part of a scene and the next. He may, for example, use the entrance of an unexpected figure to alter markedly the pace and nature of a scene's visual events in ways that help an audience understand the larger implications of the figure's arrival.[4] Consider, for example, the effect on the scene's visual dynamics of Richard's arrival in the middle of *Richard III* II.i. This is a scene in which King Edward, who is near death, attempts to heal the conflicts and rivalries that threaten the peace of his court. In the first forty-six lines of the scene, the queen and various nobles cluster about the sick king and vow to forgive one another and to live in harmony. The visual symbols of concord become the kiss and the embrace, as one courtier after another turns to his former enemies with these gestures of renewed affection.

At line forty-six Richard enters with Ratcliffe and changes everything with his announcement of Clarence's death, though not before he mouths a few pious hypocrisies about laying aside his own grudges and seeking all men's love. When he finally reveals his real message — "Who knows not that the gentle duke is dead?" (80) — the stage directions read: "*They all start.*" There are now no more embraces, no more kisses, only suspicion, disbelief, and fragmentation. The shocked king, unnerved by this announcement and by Stanley's ironic request for mercy for a servant, can no longer exercise the function of peacemaker and retires in disarray to mourn and soon to die. Significantly, Buckingham, who had shortly before embraced the queen, now stays with Richard when the others follow the king. The old factions have been reestablished, and concord has been destroyed as swiftly as it had been achieved. The visual contrasts established in the course of the scene are subtle but real, and they help to underscore for the audience the impact of Richard on his society. Before his arrival people are drawing together; after his arrival they fragment once more into suspicious, warring camps. He is the destroyer of all social concord, and not until Richmond's triumph is England again to know social peace.

Using the arrival of an unexpected figure to disrupt the visual continuity of a scene and to create visual contrasts between successive stage moments is a device Shakespeare employs in a variety of disparate scenes. In *Coriolanus* I.i, Menenius's increasingly successful efforts to calm an angry mob by humor and good sense are shattered by Coriolanus's abrupt and disruptive arrival. In *Macbeth* III.iv, the appearance of Banquo's ghost breaks the composure of Macbeth and the social harmony symbolized by the gathering of figures around the banquet table. In *As You Like It* II.vii, Orlando enters, sword in hand, to disrupt a scene of communal feasting; although in this case the pastoral community absorbs, rather than is fractured by, the intruder, and the scene ends with both his and old Adam's assimilation into the festive society briefly disrupted by his appearance. In *The Tempest* IV.i, not an actual intruder, but the obtrusive thought of Caliban's conspiracy, enters Prospero's mind and causes him to banish the festive wedding masque and send

Ferdinand and Miranda to his cell so that he can turn his attention to the punishment of Caliban and his clownish coconspirators.

In each of these cases, the pace and nature of visual events before the intruder's arrival contrast markedly with the pace and nature of succeeding visual events in ways that help the audience understand the larger significance of the intruding figure and his impact upon individuals and social structures. In each instance, pressures that have been excluded from a scene gain admittance with the arrival of the unexpected figures, and the results are often immediately apparent in the visual realignment of characters on the stage. One can multiply such examples indefinitely, but they all point to the fact that in Shakespearean drama the management of the visual spectacle is purposeful and not random; it is one means by which the audience absorbs, sometimes almost subliminally, the significance of unfolding events.

Visual contrasts, of course, can occur between scenes as well as within them; and on the Shakespearean stage a key form of visual contrast is the simple juxtaposition of dramatic segments involving many actors and those involving a few figures or even a solitary actor. These variations are possible because, by the standards of today's pinched Broadway casts, Shakespeare's plays call for a large number of actors. Sometimes one figure may be on the stage, and sometimes ten or twelve. Clearly an easy way to stimulate audience attention is to vary the number of characters onstage in successive dramatic segments. Yet such variations usually do much more than refresh the jaded visual appetite of the spectator; through them Shakespeare can create kinetic effects of great power and can control the focus of audience attention in ways that subtly contribute to the spectator's understanding of dramatic meaning.

Hamlet is one play that makes unusually sophisticated use of variations in the number of figures on the stage at any time. When one thinks of that play in performance, one often thinks first of a solitary figure speaking in passionate soliloquy. Hamlet, rivaled only by Macbeth as a speaker of soliloquies, receives his signature as a meditative man from his repeated use of this device.[5] Moreover, his soliloquies are delivered in a manner that stresses his intense isolation. Unlike those Machiavellian plotters, Richard III or Iago, Hamlet in his solo speeches does not address himself directly to an

107

audience.[6] Iago and Richard, revealing their tie to the vice of the morality play, present their villainies with a relish and beckon the audience closer to admire their handiwork.[7] By contrast, Hamlet speaks to himself. We overhear his thoughts; we are not his chosen confidants. The difference is important, because if Hamlet does not invite us to share his confidences, for that very reason we feel that his soliloquies reveal more of his private being than do the more public soliloquies of an Iago or a Richard III.

Indelibly impressed, then, on the memory of anyone who has ever seen *Hamlet* passably performed is the image of a solitary figure wrestling in his private thoughts with his fear of death, his desire for action, and his awareness of the difficulties of meaningful deeds. But the play is not all passionate soliloquy; it also contains a number of intricate public scenes (the duel, the play within the play, the funeral of Ophelia, the scene in which we first see Claudius doing business in his court) that focus attention, not upon the solitary private self, but upon men playing public roles against specific public backdrops. Claudius constantly appears amid courtiers and servants. Whether listening to reports of the actions of Fortinbras or attending a play or a duel, the king is first of all a public figure with a position and a social demeanor to maintain. His court is a very socially self-conscious place. People there are not so concerned with right action, as they are with appearing wise, obedient, cultured, kingly, vengeful, or whatever else seems required by a particular public role.

It is in part through Shakespeare's handling of the visual spectacle that he focuses attention on the gap between man viewed as private integer and man viewed as social creature in order to make the audience aware of the difficulty of integrating the two. One of Hamlet's many problems is to find a way to act in the public sphere without forfeiting his private integrity and becoming just another player of a socially defined role. Simultaneously, he must pierce through the public roles of Claudius to find—if it exists—the conscience of the private man beneath.[8] By constantly manipulating the relationship between public and private scenes, by repeatedly broadening and narrowing the visual focus of attention, Shakespeare helps his audience to feel some of the difficulties of the prince's dual task.

Scene ii of Act I provides a kind of visual touchstone for the whole play, for in it we see Shakespeare making sophisticated use of simple visual contrasts between a solitary figure and a group. The stage directions before the scene read:

> *Flourish. Enter Claudius, King of Denmark, Gertrude the Queen, Councillors, Polonius and his son Laertes, Hamlet, cum aliis [including Voltemand and Cornelius].*

These directions indicate a striking beginning for the scene. Here there is no gradual climactic buildup of characters, no slow movement from casual conversation to more urgent speech. Rather, with a ceremonial trumpet flourish, the royal entourage enters, forming a spectacle of size and imposing elegance. A particular imaginative world is evoked, one of glitter, pomp, and ceremony, and at its center stands Claudius. It is he who, visually and aurally, must dominate the scene. It is he who delivers the long speech in which, with masterful rhetoric, he assures his assembled court that—with all respect paid his dead brother—*he* is now the king and has taken queen and government into his own hands. It is he who calls forth, in turn, Cornelius and Voltemand, Laertes and Polonius, and finally Hamlet from the surrounding crowd of attendants, and, having called each forth, then dismisses each with some "business" accomplished.

The scene's visual orchestration confirms Claudius's social identity as king and his power in that context. Even the silent councillors and others who swell the scene but do not speak render more pronounced Claudius's authority. He is the center of a world-in-miniature; and Hamlet, dressed in black, speaking in asides, and forced to attend when the king commands, is clearly the outsider. We are made to realize by every visual clue at Shakespeare's disposal that the struggle of Hamlet and Claudius is not between two private and equal individuals, but between a king in a privileged public position and a prince unmistakably on the periphery of power.

My concern now, however, is to consider what follows this public encounter, with its rich orchestration of many bodies and many voices, all of which, except for Hamlet's, are willingly controlled by the presence and voice of the king. As magnificently as they entered, the court figures exit, again with a trumpet flourish, leaving only Hamlet on the stage. The trumpets are hardly silent before we are launched into Hamlet's first soliloquy, "O that this too too sullied flesh would melt" (I.ii.129). This abrupt aural and visual transition is startling. We have just been attending to a public scene of high ceremony in which rhetoric is impersonal and directed to surface effects. Claudius, at the center, is an example of accommodated man at his most self-satisfied. Suddenly we see before us the unattended figure of one person speaking private thoughts.

The transition from many figures to one figure, from public rhetoric to reflective soliloquy, happens so swiftly that it seems to call into question the reality of the glittering public pageant. The trumpets, voices of deference and authority, the brightly arrayed courtiers dancing attendance on a bejeweled king—all of these vanish in a trice, leaving only Prince Hamlet in his inky cloak. The public portion of the scene has shown how the trappings of state can confirm a social identity and protect a man such as Claudius from self-scrutiny and the scrutiny of others; but the sudden vanishing of the court suggests the insubstantial and impermanent nature of the public backdrop and so of the social identity it supports. The man standing before us after the court disappears is terribly alone and seemingly vulnerable; but he also, in his isolation, possesses an integrity and a dignity not dependent upon a retinue of servile attendants. This abrupt narrowing of the audience's visual focus, the juxtaposition of the glittering court and the solitary figure, becomes a chief means of creating in the viewer a disorienting awareness of the potential gap between the demands of social role-playing and the demands of the private self.

Throughout *Hamlet* Shakespeare continues his exploration of the difficulties this gap poses, both for the thoughtful person attempting public action or the public man driven to confront his private self. Visually, the play continues to ring changes upon the basic visual juxtapositions of I.ii, the contrasts between many figures and one figure, between public and private encounters; and nowhere are these visual contrasts more thrillingly employed than in Act III. The central public event of that act, the play scene (III.ii), is another spectacular occurrence. The whole court is present, along with the traveling players. Their old-fashioned verse mingles with Hamlet's bawdy interruptions and with the comments of Gertrude, Ophelia, and the rest. Tension is high, for the audience knows this is Hamlet's carefully chosen occasion for unmasking the king. As the trap is sprung and Claudius cries, "Give me some light. Away!" (259), confusion erupts, and polite public decorum crumbles. *The Murder of Gonzago* stops in midstream; the banter of the stage audience stops; and once again the whole court vanishes, leaving only Hamlet and Horatio behind.

This abrupt dispersal of the court and the disruption of the inner play evoke again the sense of evanescence experienced in I.ii when the court exited with Claudius; but this time some things are very different. The prince has not simply been left behind by an indifferent court and a smug king; rather, he has actively thrown the court into disarray and through the interior play has touched the private man lurking behind the public mask of king. When the play stops, it is as if a larger world of artifice has cracked open. That the man playing the role of dutiful heir to his brother's throne may be doing just that—playing a role—is suddenly, to Hamlet, a certainty and not a suspicion; and that same fact has been freshly thrust upon the king himself.[9]

The moment when Claudius cries for light and the court disappears is rightly seen as a watershed moment in the play. Hamlet has apparently found a way to act, to pierce the seemingly impenetrable wall of public appearances that his enemy has used to conceal himself. Now, it seems, private selves will be truly revealed, and the prince can move without private scruple toward the public purification of Denmark. But, of course, in this play nothing is so simple. People do not easily relinquish public position for private peace; neither does the thoughtful private man ever move without danger to his integrity into the realm of public deeds. In fact, for a brief time after the inner play crashes to a halt, Hamlet and Claudius, victim and oppressor, seem to change roles as the events set in motion by *The Murder of Gonzago* affect the two in unexpected ways and involve the audience in the complex process of reevaluating some of its own assumptions and expectations. After the public scene, Shakespeare focuses the audience's visual attention relentlessly upon a succession of intense private or semi-private encounters. The deliberate visual ironies and reversals we witness in this section of the play become an important part of a larger process by which audience expectations and moral points of reference are destabilized.

Hamlet's behavior immediately after the inner play is the first of many surprises. Before the play he had praised Horatio for self-restraint, but after the play he himself seems manically out of control: singing a song about the "strucken deer" (III.ii.261) and exposing with contemptuous ease the shabby attempts of Rosencrantz and Guildenstern to pry his secrets from him. In the same frenetic burst of energy he makes a fool of the blundering Polonius by teasing him about a cloud shape. But his euphoria quickly darkens to passionate anger. As he goes off the stage, it is to "speak daggers" (381) to his mother. What is unsettling here is how little self-possession Hamlet displays and the total lack of irony with which he adopts the bloodthirsty rhetoric of a Pyrrhus. The success of his mousetrap frees the prince to speak and act less guardedly; it also carries him far from the ideal of moderate self-control he had so recently praised in Horatio.

From Hamlet attention turns to Claudius. Rosencrantz and Guildenstern, of course, run to him for orders; but their unctuous flattery is quickly replaced by the more tortured private speech of the king. For the first time he is alone upon the stage and wrestling with a newly awakened sense of guilt. Claudius's troubled meditation seems to me to be one of the most powerful private moments of the play, in part because the scene plays havoc with the visual expectations we bring to a scene involving Claudius. Repeatedly we have seen him aloof and inscrutable against a backdrop of courtiers or engaged in public discourse with those whom he employs to serve his will. Suddenly, this man is alone—which is how we are accustomed to seeing Hamlet—and even on his knees. At least for a moment he is not paying attention to his social position but to his private soul; and, however briefly, he becomes an object of sympathy. For an instant this intensely social being has become the thoughtful private man.

But the visual ironies of III.iii are not yet over. As Claudius kneels, Hamlet appears behind the praying king and meditates revenge. This visual configuration, recalling the player's description of Pyrrhus poised to kill old Priam, suggests the new vulnerability of Claudius and the sudden power Hamlet has acquired through the play within the play.[10] But even the prince's new certitude of Claudius's guilt cannot save Hamlet from error. Deceived by appearances, Hamlet misreads, as at first does the audience, the significance of Claudius's act of prayer. The king finally cannot give up the trappings of public power — "My crown, mine own ambition, and my queen" (55) — to cleanse his private conscience; and he rises from his knees with the intention of repeating his original crime of murder by having Hamlet killed. The young prince, having foregone sure revenge on Claudius, proceeds a moment later to wreak it mistakenly on the hapless Polonius. And in one of the play's most passionate private moments, he then mercilessly castigates his mother for her real and imagined crimes while the blood of Polonius is still fresh upon his hands.

It is worth pausing to reflect for a moment on how Shakespeare's handling of the visual elements of performance contributes to the theatrical effectiveness of this arc of action extending from the play within the play to Hamlet's castigation of Gertrude. Important to note, first, is the effect upon the audience of the sudden collapse of the court world at the conclusion of *The Murder of Gonzago*. The abrupt truncation of the inner play and the disappearance from the stage of the court party suggest the fragility of the elaborate social backdrop used by Claudius to shield his private self from scrutiny. Earlier, the play had insisted, visually, upon the marginal status of Hamlet in the Danish court and upon the distance between the solitary prince, driven to assume an "antic disposition" simply to move with safety in such a court, and the king, who gathered that court like a protective mantle about him. The play scene marks the moment when that mantle is ripped from Claudius's shoulders through the action of the prince. Yet once public facades have crumbled, Shakespeare relentlessly narrows the focus of the audience's visual attention to drive home just how unpredictable and far-reaching are the implications of such an act.

After the inner play stops, Shakespeare keeps audience attention unswervingly upon figures separated from a supporting social matrix and confronting long-hidden or unacknowledged facets of the self. What we see is often neither what we expect, nor what we welcome. Claudius alone on his knees, Hamlet standing with sword in hand behind a praying man, Gertrude in penitential tears — these are potent and disconcerting images because they are unanticipated; they play havoc with our visual expectations. The easy distinction between a good prince and a corrupt power structure is shaken.[11] What we see is a king capable of self-scrutiny, if not capable of sustaining that scrutiny; a queen touched, if not transformed, by guilt; and a prince whose temporary success in the public arena causes him to lose his moral poise and reveal anger, rashness, and moral pride. Ripping the cocoon in which Claudius and Gertrude have lain wrapped in moral oblivion leads neither to their permanent transformation nor to Hamlet's successful integration of private integrity and meaningful public action.[12] In fact, quite the opposite occurs. Hamlet becomes more like his enemies without permanently transforming them.

The visual orchestration of the sequence is crucial to its theatrical effectiveness. A bold public act done, a social world in disarray, Shakespeare makes his audience look again and again at the unforeseen and disturbing consequences to the private selves in these events. With the larger social scene excluded from view, we are left to confront the mysterious and unpredictable nature of solitary man. What is the "truth" about the prince, about his uncle, or about his mother? When are their "real" selves on display? Can we recognize these real selves when we see them? As critics have long said, Hamlet's special dilemma is to live with integrity in a world of seeming, where people shift shapes like Proteus and no man is his own. The difficulty of that task comes home to the audience as it tries to keep its own cognitive and moral bearings in the succession of intensely private moments that follow the public act of "springing the mousetrap."

As the example from *Hamlet* makes plain, variations in the number of figures onstage from scene to scene, the alternation of public and private events, and contrasts between a full stage and one nearly empty are crucial elements in Shakespeare's visual orchestration of dramatic segments much longer than the individual scene. In fact, it seems to me that Shakespeare is constantly looking beyond the visual design of individual scenes to the meaningful visual orchestration of groups of scenes and of entire plays. In the next chapter I will deal in some detail with the relationship between techniques of orchestration and the theatrical coherence of groups of adjoining scenes that, taken together, form sustained dramatic movements within a play. For the moment, however, I want to focus on some of the characteristic strategies by which Shakespeare not only lends visual coherence to an entire play, but also helps the audience comprehend the significance of what it sees during an extended theatrical action.

To begin with what is simple, we can all think of works, such as *Midsummer Night's Dream, The Winter's Tale, The Merchant of Venice,* or *Antony and Cleopatra,* which make such pronounced use of discrete geographic places to structure the play's action that directors frequently establish sharp visual contrasts between, say, Belmont and Venice, or Bohemia and Sicilia, to help the audience recognize the symbolic and moral significance of each locale and of journeys between them.[13] More subtle, but equally important, are certain kinds of visual repetition that through the course of a play become important organizing motifs for the work as a whole. A well-known example is afforded by the repeated visual juxtaposition of light and dark in *Othello,* a play in which torchlight and darkness, day and night, one dark skin and many light ones, and repeated verbal images of blackness and whiteness relentlessly focus audience attention on the play's examination of opposing psychological and moral states and on the cultural clichés used to talk of such oppositions.[14]

Less discussed is the kind of visual repetition we find in *Troilus and Cressida,* a play in which the act of "looking on" becomes a central visual motif for the work as a whole. The motif first occurs in I.ii, part of which shows the parade of Trojan warriors returning from battle. Pandarus leads Cressida to a slightly elevated position (the unspecified "up here" of line 169) from which to observe the returning fighters. The parade is a dumb show, for the warriors say nothing, and their identities and significance are conveyed to us, and supposedly to Cressida, by Pandarus as he waits for the arrival of Troilus. Somewhat later, in III.ii, Pandarus is once again in the observer's role as he looks on while Troilus and Cressida kiss and court. The very next scene, however, shows other characters also involved in acts of looking on, as another parade of heroes occurs, this time in the Grecian camp. Achilles stands in the entrance to his tent while the Greek warriors pass him by with deliberate indifference. As Achilles watches the parade and is rebuffed in conversation by each warrior, he himself is watched by Ulysses, who has laid the plot to rouse him from lethargy. The act of observing an observer is repeated most spectacularly in V.ii, when Troilus and Ulysses watch Cressida and Diomedes, and all are watched by Thersites. Still later (V.iv), Thersites looks on while the final battle of Greeks and Trojans occurs; and finally Pandarus totters onto the stage to observe the last gasp of the battle and to comment upon its meaning—or lack of meaning (V.x.35–55).

Cumulatively, this motif of onlooking lends a seamy, voyeuristic feel to the play. There are few immediate and unself-conscious actions in this work; things are done to produce an effect upon an observer, as the Greeks parade before Achilles's tent to provoke his jealousy; or purposeful or private acts are made to *seem* occasions for self-display by the remarks of commentators, as when Pandarus makes the Trojans' return from battle into a perverse male beauty contest or Thersites makes the final battle into a staging ground for fools. Even the private love exchanges of Troilus and Cressida and Cressida and Diomedes become public actions by the relentless intrusion of seen or unseen observers. Surely there is a connection between the distaste this play has occasioned in critics and audiences and the repeated voyeuristic overtones of many of its major visual events. Watching the play, we feel we are seeing a world without truly private dimensions, a world in which action has dwindled to self-display, partly because the common values that should guide and inform action have been corrupted, lost, or garbled by individual egotism.[15]

The repeated visual motif of looking on also has disquieting implications for the theater audience in a more direct way, since one of the chief actions of any audience is to look on while dramatic characters act out for us certain events in their fictional lives. The play highlights the less pleasant aspects of that characteristic action by aligning the theater audience with Pandarus and Thersites, the play's chief voyeurs. If Renaissance theorists often argued that literature teaches by delight, and so the experience of the reader or audience is one of pleasure and edification, this play makes problematic and disquieting the sources of our pleasure. Clearly, for Pandarus, to look on is to feed parasitically on the lives of others;

for Thersites, it is to be confirmed, endlessly, in his own opinions, since whatever Thersites sees becomes to him an example of the knavery he assumes in everyone. Are these the options open to the theatergoer? Must watching a play be passive, parasitic, or self-confirming? One consequence of highlighting, by repetition, the visual motif of looking on is to heighten the spectator's consciousness of his own role as watcher, and to turn his attention reflexively toward the answering of those questions.

The repeated juxtaposition of light and dark in *Othello* and the repeated motif of looking on in *Troilus and Cressida* are important to the visual continuity and thematic integrity of each work. Just as critics have long identified verbal image patterns in the plays, so, too, one can certainly identify repeated visual motifs that cumulatively focus the attention of the audience on significant ideas, themes, or relationships. But there are more subtle ways in which visual repetition helps an audience keep its bearings during the course of a play. Many of the tragedies, for example, contain a "spine" of group scenes, linked together by a strong web of visual echoes, in which most of the play's key characters share the stage together. At the simplest level, such scenes help the audience to perceive visually the changing relationship of the protagonist to his society; they provide visual definition to shifts in the alignment of forces in the play's fictive world. Predictably, these group scenes often occur in Acts I, III, and V, or somewhere near the beginning, middle, and end of the work; and the visual links between them may even be rather schematically underscored to remind the spectator of prior scenes.

For example, the fight scene in Act III of *Romeo and Juliet* visually evokes the first scene of the play. In each case the setting is the public street in daylight, and in each the major event is a quarrel between Montagues and Capulets that culminates with the appearance of the prince. But the resemblances underscore important differences in the two scenes, as well. Scene i of Act III begins, not with the banter of servants, but with the quarrel of Mercutio and Benvolio; and with the rise in social class comes a corresponding rise in the seriousness of what ensues. This time the fight produces, not just words and noise, but blood and two dead bodies. Most significantly, Romeo does not wander in distractedly after the fighting has stopped, as in I.i, but he enters at the outset and, after Mercutio's death, chooses to become an active participant in the public feud between Montagues and Capulets. No longer aloof from his society's public quarrels, he in fact perpetuates those quarrels to the hazard of his own marriage. The resolution of the two lovers' troubled relationship to their society is only made clear in the final group scene of the play, V.iii, in which the deaths of Paris, Romeo, and Juliet are followed by the successive arrivals of the watch, the friar, the two families, and, for the third time in the play, the prince. Romeo and Juliet have found a way out of public feuds, but only by the most radical of routes; and their dead bodies, ringed by their families and the prince, become the sacrificial offering for their society's peace.

Each tragedy handles its spine of group scenes differently, and few are as obviously and schematically linked as the three scenes involving the prince in *Romeo and Juliet*. Nonetheless, even in a play as dramaturgically complex as *Hamlet,* the initial court scene (I.ii), the play within the play (III.ii), and the duel scene (V.ii) are visually organized to move Hamlet inexorably from the periphery to the center of the public world that has been tainted by Claudius and that it is his onerous burden to "set right." In the first of these scenes he is the proud outsider who "Know(s) not 'seems'" (I.ii.76). By his clothing, his speech, and his melancholy manner he proclaims his difference from those who now control the seats of power. In the second of these scenes he is the stage manager and indirect instigator of action, using the "seeming" of the actors to unmask the public man upon the throne and setting in train a chain of events he can neither predict nor control. The final scene places him visually at the center, rather than at the periphery, of the action. Sword in hand, he is himself a public actor, the duelist who transforms the murderous "play" Claudius has arranged into a scene of judgment.[16]

This spine of court scenes affords three concrete visualizations of Hamlet's changing relationship to Claudius in his public role as king. First Hamlet is the observer of Claudius's court, the unassimilated and seemingly impotent outsider; then the stage manager of an event that temporarily cracks the equilibrium of the court; and finally an actor who transforms his assigned role as inept duelist into the role of avenger and purifier of the court. The scenes thus are various embodiments of the play-actor metaphors running through the drama. Further, as a series of crucial public confrontations between the new king and the old king's son, they reveal changes within Hamlet himself as he moves from his alienated stance in Act I to tentative and devastating involvement in the world of seeming to the condition of readiness and humility that enables him to perform his final act in the public arena.

Of course, when I talk about these scenes in this way I am reducing their complexity. I am treating them emblematically, rather than with proper attention to their temporal unfolding and their kinetic dimensions. While they *do* focus audience attention on the changing relationships of the protagonist to his society, they do much more. In performance, because these scenes are essentially fluid, not static, their visual choreography has important kinetic consequences. I would, therefore, like to look at a spine of group scenes in *King Lear* in a way that will give full weight both to the moment-by-moment orchestration of each, as well as to the way particular visual structures are repeated in them all to tie the play together and to create kinetic effects essential to the audience's theatrical experience. Moreover, I will use my discussion of this spine of scenes to point out how the visual and aural effects I am exploring are reinforced, at every point, by Shakespeare's complementary management of the aural dimensions of performance. I will argue that in *Lear* audience response to the play's final events—Lear addressing the dead Cordelia amid a ring of courtiers and attendants—depends directly on that scene's complex recapitulation and transformation of visual, aural, and kinetic patterns the audience has repeatedly encountered in earlier parts of the performance.

By way of introducing the visual structures, in particular, that I will be exploring in *Lear*, let me say first that at one level this play has always seemed to me to be about power—the acquiring, holding, and losing of power—and about the discovery of what joy and what pain lie beyond such a preoccupation. Unlike Hamlet, who must move from the periphery to the center of his society, from the stance of detached observer to that of active duelist, Lear must make the opposite journey: out from the center to the very edges of his society and beyond to escape the selfish egotism his public position and his preoccupation with power have encouraged. Consequently, three of the major group scenes of *Lear*—I.i, II.iv, and V.iii—mark the stages of Lear's painful disengagement from the public world he has dominated for eighty years. At the same time, these scenes are orchestrated, both visually and aurally, to make palpable and immediate the grinding force of man's will to power and the cruel dialectic between weakness and strength, pain and aggression, that it is this play's special achievement to enact.[17]

It is the opening scene that first makes clear how central to the play are issues of power and how crucial is the orchestration of the visual and aural elements of the scene to the audience's understanding of these issues. Watching the opening scene, one feels the terrible need of Lear to dominate the world around him. From the moment he enters, he forces everyone to serve his will or court his wrath. Visually Lear dominates the scene. He places everyone at his beck and call, and the first casual demonstration of his power comes when he sends Gloucester to fetch Burgundy and France, followed quickly by his command that his three daughters express their love for him. Two comply.

Cordelia's refusal to obey Lear's command is underscored by the fact that her first and second speeches are asides. If the characteristic pattern of the scene is for everyone to speak to Lear, she turns toward the audience, breaking the visual and aural pattern by which Lear's dominance is expressed. However, the first character to feel the full consequences of defying Lear is Kent, whose exit at line 187 suggests good counsel's banishment by a foolish king. As Kent goes out, Burgundy enters with Gloucester, and the action of the first part of the scene is repeated.[18] France and Burgundy, like the sisters earlier, are commanded by Lear to express their affection, not for him directly, but for Cordelia, who is now dowerless. Lear clearly expects they will spurn her, and again one suitor complies with the king's wishes. France, like Cordelia and Kent before him, breaks the pattern of acquiescense by "seizing upon" the dowerless daughter. Then, in a final petty gesture of displeasure with Cordelia and France, Lear summons Burgundy to exit with him; the suitor who has flouted Cordelia is now the obvious recipient of Lear's attention.[19]

Visually, the scene is orchestrated to highlight Lear's power and to open a deep chasm between the many who seemingly define themselves by obedience to the old king's wishes and so direct their words and actions toward him, and the few who refuse him blind obedience and so turn away or are thrust from him, as Cordelia turns to the audience, France to Cordelia, and Kent to a world elsewhere. The visual and aural dynamics of this scene are clear and powerful and reinforce one another beautifully. Lear is the visual center of attention; to turn from him is dangerous and defiant. Lear is the aural center of attention; characters are to answer his requests and obey his commands; to speak to another or to answer in accents he does not expect is to chance his rage and banishment. The dramatic tension of the scene largely arises from the gap between the schematic pattern Lear would impose on every aspect of the scene and the aberrations in that pattern braved by Cordelia, Kent, and France. And it is, of course, the very marginality of Cordelia, Kent, and France that wins the audience's sympathy for their seemingly futile defiance of absolute power.

By establishing so firmly Lear's centrality and his craving for power in this complex opening scene, Shakespeare prepares the audience to recognize how utterly the lines of power shift in later scenes, beginning in I.iv, in which Goneril first refuses to heed Lear's words and tries to strip him of much of his retinue, but culminating in II.iv, the scene in which Lear vainly pleads for recognition and respect as he stands in the courtyard of Gloucester's castle. This scene is a macabre variation of the first in that, while Lear pitifully tries to reassert his initial position of dominance, he is now an impotent suppliant, and his every attempt at self-assertion is met with defiance, rather than submission.

Every detail of II.iv visually underscores Lear's powerless state. Entering to find the disguised Kent in the stocks, Lear is attended only by his fool and a nameless gentleman; no retinue and no trumpets signal his approach. Now Lear must be his own messenger, too, and after speaking with Kent he exits to seek out Gloucester for himself. No longer the dispenser of favors, but a suppliant, Lear eventually kneels to his younger daughter (149), a gesture meant to shame her, but expressing all too well his own impotence. More central to the scene's impact, however, is its overarching aural and visual design. This scene is constructed as a series of head-on con-

frontations between Lear and a succession of other people. Each
of these encounters escalates the emotional intensity of the scene;
each depends for its effectiveness upon stark aural and visual contrasts.[20] The first note of defiance to Lear's wishes is sounded by
Kent, who with cruel kindness wishes Lear to understand the truth
about his daughter and his son-in-law's intentions:

LEAR What's he that hath so much thy place mistook
      To set thee here?
KENT   It is both he and she,
      Your son and daughter.
LEAR No.
KENT Yes.
KENT No, I say.
KENT I say yea.
[LEAR No, no; they would not.
KENT Yes, they have.]
LEAR By Jupiter, I swear no!
KENT By Juno, I swear ay!

                                 (11–21)

The stichomythia, relatively rare in Shakespeare's later plays, captures perfectly the deeply antagonistic structure of all that is to
follow. Repeatedly, Lear is to say yea and to be met with vicious,
unrelenting nays.

Gloucester's is the first faint repetition of Kent's defiance, but he
is weak and would be accommodating if he could. Regan has no
such desire, and with her entrance (121) the central contest of wills
begins. When Lear kneels to her, she replies, "Good sir, no more.
These are unsightly tricks. / Return you to my sister" (152–53).
When Lear reminds her of past obligations, her answer is, "Good
sir, to th' purpose" (176). At this point, Lear has ranged before him
a host of enemies and faltering friends: Gloucester, Cornwall, Regan,
and their servants. Then Oswald enters, a known and hated enemy,
quickly followed by Goneril herself who, in taking Regan by the
hand (189), makes plain that there will be no help for Lear. Finally,
the roll call of voices mustering against Lear is climaxed by the
noise of thunder, which sounds just before Lear rushes from the
stage in anguish (278). It is as though the malice of the daughters
is echoed in a last overwhelming note by the malice of the heavens.

And while Lear's last words in I.i were to Burgundy, here they are to the fool, with whom he exits, along with Kent and Gloucester.

The aural and visual elements of Shakespeare's stagecraft here form the necessary foundation for the audience's understanding of the suffering and cruelty that constitute the naked emotional substructure of this scene. From the moment Lear finds Kent in the stocks, the audience knows the old king's reception will be a bitter one. He may deny reality, but we cannot. Consequently, each new figure who appears, each new voice raised in opposition to Lear, not only heightens *his* torment, but that of the audience as well. The aural and visual orchestration of the scene has a relentless simplicity, which produces a strong kinetic effect. The solo voice and the solitary figure of Lear are pitted against an ever more venomous succession of voices and an ever larger array of defiant bodies. As the dialogue moves relentlessly back and forth between the old king and his enemies, it is as if a heavy ball were being tossed back and forth between a line of ever stronger people on one side and a single figure on the other. Eventually, that unsupported figure must weaken; and Lear finally does, rushing from the stage crazed with grief and rage.

Bernard Beckerman has written about the essentially binary and dialectical structure of most of Shakespeare's scenes. He has said: "No matter how many characters may be on stage at one time, the action tends to follow no more than two lines of force . . . a scene may be composed of many short exchanges, each of which has a binary arrangement. Or in a longer scene involving four or five characters, the characters are likely to fall into two groups, each sharing a common movement."[21] In *Lear* II.iv, a scene involving a great many figures, this binary dialectic is sustained with extraordinary effectiveness, though the two groups are composed, not of equal numbers of figures, but of a solitary figure and a large group of enemies. The only real exception to the relentless antagonistic dialectic of the scene is afforded by the intrusions of the fool. As always, the fool's outbursts—the song about the father who wears rags or his tale of the cockney and her eels—provide relevant, if cryptic, commentary upon the scene's main events and the old king's foolishness. But here, I would argue, the fool's words are less important for their content than for the momentary checks they give to the scene's escalating rhythm of anger and antagonism. Watching the scene, the audience wants its psychological horrors to stop. The fool's intrusions articulate our desire to break the rising tension, and their failure to do so only makes each renewed repetition of abuse more painful.

This scene is, then, an excellent example of two things. First, it illustrates how one scene can recall an earlier scene to underscore changing circumstances within the play's world. In the first public scene of the play Lear stood at the center of power and only a few dared cross him. In II.iv he stands helpless before a great company; and only a few, and those the least powerful, dare follow him. Second, this scene demonstrates the role of visual and aural effects in foregrounding these changes and, more important, in conveying to a theater audience the nature of the brutality that lies at the heart of the scene. In the theater the relentless battering of the weak and the unsupported by the powerful and the cruel is not a bloodless abstraction. The audience feels kinetically this terrible battering process in every detail of the scene's visual and aural orchestration, as more and more figures mass against the old king and hurl at him the abuse he cannot escape because of his continuing fantasy that he can once more command those who so maliciously are demonstrating their power over him. In I.i Lear used his power to intimidate and control those around him, and his words and curses became weapons to beat down and drive from his sight those who were not willing to do his bidding. Now, in II.iv, as the recipient of the verbal blows, *he* is the one to be ground down and driven from the sight of those who now sit in the seat of power. And, of course, with the shifting balance of power, the audience's sympathies shift as well, for it is now Lear who is the underdog, the victim. But what is remarkable in both scenes is the extent to which the operation of a dynamic of aggression is made palpable by the creation of kinetic effects dependent upon the orchestration of each scene's visual elements and its bipolar dialogue structure.

After Act II Lear's direct involvement in the dialectical struggle for public power is snapped. Gloucester still tries, for another act, to keep his footing in the treacherous world of political intrigue; Cornwall and Albany still fence for authority; Goneril and Regan vie for the sexual mastery of Edmund; and the agile bastard grabs for power by whatever means he can; but Lear no longer has a place in the public arena. No longer the inhabitant of "grac'd" palaces, he wanders onto heaths and rocky beaches, finds shelter in hovels and farmhouses. His brutal expulsion from power is just that—brutal; yet it is also, obviously, his route to a freedom he has never known. As Robert Egan has recently suggested, in the middle portions of the play Lear undertakes a dialogue with the cosmos that is as grand and as daring as the gestures of any of Shakespeare's tragic protagonists; it is a dialogue that can only be undertaken when Lear's energies are not wholly consumed in the fight to maintain a public position of authority.[22] In acts III and IV Lear is vulnerable and open—open to the rain and the wind, to the misery of naked wretches, to the wisdom of his mad philosopher, and to his own overwhelming anger and guilt.

Finally, of course, Lear passes through this purgatory to a moment of bliss with Cordelia when his rage is stilled and he finds, instead of the joy of public adulation he has lost, the joy of mutual love. In this state *mine* and *thine* no longer exist, and there is no room for the structures of domination and subservience Lear had spent a life upholding and that, at first, he instinctively reasserts even with Cordelia, as he kneels and begs for the poisoned cup, placing himself in the role of suppliant in which he had so often placed others. Certainly Lear deserves to kneel—deserves this gesture of abasement—yet Cordelia knows, as well as Hamlet, that if you treat every man as he deserves, none will 'scape whipping. The charity of her "no cause, no cause" (IV.vii.75) wipes away those categories of guilty and sinless, inferior and superior, weak and powerful upon which are erected the world's hierarchies of power.

Yet, to dwell upon the reunion of Lear and Cordelia always risks sentimentalizing and distorting this play, a point to which I shall return later. It is an understatement to say that acts III and IV do not primarily present us with images of beatitude. On the contrary, in the world of the castle they show us a continuing and bestial struggle for domination; and in the world of the heath we experience, primarily, the pain and torment of a man cut loose from familiar structures, of a man who has lost one sense of his identity but has not yet found another to take its place. And because this man is the king, his fall into the abyss is more than a personal calamity; it also shatters larger frames of coherence. In part, and here as elsewhere I simplify to make a point, Shakespeare's task is to find a theatrical idiom in which to express the chaos and pain that result when the king is dethroned, his personal sense of self shattered, and old patterns of deference and authority emptied of significance. One way of dramatizing such a world turned upside down is to create scenes the performance structure of which is the antithesis of the tight dialectical pattern we examined in I.i and II.iv. In these long and important scenes, Lear's centrality was underscored by a relentless performance dialectic in which he always figured as one term. Whether the figure to be obeyed or, when power had shifted, the figure to be opposed, Lear constituted one pole of a powerful binary structure which Beckerman has identified as a defining feature of Shakespeare's stagecraft. By contrast, when Lear has reached Gloucester's farmhouse at the end of Act III, the scene is orchestrated to suggest how very close the king, his world, and the play's scenic structures are verging on incoherence and fragmentation.

For much of the farmhouse scene, visual prominence is given to two empty jointstools, emblems of the unkind daughters who have caused such psychic and social havoc. About these stools circle the deranged king, the frightened fool, and the mock lunatic, Poor Tom. Rather than the dialogue following a clear back-and-forth rhythm, it leapfrogs from one figure to another so that the audience has trouble even seeing how one speech connects logically to what precedes and what follows.[23] The result is a wild whirling of antiphonal voices, expressing, in various idioms of foolery and madness, a world turned upside down and offering the audience not even the consolation of coherence.

> EDGAR Frateretto calls me, and tells me Nero is an angler in the lake of darkness. Pray, innocent, and beware the foul fiend.
>
> FOOL Prithee, nuncle, tell me whether a madman be a gentleman or a yeoman?
>
> LEAR A King, a King.
>
> FOOL No; he's a yeoman that has a gentleman to his son; for he's a mad yeoman that sees his son a gentleman before him.

LEAR   To have a thousand with red burning spits
           Come hizzing in upon 'em —
[EDGAR The Foul fiend bites my back.
FOOL   He's mad that trusts in the tameness of a wolf, a horse's
           health, a boy's love, or a whore's oath.]
                                    (III.vi.6–19)

What is important here is the impression of fractured logic and discontinuity created by this wild babble of voices. Edgar's words about the foul fiend and Nero are followed up by no one. Instead, the fool offers a riddle about the social standing of madmen. For a moment, Lear seems to follow the fool's lead. By answering that a madman is neither a peon nor a gentleman, but a king, he shows that he has given the fool's words a strikingly personal interpretation. The fool goes on to give the "correct" answer to his riddle, but Lear has lost interest, trying instead to put out the eyes of imagined enemies with burning spits. Then Edgar cries out again, "The foul fiend bites my back." His words do not follow logically from what has gone before, but they echo emotionally the general outpouring of rage and suffering to which each individual voice adds its particular contribution. The fool follows up with a bitter maxim about the folly of trusting what is innately untrustworthy, and suddenly Lear becomes obsessed with the idea of calling his daughters to trial. But even as Lear enacts their arraignment, the dialogue continues to jump, like a spark, from one figure to another so that the scene seems to follow the frightening associational logic of a nightmare rather than the analytical logic of the waking world. Only the words of the listening Kent (33–34, 57–58, 80) and the asides of Edgar (59–60) offer a counterpoint to this scene of whirling madness and remind us of a contrasting world of reason and coherence.

In writing about this scene, Harley Granville-Barker has called it an example of "pure drama," by which he means that "the sound of the dialogue matters almost more than its meaning."[24] I would argue that this scene is no more an example of pure drama than the scene in Gloucester's courtyard, though the seeming illogicality of much of the dialogue here turns our attention more immediately to the scene's aural, visual, and kinetic elements. These elements, however, are always integral to any of Shakespeare's scenes. In II.iv the visual massing of figures against Lear and the relentless back and forth progress of the dialogue between Lear and a series of opponents underscore for the audience Lear's impotence and create the overwhelming kinetic effect of weakness being borne down by cruel strength. Conversely, in the farmhouse, speech flies erratically back and forth among figures ranged in a whirling circle, all order gone. The leapfrogging movement of the dialogue contributes, kinetically, to the impression of randomness and lack of structure so central to the scene's primary concern: the depiction of psychic and social chaos. The lack of visual patterning in the scene and the pure sound of the dialogue, the cacophonous babble of madmen and fools, also contribute to the scene's special effectiveness as a dramatization of madness.

Yet no more here than in II.iv is the *content* of speech irrelevant. As Sheldon Zitner and others have argued, there is always sense in Lear's madness, the fool's riddles, and Poor Tom's mock insanity.[25] The mock trial is an important step in Lear's psychic journey, as he gives way utterly to the craving for revenge that is only removed when Cordelia's "no cause, no cause" (IV.vii.75) releases him from his wheel of fire. The point is simply that Shakespeare is always attentive to the sound as well as the sense of speech, to the patterned or seemingly patternless movement of dialogue, to the importance of gesture and the configuration of bodies upon the stage. The scene in Gloucester's castle may make us newly attentive to his handling of these elements of "pure drama," but its primary effect should be to awaken our senses to his continual orchestration of such elements in scenes where the "sense" of the words may assume undue prominence in our critical assessments of what makes a scene theatrically meaningful to the audience.

Of course, Lear does not end the play in the farmhouse; neither is the play's final vision that of a world given over to the unstructured, cacophonous babble of madmen. Eventually Lear is united with Cordelia and briefly finds a world seemingly set apart from the public struggles for power. But the play does not end there, either, with the depiction of an otherworldly state of blessed mutuality. What has been found must again be lost, if only so that the hero can come to terms, finally and profoundly, with the public world whose demands led to Cordelia's original banishment and whose blandishments Lear can so easily ignore once he has found that daughter again. Lear's desire to sing with Cordelia like birds in a cage expresses his newfound disesteem for worldly things and also his willed ignorance of the world's power. At this point, Lear always reminds me of Marvell's nymph who tried to find in an enclosed garden, with a guileless fawn, a safe haven from the wanton troopers of the world. Cordelia is tougher than Lear in this regard. In wanting to see "these daughters and these sisters" (V.iii.7), she makes plain her awareness of the world beyond the cage in which Lear would find an unproblematic haven.

In the last scene of the play, Lear once more confronts the public world and holds in his arms a testament of the world's power to destroy all safe havens. Particularly striking in this scene, however, is the way Shakespeare suggests to the audience the nature of Lear's final relationship to that public world—the significance of his final renunciation of it, a renunciation more profound and more final than could occur while Cordelia lived. In part, as I have been suggesting throughout this book, what this final scene means is largely determined by Shakespeare's handling of those elements of "pure drama"—gesture, sound, kinetic effect—by which dramatic idea attains theatrical expression. Of special importance is the way this scene recapitulates, only to alter, certain performance structures prominent in earlier scenes, particularly the dialectical public scenes of acts I and II.[26]

First, what we sometimes forget is that most of the last scene of *Lear* occurs without the title character on stage. Lear's appearances at the beginning and end of the scene, first with the living and then with the dead Cordelia, frame this scene's long central section, which enacts the quarrels within the victors' camp and Edgar's defeat of Edmund in single combat. The actions that occur in Lear's absence from the stage highlight for one last time the destruction brought about by the libidinal appetites and will to power so often set forth in this play. The battle against Cordelia and Lear won, the evil sisters now compete for mastery of Edmund, who in turn fights the disguised Edgar. Even this Edgar, who channels his aggression into the socially sanctioned form of a ritual combat, is not presented without irony. Even as power once more shifts and the good son defeats the evil son, Cordelia is being hung offstage.

When Lear closes the scene by entering with the body of Cordelia, he bears in his arms the fruits of the cycle of aggression, blow and counterblow, which he set in motion by his own acts. And, in striking ways, the visual orchestration of the play's final moments seems deliberately to recall its beginning. Again Lear is the center of attention; again he stands amid a ring of deferential courtiers; again there are gathered, living and dead, the central actors in this play's tragic events. But now everything has changed; and for me, Shakespeare most forcefully conveys what has changed by his handling of the movement of dialogue in these final moments. Those onstage who encircle Lear yearn to reestablish the binary dialectic of scene i. With every good intention they attempt to put Lear back in the seat of power he held in the opening moments. They turn to him, not only because they honor him, but also because they, like most of us, need a master. They cannot imagine a world without a controlling center of power, a world without a necessary structure of authority and deference, despite all that the play's events have shown them and us about the horrible perversions of humanity such a structure can spawn. With well-meaning cruelty, those onstage assault Lear with their insistence that he assume a place in a structure of dialogue and in a system of social organization in which he now has no interest, though he can no longer retain any illusions about his invulnerability to the destructive power of the world beyond the self.

Watching the scene, what the audience *sees* is an old man bonded only to a corpse—"look there, look there" (V.iii.312)—but surrounded by people who want him to be bonded to them. What the audience *hears* is the repeated frustration of an expected pattern of question and reply, statement and rejoinder, which fuels the binary dynamic of stage speech. But now Lear cannot—or will not—focus on what others want him to do, know, recognize.

KENT   O my good master.
LEAR   Prithee away.
EDGAR   'Tis noble Kent, your friend.

LEAR   A plague upon you murderers, traitors all;
          I might have saved her; now she's gone for ever.
          Cordelia, Cordelia, stay a little. Ha,
          What is't thou say'st?

                                      (268–73)

What we hear in essence is two fractured dialogues held in counterpoint: Lear's impassioned, one-sided conversation with the dead Cordelia, the only object that seems to have any substantial reality for him; and the vague and faltering dialogue of Lear with the living figures around him. They speak with urgency, but he cannot answer in the accents they expect, just as Cordelia once could not answer him in the tones he required. There is no longer pressure emanating out from Lear toward those around him by which the comforting rituals of deference and authority, power exerted and obeyed, can be sustained.[27] For Lear the discourse of power is at an end. When he turns his back upon his retainers to cling to the dead body of Cordelia, he moves to a still place we can only understand as the antithesis of the incessant motion of appetite and will to power that has informed the world of the play from first to last and found expression in the relentless verbal and visual dialectic enacted in scene after scene.

For me the ending of *Lear* is both painful and exhilarating: painful in its insistence on the intensity of Lear's pain, exhilarating in its dramatization of his transcendence of the worldly preoccupations and the egotism that led him to this pass. But what I wish to emphasize is the role of the scene's visual orchestration in expressing its meaning in fully dramatic terms. Not only is Lear's entrance with Cordelia in his arms—a reversal of the traditional Pieta configuration—a striking and resonant visual emblem; not only does the final massing of figures on the stage—figures Lear either does not recognize or upon whom he cannot focus—paradoxically foreground for the audience his essential aloneness, his final tragic isolation, more than if he were unattended; but also this visual coming together of the play's chief characters ironically casts our minds back to earlier scenes in which Lear desperately wanted to stand in a position of command in such a gathering—an aim to which he is now profoundly indifferent.

In addition, the very gap between his interlocutors' verbal gestures and Lear's responses becomes, in the play's final moments, kinetically expressive. We feel, palpably, the loosening of the taut dialectical structures that have informed so much of the play's dialogue and action. Lear is drifting inexorably toward silence and stasis. He no longer functions as one term of an ongoing bipolar dialectic of power exerted and obeyed. The world may again pick up its familiar rhythms, but henceforth without Lear as its driving engine. Whether it is weariness, pain, or wisdom that leads the old king to the stillness of his moment of death we may never know for certain; but what we feel in the theater is the finality of his renunciation of worldly ties. And it is *only* in the idiom of the theater that that renunciation is most fully expressed and felt as Shakespeare's sustained orchestration of the sensory dimensions of this play's key scenes gives form and meaning to the audience's theatrical experience and helps it see feelingly the hard truths of this fiction.

In all I have said about *Lear*, of course, I have not confined myself to speaking solely of the orchestration of visual elements of the implied play. This choice has been deliberate. My purpose has been to show, not only that there is a meaningful and recurring visual design apparent in certain major scenes of the play, but also that fluid visual progressions create kinetic effects reinforced by the aural patterning of the dialogue. In this play, as in his others, Shakespeare's orchestration of the visual spectacle works in tandem with his aural strategies and both have kinetic consequences. In the two chapters which follow I will increasingly focus on the way many aspects of the performed play are orchestrated concurrently and in mutually reinforcing ways.

NOTES

1. See Rose, *Shakespearean Design*, esp. 1–26; Dessen, *Elizabethan Drama and the Viewer's Eye;* and Reibetanz, "Theatrical Emblems in *King Lear*," in *Some Facets of "King Lear*," ed. Colie and Flahiff, 39–57.

2. The critic who most successfully deals with the dynamic elements of Shakespeare's visual stagecraft is J. L. Styan, in *Shakespeare's Stagecraft*, esp. 53–138.

3. Robert Heilman discusses the symbolic implications of darkness and clamor in *Magic in the Web,* esp. 64–73, 113–21.

4. James Hirsh, in *The Structure of Shakespearean Scenes* (New Haven: Yale University Press, 1981), at several points discusses the way in which messengers or other new arrivals to a scene can change its orientation and direction. See, for example, 31 and 123–24.

5. Colie, *Shakespeare's Living Art,* esp. 213–18.

6. Wolfgang Clemen, in *Shakespeare's Dramatic Art,* 147–62, discusses various functions of the Shakespearean soliloquy besides that of self-expression.

7. Spivack, *Shakespeare and the Allegory of Evil,* esp. 31–33, 41–42.

8. For a classic discussion of the reality-appearance theme in the play and the difficulties confronting Hamlet as a result of living in a world of "seeming," see Mack, "The World of *Hamlet,*" 502–23.

9. Nigel Alexander (*Poison, Play, and Duel,* 117) tellingly discusses the inner play as Hamlet's attempt to use "the weapons of words to unmask Claudius." The irony of the play's aftermath, as Alexander so clearly sees, is that while the play temporarily unleashes Claudius's memory and conscience, it also reveals to the audience new dimensions of the prince. The unmasker of Claudius is unmasked to us, the audience, by his response to the success of his "mousetrap."

10. For a quite different reading of this sequence more favorable to Hamlet, see Styan, *Shakespeare's Stagecraft,* 96–97.

11. I certainly do not agree with G. Wilson Knight's view, expressed in *The Wheel of Fire: Interpretations of Shakespearian Tragedy with Three New Essays,* 4th ed. (1949; reprint, London: Methuen, 1974), 17–46, that Claudius is more "human" than Hamlet and that it is the cynicism and sickness of the young prince that poisons the atmosphere of Elsinore. My point is simply that the events following the inner play make the audience pointedly aware of the genuine failings of the protagonist and of the latent moral sensitivity of the king. Neither is quite what he seemed.

12. For a discussion of memory as an antidote to moral oblivion, see Alexander, *Poison, Play, and Duel,* 30–57.

13. C. L. Barber, in *Shakespeare's Festive Comedy,* makes much of the opposition between a "green world" and the world of the "town" or "civilization" in Shakespeare's comedies; and critics such as Alvin Kernan, in his introduction to the Signet *Othello* (New York: New American Library, 1963), xxiii–xxxv, suggest the importance of symbolically opposed geographical places (such as Venice and Cyprus) to the meaning of plays in which geographical distinctions are less overtly emphasized than they are in, say, *As You Like It.* In production, highlighting the differences between

distinct locales is just the most obvious way of directing audience attention visually to significant polarities in the play.

14. Colie, *Shakespeare's Living Art*, 135–67.

15. Richard Fly, in *Shakespeare's Mediated World* (Amherst: University of Massachusets Press, 1976), 27–51, provides a provocative discussion of the central role of the go-between in *Troilus and Cressida* and of the metadramatic implications of the play's emphasis on mediation for one's understanding of Shakespeare's view of the purpose and nature of his art.

16. Lawrence Danson, in *Tragic Alphabet: Shakespeare's Drama of Language* (New Haven: Yale University Press, 1974), sees Hamlet's essential task as that of becoming a true player, that is, of "uniting the proper action with his words, of informing his words with meaning through gesture" (45). Consequently, "the act of revenge is conceived, by Hamlet and his creator, as an expressive act, a fully meaningful linguistic and gestural expression to be undertaken in a world where words and gestures have become largely meaningless. It is thus a creative as much as a destructive act" (48). In the final scene, as duelist, Hamlet becomes such a true player.

17. Michael Goldman, in "The Worst of *King Lear*," *Shakespeare and the Energies of Drama*, 94–108, discusses *Lear* as a play that batters, but does not numb, its audience. It becomes in performance a perverse kind of endurance contest, in which the audience's ability, as well as Lear's, to respond to pain that lies beyond "the worst" is constantly tested. My intent in what follows is to discuss some of the dramaturgical features of the play that create such a harrowing audience experience.

18. For a slightly different way of approaching the structure of I.i, see Mark Rose, *Shakespearean Design*, 35–39.

19. For a discussion of this and other uses of symbolic entrances and exits, see Mack, "The Jacobean Shakespeare," 11–41.

20. Styan, in *Shakespeare's Stagecraft*, 184–86, discusses the way the emotional pressure of this scene is increased in graduated stages.

21. Bernard Beckerman, "Shakespeare's Industrious Scenes," *Shakespeare Quarterly* 30 (1979): 138–50, at 144.

22. Robert Egan, "Kent and the Audience: The Character as Spectator," *Shakespeare Quarterly* 32 (1981): 146–54, at 152.

23. In the folio version of the play this scene is much shorter than in the quarto, but the central impression of unstructured cacophany and madness remains.

24. Granville-Barker, *Prefaces to Shakespeare*, 1:294.

25. Zitner, "*King Lear* and Its Language," 3–22.

26. Throughout this chapter my emphasis on the way scenes are struc-

tured to echo one another reinforces James Hirsh's thesis that similarly constructed scenes in a Shakespearean play often are meant to comment on one another. For a summary of this position, see Hirsh, *The Structure of Shakespearean Scenes,* 208–10.

27. Walter C. Foreman, Jr., in *The Music of the Close: The Final Scenes of Shakespeare's Tragedies* (Lexington: University of Kentucky Press, 1978), 113–58, makes some instructive remarks on the absence of egotism in Lear's final speeches and his failure to "shape" his death as do other Shakespearean tragic heroes. See esp. 156–58.

CHAPTER 6

Orchestration
and Theatrical Structure

For VERY GOOD REASONS the individual scene—defined as the dramatic action occurring between two complete clearings of the stage—is now often viewed as the most important unit of construction in Shakespeare's plays. In this book I myself have spent a good deal of time exploring the implicit performance design of the individual scene and its effects upon the audience. But I also believe that Shakespeare, in constructing his plays, often looked beyond the single scene to larger theatrical sequences consisting of several adjoining scenes orchestrated as a single unit and designed to be experienced as such by the viewer. Often, these sequences of linked scenes are orchestrated to gain power from one another and to achieve, collectively, an emotional and intellectual resonance no single scene could attain by itself. In this chapter I want to explore how Shakespeare's handling of the sensory aspects of performance helps the audience to discern these larger theatrical units and to experience their full complexity.

A major question is, of course, What constitutes the principle of coherence in these scenic groups? My answer is, it depends. Sometimes adjoining scenes are linked thematically, or together produce a sustained emotional effect, or enact successive stages of a single narrative development. But often the visual, aural, and kinetic orchestration of the sequence is what gives it its primary theatrical integrity. Just as Shakespeare carefully orchestrates the individual scene and just as he may orchestrate a spine of widely separated scenes in order to establish visual or kinetic echoes, so, too, he carefully orchestrates groups of linked scenes to create a sustained and complicated audience experience. If critics, in dealing with the structure of Shakespeare's plays, focus solely on plot structure, they overlook all that goes on in these dramas which has no bearing on plot; and they overlook, as well, the fact that on the stage it is the continuum of sights, sounds, and movements to which the dramatist must first give articulate form if effective theater is to result.

Before I talk about some of the principles controlling Shakespeare's orchestration of scenic units, however, I want to review briefly some of the ways in which previous critics have approached the question of Shakespeare's dramatic structure. I do this to make clear my debts to others and also to make plain why I find inadequate or partial those accounts of dramatic structure which pay no attention to the performance design of the implied theatrical event or which focus too narrowly on the individual scenic unit.

In search of the principles underlying Shakespeare's dramatic structure, many critics have run afoul of the act and scene divisions incorporated into his texts by a variety of editors.[1] T. W. Baldwin has been the strongest proponent of the idea that the present act divisions actually correspond—perhaps with minor adjustments—to Shakespeare's intention to divide, particularly the early plays, into five parts as a study of Roman drama would have taught him.[2] Baldwin is concerned almost exclusively with the structure of the plot and with the effect of classical precedents upon Shakespeare's practice. The problem is, of course, that Shakespeare's plays in actuality do not seem to imitate classical models very closely, and a slavish faith in the primacy of a five-act structure may inhibit critics from seeing even the basic plot structure of a play clearly.[3]

More flexible than Baldwin, but also dedicated to the notion that a play's structure equals its plot structure, is A. C. Bradley. In his classic consideration of the structure of Shakespearean tragedy, Bradley divided the action of the play into three parts roughly corresponding to Act I, Act II–Act IV, and Act V. The terms he employs to describe these divisions are the ancient ones of exposition, conflict, and catastrophe, with stress on the third act crisis and the lull in action in Act IV before the tragic conclusion in Act V.[4] While suggesting that the action of most Shakespearean tragedies follows the above paradigm (*Othello* is an exception), Bradley is not insistent that these divisions of the action correspond in any strict way to act divisions.

In regard to Shakespearean comedy, the most influential remarks on Shakespeare's comic structure in the last several decades have undoubtedly been those of C. L. Barber and Northrop Frye, both of whom trace the symbolic design of the comic plot: the movement from a blocked or repressive society to the chaos of Saturnalian upheaval to the restoration of order and the renewal of a society now purged of its repressive aspects and so transformed.[5] Again, neither critic attempts to link these sequential stages of the plays' symbolic action to specific act and scene units, so they, too, are more flexible than Baldwin in how they talk about structure. On the other hand, neither pays much attention to the ways in which comic plot is translated into specifically theatrical form, and their remarks on comic structure are often as applicable to nondramatic as to dramatic texts.

It was really with the pioneering work of Harley Granville-Barker that attention to the structure of Shakespeare's plots was first fully supplemented by attention to his structuring of the theatrical event. Granville-Barker was insistent that our present act and scene divisions tell us little about the real structure of the plays.[6] He was a strong proponent of the idea that the flow of action upon the Shakespearean stage was largely continuous, partly because there was little or no scenery to change.[7] Instead of seeing the plays divided into a number of discrete acts and scenes, he felt they were divided at most into two or three segments within each of which stage action was continuous and fluid. And for Granville-Barker, the integrity of these segments was largely determined by their theatrical coherence established as much by atmosphere, acting rhythms, and visual design as by plot. For him, the plays were theater pieces. Breaks came when one discrete phase of the theatrical experience was over, not necessarily when the plot advanced another step.

Granville-Barker's comments on the structure of Shakespeare's plays, by stressing the rhythm of stage action as a determinant of their stage structure, are a vital corrective to those who, in discussing structure, ignore that Shakespeare wrote for the stage and was concerned about much more than clear plot delineation. On the other hand, Granville-Barker did not offer clear principles, other than the prompting of his own theatrical sense, for deciding where the flow of stage action reached its "natural" resting points. I will build on Granville-Barker's work in this chapter by defining at least a few of the recurring techniques of orchestration by which Shakespeare imparted a discernible rhythm and structure to the flow of stage actions in particular scenic units.

By focusing on the orchestration of groups of scenes, I do not intend, however, to deny that for Shakespeare the individual scene was an important theatrical building block. Clearly it was, and recently three critics in particular—Emrys Jones, Mark Rose, and James Hirsh—have helped us to see that this is so, though they differ markedly in the attention they pay to dramatic units *larger* than the single scene. James Hirsh, for example, believes so strongly that the scene is the most significant unit of construction for Shakespeare that he proposes removing all act divisions from modern editions of the plays and simply numbering all scenes consecutively.[8] He provides a typology of Shakespearean scenes based on the number of characters present in each and on the number of exits and entrances that occur in the course of a scene; and while he argues that particular types of scenes in a given play are meant to echo one another structurally, he devotes little attention to possible ways in which adjoining scenes might be linked to one another.

Emrys Jones, too, directs most of his attention to the structure of the individual scene. He shows how Shakespeare used certain types of scenes—usually with increasing sophistication—from his earliest to his latest plays. He proposes, for example, that one model for the closet scene in *Hamlet* is Faulconbridge's confrontation with his mother in *King John* I.i.220–76.[9] While in this instance Jones has simply identified a certain situation Shakespeare repeatedly dramatized, elsewhere he discusses recurring scenic structures, such as "frame" and "ensemble" scenes.[10] Furthermore, while he generally accepts the cleared stage as indicating the boundaries of a scene, he notes that certain adjoining scenes may be regarded as a unit because they portray aspects of one action. For example, *Othello* III.iv, IV.i, and IV.ii constitute such a unit because here we see the sustained effects of Othello's jealousy in his behavior toward Desdemona. In the first scene Othello angrily demands the handkerchief, in the second he strikes Desdemona before Lodovico, and in the third he calls her a whore in their private encounter.[11] In addition, Jones argues that many of Shakespeare's plays have a general two-part structure with the break occurring most often near the beginning of Act IV. While Jones most often examines individual scenes, he clearly does pay some attention to larger dramatic units.

It is Mark Rose, however, who explores most fully what interests me: the possibility that there may be strong links between scenes presently designated as separate entities. Rose argues that Shakespeare inherited the didactic tradition of medieval morality drama and constructed his plays as a succession of "speaking pictures" meant to instruct as well as to delight. He suggests that we view the plays as a series of deliberate juxtapositions of episodes with related themes.[12] For Bradley's interest in plot, he substitutes a concern with thematic contrasts and correspondences among adjoining visual units. Pauses or breaks, he feels, should occur between these diptych or triptych units and not necessarily between present act and scene divisions.

One problem, of course, is how attention is directed to these thematic contrasts and correspondences and how, in the theater, we feel the integrity of these diptych or triptych structures. Theatrical meaning, as I have been arguing throughout this book, rarely depends solely on the semantic content of dramatic speech. It also depends upon the interplay between language and visual spectacle and upon the particular sequence in which we perceive changes in the tempo, aural texture, and visual features of the plays. Intentionally or not, Rose's metaphors, drawn from the visual arts, suggest that the plays are composed of static thematic units, the coherence of which is discerned retrospectively. I would argue, however, that Rose's diptych and triptych units are usually temporally orchestrated in such a way as to give each unit a kinetic, visual, or rhythmic coherence — in other words, a theatrical coherence — which releases or underscores their thematic meaning.

Consider, for example, the orchestration of the opening of Act II of *Romeo and Juliet*. The act begins with a formal sonnet spoken by the chorus, followed in II.i by Mercutio's bawdy catcalls outside Capulet's orchard, which in turn is followed by Romeo's famous balcony scene with Juliet (II.ii).[13] The chorus, in a detached and formal manner, begins the act by summarizing and simplifying what we are next to see enacted, Romeo's movement from one passion to another.

> Now old desire doth in his deathbed lie,
>   And young affection gapes to be his heir;
> That fair for which love groaned for and would die,
>   With tender Juliet matched, is now not fair.
>
> (II.Cho.1–4)

But what this shift of affection *means* is not clear until the next two scenes unfold. As it turns out, Romeo is not simply exchanging one woman for another, but extending his emotional range and progressing toward a richer emotional experience than he has known. The two ensuing scenes suggest a progress from boisterous and unrefined emotion to restrained lyricism. We move from the realm of simple sexuality and adolescent infatuation, expressed in Mercutio's bawdy conjuration of Rosaline, to the more complex passion expressed in Romeo's hushed praise of Juliet. The aural shifts between the two scenes are pronounced. Bawdy jests and shouts give way to whispered praise: "earthbound" images of thighs and medlars give way to "heavenly" images of skies, sun, moon, and stars. Simultaneously, the audience's visual attention is being directed upward — toward the balcony upon which Juliet appears and toward which Romeo climbs. We are watching, and being invited to share, an "ascent" of a very complex sort.

These two scenes do not simply juxtapose, as one critic has suggested, Mercutio's Ovidianism to Romeo's Petrarchanism.[14] Rather, the former is palpably eclipsed by the latter as attention shifts from bawdy jests to adoring praise, from shouts to whispers, from earth to air, so that the refining power of the new love Romeo and Juliet are experiencing can be made palpable to the audience. We begin this theatrical movement on the ground with the chorus; we end it on the balcony with Romeo; and the sensation of ascent this sequence evokes is furthered by all the devices of stagecraft at Shakespeare's disposal. The orchestration of the sequence both gives it theatrical coherence and helps the audience to participate in the sense of emotional elevation genuine love brings in its wake.

What is true in this theatrical sequence, I submit, is true in all of Shakespeare's plays. They are designed for effective stage presentation; and, while no two plays exemplify the same theatrical structure, each presents to the audience a succession of coherent, carefully orchestrated movements within which several of our present scenes may be subsumed. The most meaningful unit to consider in talking about a play's structure is therefore not always the individual scene, defined as the action occurring between one cleared stage and the next, but rather several such scenes linked together to create sustained and coherent emotional, sensory, or cognitive effects. In all cases the import and coherence of a theatrical movement depends as much upon the skillful orchestration of its visual, aural, and kinetic elements as upon its thematic or plot coherence. Only a critic wearing blinders would deny that our sense of the structure of Shakespeare's plays arises from a combination of factors. But in what follows I will highlight the crucial role played by Shakespeare's art of orchestration in imparting to the audience a sense of the coherence and meaning of successive theatrical movements.

To establish some of the ways Shakespeare orchestrates the sensory elements of performance to give theatrical coherence to discrete groups of scenes, I want first to examine the two opening movements of *Julius Caesar*: scenes i and ii of Act I, and then scene iii of Act I in conjunction with scenes i and ii of Act II. I pick these scenic groups because their orchestration is relatively simple and yet representative of one way in which Shakespeare often gives theatrical coherence to a scenic group. The theatrical unity of each depends heavily upon particular kinds of aural and visual repetition. Such repetition helps to create a particular atmosphere or mood within each segment and to make possible strong and effective contrasts between them.

Scenes i and ii of Act I are both public and occur in the streets of Rome. Each reveals dissension in the body politic; and in each that dissension is given repeated visual, as well as verbal, articulation. The play begins with a tribune castigating the plebeians:

> Hence! home, you idle creatures, get you home!
> Is this a holiday? What, know you not,

Being mechanical, you ought not walk
Upon a laboring day without the sign
Of your profession? Speak, what trade art thou?
                                        (I.i.1–5)

The tribunes are angry that the plebeians, celebrating Caesar and decorating his statues, have forgotten about the former triumphs of Pompey. The tribunes fear Caesar's swelling greatness, that he "would soar above the view of men / And keep us all in servile fearfulness" (74–75). The workingmen of Rome seem neither sophisticated nor determined in their defense of Caesar. They skulk away when faced with the tribunes' wrath. Nonetheless, the scene suggests a public world divided—some are for Caesar and some are against him. Visually the division is signaled by the standoff between the group of plebeians and the two tribunes who are eventually left alone on stage.

The next scene also takes place in the public streets and repeats the basic visual opposition between a crowd and several figures who markedly and repeatedly separate themselves from that mass. The two scenes are loosely linked narratively. Caesar, who has just been discussed by the tribunes, now appears onstage at the head of a public procession. The power so feared by the tribunes is evident at once in the way this enormous crowd gravitates about Caesar. When he speaks, all words and music cease. "Peace, ho! Caesar speaks" (I.ii.1). "Bid every noise be still. Peace yet again!" (14). Because we have already heard how Caesar's greatness is feared, we watch with special attentiveness his imperious conduct and the obsequiousness of those around him: "When Caesar says 'Do this,' it is performed" (10). Moreover, we are prepared for the discontent of Cassius. When Cassius and Brutus stand aside from the procession, it is a visual statement of their dissent and a visual echo of the tribunes' separation from the plebeians. Moreover, all the time Cassius is conferring with Brutus, offstage shouts, holding out the possibility that Caesar is being crowned king, are an aural reminder of the mass of people who hold less critical views of Caesar's power than do the two men before us.

The return of Caesar's train once more calls attention to the division in Rome. Caesar, angry, casts a cold eye on the "lean and hungry" Cassius, who in his turn continues to deprecate Caesar and to work upon Brutus and Casca to join in a conspiracy against him. The first scene ended with the tribunes alone upon the stage after the plebeians, Caesar's supporters, had skulked away; the second scene ends with three more powerful enemies of Caesar left upon the stage after his train finally passes from view. Together, the two scenes constitute the opening movement of the play. Both are public, daytime scenes occurring in the streets of the city. Both, through sharp visual oppositions, show a Rome divided against itself. Both focus attention upon conflict between Caesar and a few men who, for reasons of principle or simple jealousy, are deeply troubled by his growing power.

Scene iii of Act I begins the second major theatrical movement of the play. It is orchestrated in a way that both creates a sharp contrast with the first movement and also enhances the audience's awareness of the unity and significance of this second scenic group. Temporally, the scenes now designated I.iii, II.i, and II.ii represent the evening, the deep night, and the dawn that precede Caesar's murder.[15] In contrast to the public nature of the first two scenes, they show us private encounters or the privacy of homes invaded by figures and pressures from the public realm.[16] Most important, they are dominated by an oppressive atmosphere of fear and fore-boding that cumulatively suggests the external and internal turmoil which precedes the acting out of that great event, Caesar's murder.

The first of the three scenes is important for establishing the atmosphere that is to dominate the others. It is the ground against which the next two scenes are figured; and, although I.iii is relatively unimportant in terms of plot, it is the key to establishing expec-tations about what is to follow. Commonly Shakespeare introduces a theatrical movement by some striking aural or visual departure from prior events, thereby helping the audience to reorient its at-tention. This scene enacts such a decided break with previous action. After two scenes that show crowds moving through Rome's streets in the daytime, I.iii opens in darkness with only two people onstage. Moreover, a prodigious storm is in progress, and in this and the next two scenes it is referred to repeatedly. Casca, who in the former scene spoke so sarcastically of Caesar's behavior in the forum, now assumes a new voice, one thrilled with terror and fear.[17] Sword in hand, he says to Cicero:

> Are you not moved when all the sway of earth
> Shakes like a thing unfirm? O Cicero,
> I have seen tempests when the scolding winds
> Have rived the knotty oaks, and I have seen
> Th' ambitious ocean swell and rage and foam
> To be exalted with the threat'ning clouds;
> But never till to-night, never till now,
> Did I go through a tempest dropping fire.
> Either there is a civil strife in heaven,
> Or else the world, too saucy with the gods,
> Incenses them to send destruction.
>
> (3–13)

A portentous atmosphere, "most bloody, fiery, and most terrible" (130), is quickly established. It is in this atmosphere that we watch the furtive comings and goings of the conspirators. Not even Cassius's bravado, as he laughs at Casca's fears, can dispel the feeling of terrible foreboding created by this wild night. Cassius interprets the storm as a warning against Caesar's prodigious power, though quite clearly it can be interpreted as a warning against his own plot to topple this colossus. During the fearsome night many men try to construe events according to their own ends and desires: Brutus interprets murder as a sacrifice;[18] many try to interpret Caesar's dream. But the unnatural events in the heavens seem to mock each man's certainties.

The events in Brutus's orchard in the following scene are colored by the same disturbing atmosphere. It is still night, and we hear references to "whizzing" exhalations in the heavens. Though there are fewer overt signs of the storm, the conspirators, with their muffled faces and shrouding cloaks, bring reminders of the terrible night into Brutus's private sanctum as his domestic solitude is violated by their knocking (s.d. following II.i.59). More to the point, however, the external storm that so dominates I.iii prepares for, and becomes by implication a reflection of, the psychic and emotional storm raging within Brutus even before the conspirators arrive. We first see him in this scene debating with himself the question

145

of Caesar's dangerous power. Then, further troubled by the message thrown in his study window, he describes the anguish of decision:

> Since Cassius first did whet me against Caesar,
> I have not slept.
> Between the acting of a dreadful thing
> And the first motion, all the interim is
> Like a phantasma or a hideous dream.
> The genius and the mortal instruments
> Are then in council, and the state of a man
> Like to a little kingdom, suffers then
> The nature of an insurrection.
>
> (II.i.61–69)

A phantasma or a hideous dream is exactly what is imaged for the audience by this night of storm and prodigies.

Furthermore, after the conspirators leave, Brutus's touching conversation with Portia makes more clear how thoroughly his domestic and internal peace have been disturbed. The conversation between husband and wife, already overshadowed by uncertainty and foreboding, is interrupted by yet another knocking at the outer door (s.d. following II.i.303). Portia must yield to another would-be conspirator. Aurally, the knockings at the door become a sensory symbol of lost peace as surely as do the rumbles of thunder.

This scene is linked aurally to the following one by the crash of thunder that closes II.i and opens II.ii. Again we see a deeply troubled husband and wife striving to put an interpretation upon the night's events. Again this private realm is invaded by figures from without, first Decius, then the whole band of conspirators. The audience at this point knows the day to come promises death to Caesar and the destruction of Calphurnia's domestic world. The atmosphere of foreboding hovering over the entire dramatic movement is about to erupt into actual and unpredictable violence.

In the broadest terms, it is the pervasively private nature of these scenes, the prevalent darkness, the repeated sounds of the storm, and the atmosphere of foreboding that give them their theatrical coherence and distinguish them sharply from the public daytime scenes that go before and also come after. The three scenes bridge the time between the first "motion" placed in Brutus's mind by

Cassius that they move to curb Caesar's power and the actual acting of the deed. Collectively, they suggest to the audience some of the frightfulness of the waking dream that has engulfed Brutus in this interim. To break the continuity of these scenes by pausing at the traditional act division following I.iii would shatter entirely our sense of the outer storm as a carefully orchestrated prelude to the inner turmoil of Brutus and our sense that a prodigious upheaval threatens his peaceful domestic life, as surely as that of Caesar and Calphurnia. Subsequently, the brief scenes involving Artemidorus (II.iii) and Portia (II.iv) form the bridge leading us to the next movement of the tragedy as we once more move into the public streets and toward the acting of the deed so long debated.

The theatrical unity of a succession of scenes is not always as easy to perceive as in *Julius Caesar* I.iii–II.ii in which aural and visual repetition—darkness, storm, private homes laid open to disturbing intruders—binds together the individual scenes and reinforces their narrative and thematic coherence. Often, however, we encounter in Shakespeare's plays a succession of scenes that seem narratively, thematically, tonally, and visually discrete. They do not glide easily into one another; they do not share a dominant mood or atmosphere. In such cases, should we not simply treat each scene as a separate and complex entity and give over the search for an overarching unity? Sometimes, undoubtedly, yes; but often, I would argue, even such an apparently disjunctive sequence may be orchestrated to evoke from the audience a sustained and, ultimately, unified response. To consider each scene solely as a self-sufficient dramatic unit would ignore the total effect they produce when experienced as a sequential whole.

For illustration I want to look at the complex series of seemingly discrete scenes that constitute the opening movement of *Hamlet,* scenes i–v. Here the abrupt aural and visual changes that accompany the transitions from scene to scene help to create in the audience sustained feelings of disorientation and bafflement. One perspective upon reality collides sharply with another, drawing attention toward a whole range of implicit conflicts and contradictions between man seen as a social creature and man as a solitary being, between sincerity and "seeming," between self-assurance and self-doubt, between the rational dimensions and the irrational emotional aspects of human experience. The return to the battlements at the end of this movement imparts a sense of closure to it, partly because the recreation of the mood of the opening moments makes us feel that we have come full circle through a maze of contradictions, partly also because the second battlements scene offers a partial resolution to some of the tensions and conflicts arising from the preceding events. The orchestration of the whole movement, with its abrupt transitions from episode to episode, leads the audience to experience with Hamlet the sense of being caught in a world of "seeming" and of deceptive surfaces.

To show how this movement produces a growing sense of unresolved tension and disorientation, I wish to consider briefly the transition points between scenes and how they are orchestrated. The compelling atmosphere upon the battlements has often been noted.[19] The darkness, the questions that fly back and forth, the chilling appearance of the ghost who will not speak, Horatio's account of the prodigies that occurred on the night of Caesar's death, his lyrical description of the morning—these factors, taken together, evoke feelings of wonder, fear, and mystery. Then, abruptly and without narrative preparation, we move to the bright and crowded court of Claudius. We do not move gradually into this court world; rather, with trumpets and pomp, the court surges into view, and Claudius immediately begins a long and artfully polished speech. The suddenness of the visual and narrative transition leaves us groping for continuity. What have the mysteries of darkness and ghosts to do with this elegant and ceremonious world?

The very existence of the first scene colors and complicates our responses to the second. After the mysteriousness of that midnight world, the commanding self-assurance of Claudius invites confidence and seems to hold the promise of stability and order. In this lighted room, at least, reason rules. Yet, after the troubling prelude on the battlements, the king's rhetoric seems suspiciously slick and his self-assurance presumptuous. The ghostly image of the dead king—an epic figure, remote, held in obvious awe when alive, and now even more awesome when dead—lingers in our mind to mock the prosiness of the living king. Somewhere beyond this circle of light, darkness and disquietude exist, a fact that is constantly recalled by the brooding presence of Prince Hamlet. Our attitude toward him at this point must be one of bafflement; we are poised between sympathy and distrust. Viewed only from the "reasonable" point of view represented by Claudius, Hamlet's melancholy must seem "most absurd" (I.ii.103). On the other hand, the opening scene has suggested that there are more things in heaven and in earth than mere reason can comprehend.

Further visual and aural contrasts follow. The court vanishes as quickly as it appeared, leaving Hamlet alone on the stage. His soliloquy invites us to share his perspective more fully, even as it underscores more completely the gulf between the private man and the society from which he is alienated. The arrival of Horatio and his friends again changes our perspective. They surround the solitary prince with kindness and deferential solicitude, suggesting that he is not so alone and unsupported as he first appeared. Though the play is full of false friends and spies, the loyalty of Horatio, and here of Bernardo and Marcellus, implies that all friendship need not be seeming. Though these figures cannot share Hamlet's grief completely or fulfill the commands soon to be laid upon him by the ghost, they reach toward him with sympathy, and their language carries with it none of the odor of court hypocrisy.[20] When Hamlet asks Horatio why he is in Denmark, his friend replies:

HORATIO My Lord, I came to see your father's funeral.
HAMLET I prithee do not mock me, fellow student.
I think it was to see my mother's wedding.
HORATIO Indeed, my lord, it followed hard upon.
(I.ii.176–79)

Horatio, with great simplicity, will say what those who rotate around Claudius will never admit. He then goes on to tell Hamlet of the appearance of the ghost.

But before we return to the sentries' world, yet another sharply disorienting scene intervenes. Through a striking change of key we are projected into an atmosphere of middle-class prudence and domesticity, as Ophelia, Laertes, and then Polonius appear on the stage. Though we learn from I.iii that Hamlet is, or has been, a suitor to Ophelia, what is most striking is the scene's tone of unruffled self-assurance and worldly wisdom. We are invited to see the world, not from the perspective of Hamlet's troubled doubts and questions, but from the vantage point of men who are certain they can tell the difference between the surface appearance of things and the underlying reality.

> LAERTES For Hamlet, and the trifling of his favor,
> Hold it a fashion and a toy in blood,
> A violet in the youth of primy nature,
> Forward, not permanent, sweet, not lasting,
> The perfume and suppliance of a minute,
> No more.
>
> (5–10)

Though Laertes's language is less overtly platitudinous than his father's, the son is much like the father in the self-assurance with which he dispenses his advice. This is not to say that real affection and a desire to help do not underlie his words. But after the troubled anguish of Hamlet, Laertes's diagnostic prescriptions slide with unthinking ease from his mouth. There is no probing here for what Hamlet's love may mean to his sister or to Hamlet himself, simply the assumption that "best safety lies in fear" (43). The tone of prudence and self-assurance that dominates the scene has, to be sure, a seductive charm. Even Polonius's advice can be taken in part at face value. But implicitly we are asked to compare Hamlet's restless questions with these prudent saws. Can life truly be comprehended by such packaged wisdom? The very existence of the scene throws into higher relief the more desperate search for answers that Hamlet undertakes upon the battlements.

His arrival there, by recreating the special ambiance of the opening scene, signals the closure of the play's first movement. All the events within it are bracketed between the mysterious darkness of the midnight world. We have moved from darkness to light and back to darkness, with the uneasy suggestion that all may be morally dark in the lighted court. Even in I.iv as Hamlet and the sentries stand in anticipation of the ghost's return, the sound of trumpets and cannon applauding Claudius's revels provides an instance of aural counterpoint that reminds us of the sumptuous and self-indulgent court within and of the hackneyed wisdom of both king and councilor. As the revels proceed within the court, Hamlet, without, hears from the ghost confirmation of his worst suspicions: the new king murdered the old.

The orchestration of the whole movement keeps the audience searching for a stable point of reference, for a voice of true authority to separate out from those whose certitude masks guile or signals complacence. We search, like Hamlet, for a perspective we can trust. Against this background, the words of the ghost ring with gratifying simplicity: "The serpent that did sting thy father's life / Now wears his crown" (I.v.39–40).

> Let not the royal bed of Denmark be
> A couch for luxury and damnèd incest.
> But howsomever thou pursues this act,
> Taint not thy mind, nor let thy soul contrive
> Against thy mother aught.
>
> (82–86)

The command seems simple and at first appears to offer a clear guide for action, just as the return to the midnight world on the castle walls implies closure to this theatrical movement. The mystery in Elsinore has been explained — or has it? The whole orchestration of Act I militates against certainties. No sooner is one perspective upon reality established than it is undermined or juxtaposed to a contrary perspective. In such a context, we must wonder, as Hamlet comes to wonder, whether even the ghost offers a reliable point of reference.

The opening movement of *Hamlet* thus serves as a powerful theatrical introduction to the complexity of the dramatic world Shakespeare explores in this play. The abrupt transitions from episode to episode constantly unsettle our perspective upon events while helping to suggest a network of unreconciled tensions, not only, for example, between the melancholy prince and the patronizing king, but between the doubts of Hamlet and the bland certainties of Polonius, between the mysteries of the battlements and the seemingly unshakable "order" represented in Claudius's court. Our cumulative struggle to obtain a trustworthy perspective upon events leads us ultimately to experience something of Hamlet's own baffled uncertainties in the serpent-infested garden of Elsinore.

What bears emphasis, moreover, is the role of aural, visual, and kinetic events in creating the cumulative power and meaning of the sequence for the audience. We are manipulated by a deliberately disjunctive stagecraft to feel, through stark juxtapositions of light and dark, unctuous and ironic rhetoric, crowded stages and solitary figures, the unmediated tensions in Elsinore and the difficulty of winning through to a unifying truth amid multiple and competing frames of reference. Ironically, the theatrical unity of the movement comes largely from the cumulative effect of its inner discontinuities—discontinuities accented first on the sensory level. Even the end of the movement, with its return to the setting and atmosphere of scene i, does not bring about the strong sense of closure one might expect, so powerful has been the entire movement's suggestion of an unstable, deceptive, and discontinuous theatrical universe. Act I can certainly be seen as a series of discrete scenes, but I think there is much merit in seeing how these separate scenes are orchestrated to evoke sustained feelings of disorientation and doubt in the viewer, effects lost to sight if we atomize the theatrical experience too finely.[21]

That Shakespeare deliberately orchestrated groups of scenes to enhance their cumulative theatrical impact and to parse the theatrical experience into meaningful units for the audience is the central thesis of this chapter. Nowhere is this thesis more clearly demonstrated than in Shakespeare's orchestration of sustained climactic or crescendo effects by which the audience, through the handling of stage events, is caught up in a rising tide of tension, fear, or anticipation. Again, such crescendo effects depend, not upon plot events alone, but also upon Shakespeare's management of the sensory elements of the theatrical experience.

In some plays, certainly the tragedies, what I call crescendo effects are more central to the work's orchestration than in others. Plays such as *Henry IV, Part I,* and *As You Like It,* for example, lack a narrative or theatrical climax in Act III of the sort we find in *King Lear* or *Hamlet.* The climactic effects of the former plays depend upon what Paula Johnson has called "terminal heightening," a bringing together at the play's conclusion of nearly all its characters—at Shrewsbury and at the forest wedding—to create the impression of a climactic end toward which all these figures have been inexorably moving.[22] But the body of these plays is structured, theatrically, by a primarily nonclimactic pattern of repeated contrasts among different stage groups. In *As You Like It,* the various pairs of lovers, and in *Henry IV, Part I,* rebel, court, and tavern figures by and large do not mix until the plays' conclusions; dramatic tension is sustained by repeated juxtapositions of idiom and outlook among the various stage parties as a theme or group of themes is elaborated from different perspectives in a succession of adjoining scenes or episodes.[23]

In the next chapter I will look in detail at the orchestration of a single comedy, *Twelfth Night,* in which climactic theatrical structures mix with nonclimactic structures of contrast and variation. For the moment, however, I wish to examine sustained crescendo effects as they are variously orchestrated in several tragedies and then to look at the decided lowering of tension—the meditative lull—that often follows climactic sequences and constitutes, in its turn, a distinctive and functional theatrical movement.

Individual scenes, of course, are often orchestrated climactically. As early as the writing of *Titus Andronicus,* Shakespeare was creating, in the little space of a single scene, perfect climactic structures. I want briefly to examine one of these scenes—*Titus Andronicus* III.i, in which Titus pleads in vain for the lives of his two sons and then learns, in succession, of a host of further cruelties done to him or to his family—to identify some of the techniques by which Shakespeare orchestrates crescendo effects, not just in single scenes, but in much larger dramatic units.

Titus Andronicus III.i depends structurally on the repetition of a basic visual and narrative situation: Titus confronted by a messenger bearing bad news.[24] That the scene creates the impression of escalating emotional tension, rather than numbing sameness, is largely due to the increasingly horrible visual tableaux incorporated in the scene and to Shakespeare's careful graduation of Titus's responses. The scene opens with a striking visual rendering of Titus's impotence and humiliation. While Roman judges and senators pass in procession to execute Titus's two sons, he pleads for their lives, even throwing himself on the ground and continuing to beg after the procession has passed from the stage. But the sight of Titus on the ground is not the worst of the scene's visual shocks. The audience has already seen the ravished Lavinia, but Titus has not;

Marcus brings her, lacking both hands and tongue, to her father (33). Later, we see Aaron cut off Titus's hand (191); and, finally, a messenger brings that hand and the heads of his two sons onto the stage (233). There seems to be no worst in such a scene. It ends with a grotesque visual parody of the procession with which it opened. Marcus exits carrying one son's head; Titus bears the other head in his one remaining hand; Lavinia carries her father's other hand in her teeth.

At the same time that the audience is assimilating these escalating visual shocks, Shakespeare is carefully escalating Titus's own emotional rhetoric. After the procession of Roman senators passes by, Lucius enters to tell his father that he, the remaining son, has been banished. To this news Titus reacts with ironic joy, for Rome is but a "wilderness of tigers" (54), and to be banished from it is to be saved from destruction. However, the next newsbearer to appear is Marcus, who brings the mutilated Lavinia onstage. Seeing her, Titus realizes that his former grief for his sons was not the worst he must bear:

> What fool hath added water to the sea
> Or brought a faggot to bright-burning Troy?
> My grief was at the height before thou cam'st,
> And now like Nilus it disdaineth bounds.
>
> (68–71)

His subdued, ironic reaction to Lucius's banishment is replaced by a wild outpouring of grief. Moreover, throughout the central part of this scene, the growing extremity of Titus's passion is made perceptible by the counterpoint between his voice and the more "reasonable" voice of Marcus. For example, having been led by Aaron into cutting off his hand, Titus desperately laments his condition, while Marcus tries to moderate his grief.

TITUS   O, here I lift this one hand up to heaven,
             And bow this feeble ruin to the earth.
             If any power pities wretched tears,
             To that I call!
             [To Lavinia] What, wouldst thou kneel with me?
             Do then, dear heart; for heaven shall hear our prayers,

> Or with our sighs we'll breathe the welkin dim
> And stain the sun with fog, as sometime clouds
> When they do hug him in their melting bosoms.
>
> MARCUS O brother, speak with possibility,
> And do not break into these deep extremes.
>
> TITUS Is not my sorrow deep, having no bottom?
> Then be my passions bottomless with them!
>
> MARCUS But yet let reason govern thy lament.
>
> TITUS If there were reason for these miseries,
> Then into limits could I bend my woes:
> When heaven doth weep, doth not the earth o'erflow?
>
> (206–21)

Titus is beyond consolation, but what he does not know is that Aaron has deliberately tricked him into severing his hand. When a messenger appears with that hand and his sons' heads, Shakespeare uses a device discussed in chapter 4, a sudden unexpected silence, to signal the further escalation of Titus's woe. It is now Marcus who adopts the raging rhetoric previously employed by Titus.

> Now let hot Etna cool in Sicily,
> And be my heart an ever-burning hell!
> These miseries are more than may be borne.
>
> (241–43)

Only after Marcus and Lucius have both spoken does Titus simply say, "When will this fearful slumber have an end?" (252). The nightmare that has overtaken Titus beggars speech. His brother cannot understand Titus's silence. He says that now the time has come to give full voice to grief, but for answer Titus merely laughs (264). He has passed beyond the boundary where language or tears can encompass his grief. That Marcus will now rage simply shows that his emotions remain at one remove from his brother's.

This scene, occurring in a relatively early play, shows Shakespeare's skill in using visual and aural effects to escalate emotional tension. The gradual filling of the stage as "messenger" after "messenger" appears, the succession of visual cruelties, the careful gradation in Titus's own expressions of grief, the use of Marcus as foil—all these elements work together to convey to an audience some sense of the growing nightmare of suffering that overtakes the protagonist.

What I would now like to suggest is that the crescendo effect perceptible in such a single scene may be sustained through several and so, in performance, may lend theatrical continuity and enhanced meaning to what may appear, in reading the plays, as a succession of discrete events. *King Lear* offers a particularly rich field for exploring such sustained crescendo effects, and I wish here to consider the differing techniques of orchestration informing two of them. Neither depends as blatantly as does the *Titus* scene on a succession of horrid visual shocks; each does borrow and elaborate on other devices apparent in that earlier scene.

The first and simpler crescendo effect is achieved by scenes ii, iii, and iv of Act II. Modern editors have divided this sequence into three scenes, though in the First Folio they form one. Kent, asleep in the stocks, should be visible onstage throughout Edgar's monologue (II.iii.1–21). Present scene divisions obscure this visual continuity and can lead the audience to assume an unnecessary disjunction between the three events with which the sequence deals: Kent's reception at Gloucester's castle, Edgar's monologue, and Lear's reception at the same spot. Mark Rose has suggested that the three scenes are clearly related in thematic terms, each portraying a "good man unjustly shut out in the cold, excluded from the castle."[25] This is surely true, but such a description only partially describes what goes on in this sequence and how these acts of exclusion are orchestrated to affect the audience.

More is involved in these scenes than the underscoring of theme. The events that comprise the sequence are orchestrated to gain energy from one another and to involve the audience in an inexorable escalation of emotional tension. As Rose has pointed out, the three scenes enact the same basic event, but each repetition is pitched at a higher level of intensity. As a result, the audience feels it is caught in a world in which savagery grows and feeds on itself. At the same time, the segments involving Kent and Edgar provide a ground for Lear's suffering that helps the audience perceive the greater magnitude of the old king's torment. Like Marcus in the scene from *Titus Andronicus* just discussed, Kent and Edgar provide a yardstick by which the audience can implicitly measure the dimensions of heroic emotion. These three "good men" *are* in somewhat parallel situations, but they do not respond to that situation in exactly the same way.

The Kent episode is sparely handled. He and Oswald arrive almost simultaneously at Gloucester's castle bearing messages for Gloucester and Regan. Kent immediately castigates the feckless courtier, finally thrashing him until he bellows for help. At this point Edmund enters, sword drawn, followed by Gloucester, Cornwall, Regan, and a retinue. Kent suddenly finds himself faced with not one opponent, but many; and while Oswald rather comically tries to avoid his wrath, Cornwall is all too ready to match words and power. The blunt Kent has not much more respect for Regan's husband, however, than for Goneril's miserable servant; and in good round language he continues to abuse Oswald, even as he gives offence to Cornwall.

> Sir, 'tis my occupation to be plain:
> I have seen better faces in my time
> Than stands on any shoulder that I see
> Before me at this instant.
> (II.ii.87–90)

The comic confrontation between Oswald and Kent has escalated into a more dangerous standoff between the king's messenger and the offended duke. For his plainness, Kent is unceremoniously clapped in the stocks.

Here, as elsewhere in *Lear*, the scene is designed, aurally, visually, and kinetically, to pit a solitary figure against a group of opponents so that the bearing down of the weak by the strong can be tangibly enacted for the audience. But this episode puts sharp limits on the viewer's fear and pity. Kent throughout maintains a sense of rueful humor. There is comedy in his attacks on the goose-fearful Oswald, humor in the outrageous way he baits the angry Cornwall, especially when he switches (100) from blunt plainness to unmistakably fulsome flattery. The point is that Kent acts from the firm position of a loyal servant. He never wavers from that role. Even though he ends up in the stocks, he manages to make a monkey of Oswald and even of the fiery duke by forcing him to spend his fury on a man who is obviously his social inferior but refuses to be awed by his authority. Kent does not expect to command respect in and of himself, only in his role as messenger of the king:

> I serve the King—
> On whose employment I was sent to you;
> You shall do small respect, show too bold malice
> Against the grace and person of my master,
> Stocking his messenger.
>
> (123–27)

The physical discomfort of being put in the stocks is his; but the disgrace, in every important way, is Lear's.

If Kent's ironic humor somewhat mitigates our pity for his plight, Edgar's situation is more immediately terrifying, especially if—as is often done in performance—he actually transforms himself visually during his monologue from courtier to bedlam beggar by ripping off his clothing, griming his face, disheveling his hair, and sticking "pricks" into his skin.[26] The vulnerability of man naked, stripped of his accommodations, is painfully evident, and after Kent's self-possessed irony, Edgar's language is anything but detached. He is a man in flight and clutching at whatever disguise can save his life. While Kent at least retains a kind of integrity in his role as loyal servant, Edgar loses his social identity before our eyes, reduced to the poorest of human states. His transformation, however, is achieved with emblematic swiftness and finality. He *was* the pampered elder son of a respected court figure; now, by a turn of Fortune's wheel, he *is* a pariah. Kent, even in the stocks and even in disguise, is still what he was—Lear's faithful follower. Edgar's transformation is more stunning and absolute. Yet even at this point Edgar does not despair. "Poor Turleygod, poor Tom, / That's something yet: Edgar I nothing am" (II.ii.20–21). He can accept his transformation, and he can go on.

For the audience, the worst is still ahead. Anticipation plays an important role in the audience's rising dread at this moment. Having seen Kent abused and Edgar driven to doff his clothes, his social identity, and his very name, we cannot really hope that Lear will fare better with those who now hold power. When the old king arrives at the very spot before the sleeping Kent where Edgar has stood, we expect, not surcease from suffering, but its exacerbation.

And we are right. But what makes this scene so much more terrible than what has gone before is that Lear can neither defend himself from humiliation by ironic self-composure nor accept his lot. Edgar cast off his old self in twenty-one chilling lines. Lear hopelessly tries, through most of the 304 lines of II.iv, to maintain his old identity as king and honored father. While the Edgar episode is compressed and starkly emblematic, that involving Lear is drawn-out and acutely psychological. It lays bare, in excruciating detail, the futile strategems of Lear to retain his power and the ruthless frustration of those designs by a series of cruel opponents.

What I wish to emphasize is how the Kent and Edgar episodes wind up, in stages, the emotional tension as the audience approaches the Lear segment. Taken together, the events in Gloucester's court-yard suggest a sustained crescendo movement orchestrated in three parts. Each shows a single figure in some way humiliated and over-powered by the faction of Goneril, Regan, and Edmund. But the Kent episode suggests none of the terrible wrenching apart of the self that is so much a part of Lear's agony. Its mounting tension results from the fact that Kent's bluntness is directed against ever more powerful figures capable of increasingly brutal retaliation, but he bears with equanimity all they can do. Edgar responds more radically to the shifting contours of his world. As he takes off his clothes, he shows how vulnerable is unaccommodated man and how fragile his social identity. But only with Lear's entry does the audience see the inner cost—to a man of fourscore years—of having his sense of self destroyed. Kent and Edgar's experiences predict Lear's, but do not encompass it. Lear's grief and rage are greater than theirs, his resistance more fierce. Yet it is only because his experience is foregrounded against theirs that its intensity is so plain to the beholder.

The crescendo effect achieved in scenes II.ii to II.iv depends upon the repetition, at varying levels of intensity, of a basic action by several characters successively. Not only are all three good men shut out of the castle, but all must face a loss of identity, position, and authority. The sequence climaxes when Lear, humiliated past bear-ing, foresees his madness and rushes out into the storm. The ques-tion, of course, is what can follow such a sequence? Isn't it time for the play, and Lear's suffering, to end? The answer is, of course, no; though how Shakespeare can contrive to sustain and even en-hance the emotional pressure on the stage and in the audience is a crucial theatrical question.[27]

Like scenes ii to iv of Act II, scenes i to vii of Act III form an integral theatrical movement orchestrated climactically. But Shake-speare finds a new way to build, for the audience, the emotional pressure of the sequence. In *Titus* III.i and the second act of *Lear*, a sense of climax grows from repetition of a basic situation at greater levels of intensity. In Act III of *Lear*, repetition works in tandem with contrast. Geographically, the act moves with patterned precision between two locales: heath and castle. Each locale is a symbolic one; each embodies certain values; and it is through aural and visual contrasts that Shakespeare first directs audience attention to these differences. Moreover, what the audience sees going on in the castle scenes influences how that audience responds to the heath scenes. The castle episodes do more than provide opportunities for the actor playing Lear to rest his voice, though they certainly do serve that pragmatic purpose. More crucially, they define a growing threat to Lear and to civilization itself; and the audience's deepening awareness of that threat enhances its fear and terror for the ragged band cast out into the storm.[28]

This theatrical movement opens with a straightforward "stepping-stone" progression from a conversation between Kent and a gentle-man to Lear's impassioned "Blow, winds, and crack your cheeks!" (III.ii.1).[29] The two attendant figures, appearing first, convey infor-mation about the political situation and also describe Lear's present state as he runs "unbonneted" on the heath, crying to the heavens. Though they speak with urgency and compassion, their language provides detachment and exteriority against which we measure the intensity and interiority of the king's speech. While both the First Folio and the modern editions mark a scene division when Kent and the gentleman exit, a powerful sense of continuity actually binds the two scenes, partly because Kent describes the very thing we next see—Lear on the heath, partly also because we are carried forward on a rising emotional tide from passion described to passion enacted. This is a familiar pattern of graduated emotional intensi-fication.

With scene iii, however, the orchestration of the sequence changes. Twice more we are to return to witness the various states of rage, resignation, and madness through which Lear passes in his purgatorial night on the heath; but the important thing is that we do not focus only upon the king and his followers. Interspersed with the Lear scenes are others involving those who now are in possession of Gloucester's castle. These "interruptions," however, do not dilute, but progressively heighten, the terror and pity with which we observe Lear.

At the simplest level, the presence of the castle scenes make each return to the heath a newly painful shock. Lear's torment and our exposure to it never seem to end. But the castle episodes are more than diversions from which we are repeatedly launched back into Lear's suffering; they also cumulatively define a world of naked power and ruthlessness that threatens to destroy all true civility. Heath and castle become opposing moral worlds, and the disjunction between them is first cued on a visual and aural level. There is cacophony and storm on the heath, calm in the castle; jagged lightning without, steady torchlight within; mad raging opposed to "reasonable" calculation; rain-drenched, bedraggled figures set against fur-gowned courtiers. But while the castle world seems, at first, by these contrasts to embody order and stability, eventually a terrible irony is underscored. In this topsy-turvy world, it is only on the tempestuous heath that humane values survive. The calm of the castle thinly veils a stark bestiality. Part of the escalating power of this theatrical sequence comes from the audience's growing recognition of just what depravity furred gowns can hide.

To see how the dialectic between heath and castle functions, consider III.iii, the first occasion in which the audience's attention is directed back to the castle. Gloucester is speaking to Edmund. The cacophonous noise of the storm, Lear's raging, and the fool's babbling "prophecy" give way to quieter speech. Gloucester is plotting to deceive the duke and aid Lear, having learned of Cordelia's plan to revenge her father. His principles have won out over his timidity. Though not daring to side openly with Lear, he is now ready to aid him secretly. When he leaves, Edmund speaks these chilling lines:

> This courtesy forbid thee shall the Duke
> Instantly know, and of that letter too.
> This seems a fair deserving, and must draw me
> That which my father loses—no less than all.
> The younger rises when the old doth fall.
>   (19–23)

With impeccable logic, Edmund schemes to make his fortune by betraying his father. There is madness in such "reason," and clearly to be sane is not synonymous with being kind. Ordinarily we regard the world of order represented by civilized society as a bulwark against anarchy. Here, however, this assumption is turned on its head. What we see is a foul perversion of order and reason by a callous and ambitious figure.

By contrast, amid the howling storm upon the heath, deeds of loyalty and kindness are repeatedly done. After Edmund's monologue we see Kent gently trying to get his master to enter a hovel, and we hear the king's prayer for the naked wretches "That bide the pelting of this pitiless storm" (III.iv.29). The outcasts, in their torment, have retained, or attained to, some of the values of a truly civilized order. To be sure, in his madness and frustration, Lear continues to rage and curse his daughters, but he has kindness for his fool and his "philosopher"; and Kent is a constant reminder of the human ties of love and loyalty that bind man to man and keep them from becoming beasts of prey.

As the act proceeds, the alternation of scenes makes us increasingly aware of the ageless opposition between cruelty and kindness, self-aggrandizement and selflessness, hypocrisy and truthfulness. Of course, within the castle, Gloucester and later Cornwall's servant take their stands against the ruthless viciousness that is dominant among those in power. But in taking vengeance upon them, Cornwall and Regan are indirectly attacking Lear and all those tied by bonds of love and loyalty to him. Cumulatively, the audience's horror grows as it is made to see how thoroughly goodness is threatened by the schemers who control the castle.

While Lear's personal ordeal reaches a climax in his madness in Gloucester's farmhouse, the audience must see more. The theatrical movement ends with the blinding of Gloucester, a physical echo of the psychic mutilation of Lear. While the first two scenes in the castle are brief, this one is long and brutally explicit in its violence. Though Gloucester and Lear are made to suffer in different ways, this distinction is probably secondary in the minds of the audience to the overwhelming impression of endless and growing torment that the entire movement has produced.[30] Were the castle scenes not intertwined with the heath scenes, the audience would not so strongly feel the ironic reversal by which the lawless heath becomes the refuge of goodness, the orderly castle the seat of evil. At the same time, the movement would lose much of its climactic power. By progressively revealing the growing strength and viciousness of the anti-Lear faction, the castle scenes make us care more deeply and fear more strongly for that tattered band out in the storm.

I have taken a good deal of time to discuss various ways in which crescendo effects are achieved, because they constitute an important aspect of an audience's experience of many of Shakespeare's plays, especially the tragedies. Whether orchestrated within a single scene or sustained through several, crescendo effects reveal one powerful technique by which a series of scenes may be welded together to form a coherent theatrical movement, the total effect of which is greater than the sum of its parts.

Usually, the most pronounced crescendo effects in a play occur at the midpoint of a play and direct audience attention toward the narrative climax. For example, in *Julius Caesar* the fearsome night of anticipation already discussed gives way to the violent events in the capitol and the forum. It is as if passions long held in check suddenly erupt in ways not altogether predictable, as the planned violence of Caesar's murder is followed eventually by Antony's manipulation of the Roman mob and then their attack on the hapless poet, Cinna. In *King Lear* the crescendo effect builds in a series of waves, leading toward the central agony on the heath, as we watch Lear's initial dispute with Goneril in her castle (I.iii–iv), then the whole sequence of events in Gloucester's courtyard (II.ii–iv), and finally the events just discussed. Cumulatively, the experience involves us in a seemingly endless exposure to human suffering.

Frequently, such crescendos bring in their wake a decided lowering of emotional tension. The strong emotional climax produced by the forum events in *Julius Caesar,* by Lear's night on the heath, or Coriolanus's banishment is followed by a perceptible slowing of tempo, a more subdued stage atmosphere. Often the transition is signaled by a change of key, a shift from public events to private. After Lear's purgatorial night on the heath and Gloucester's blinding, Act IV opens with the solitary figure of Edgar on the stage, soon joined by Gloucester himself, led by an old man. The noise of the storm, Gloucester's cries as he is blinded, the din of Cornwall's fight with his servant — these have all passed.

In one production of the play that I saw, much was made of this transition from cacophony to calm, dark to dawn.[31] As Edgar appeared, the stage was bathed in soft morning light, and one could hear the chirp of birds. The audience was suddenly released from a long nightmare into a world seemingly transformed. Nature now showed herself as gentle as the old peasant who offered Gloucester his help. Later, this new mood of gentleness and healing was echoed in Cordelia's invocation of the healing powers of nature's herbs (IV.iv.15–20) and in the sound of soft music that wakes a renewed Lear from sleep (IV.vii.24). Of course, the horrors of the play were not over, but for a moment a tenuous calm had prevailed.

Bradley saw the portion of the tragedies following the narrative climax as a potential weak spot in their structure, for there the pace of action slows.[32] It is my contention, however, that, since plot alone is seldom Shakespeare's primary concern, these narrative lulls can and do constitute coherent theatrical movements as important as any other for our fullest understanding of the plays. Within them, delicate tonal modulations help the audience to assimilate by indirection some of the changes brought about by previous events. Emotions surface that are new to the plays and turn attention toward a transformed dramatic landscape, chastened by grief and loss. The audience is given a necessary opportunity for assimilation and reevaluation.

The slowing of the action after the central crescendo movement of a tragedy enables the audience to count the cost — to protagonist and bystander alike — of previous events. Private moments come to the fore, and an elegiac tone is often established, enabling us to realize that things of great worth and beauty have been, or are about to be, destroyed. We can think, for example, of Desdemona preparing for bed on the night of her murder and singing the willow ballad (*Oth.* IV.iii). Her purity is never more evident, but she—and the promise she has held out for the entire play of love's transforming and refining power—is about to be destroyed. Just so, Ophelia in her madness (*Ham.* IV.v) reminds us of the destruction of innocence that is one by-product of the great conflict between Claudius and the prince. So also the announcement of Portia's death in *Julius Caesar* IV.iii recalls a world of domestic tranquility forfeited amid civil strife, even as Brutus's quarrel with Cassius makes clear the compromises and shabby wrangling that have diminished his high-minded "sacrifice" of Caesar.

In fact, the three scenes that follow the mobbing of Cinna in that play make very plain Shakespeare's concern with the spiritual consequences of acts, rather than their practical or overt consequences. The most obvious result of Caesar's death is civil war and the eventual triumph of the triumvirate. But before the battles of the last movement of the tragedy lead us to that final consequence, the action pauses, and more subtle consequences suggest themselves.

ANTONY These many, then, shall die; their names are pricked.
OCTAVIUS Your brother too must die. Consent you, Lepidus?
LEPIDUS I do consent—
OCTAVIUS   Prick him down, Antony.
LEPIDUS Upon condition Publius shall not live,
         Who is your sister's son, Mark Antony.
ANTONY He shall not live. Look, with a spot I
                damn him.

(IV.i.1–6)

After a series of public scenes, we see a private encounter; after passionate rhetoric and shouts, we hear quiet voices dispassionately condemning brothers and nephews to die. A ruthlessness has been born, far worse than the mindless violence of the aroused plebeians. Civil war has provided the excuse for the political mentality of a police state.

This scene, with its altered tone, is prelude to the subsequent quarrel between Brutus and Cassius. Though less coldly repulsive, their meeting reveals that here, too, there has been a "falling off" from past ideals. In the privacy of Brutus's tent, the two snipe at one another like schoolboys.

CASSIUS   Brutus, bait not me!
            I'll not endure it. You forget yourself
            To hedge me in. I am a soldier, I,
            Older in practice, abler than yourself
            To make conditions.
BRUTUS   Go to! you are not Cassius.
CASSIUS I am.
BRUTUS I say you are not.
CASSIUS Urge me no more! I shall forget myself.
            Have mind upon your health. Tempt me no farther.
BRUTUS Away, slight man!

                                                        (IV.iii.28–37)

At the root of their quarrel is a struggle between honor and expediency. The conspirators now head an army, and an army needs money and allies. Cassius would win friends and raise money in any way he can; Brutus would do all honorably. But Brutus asks Cassius for the money he will not raise or seize for himself. The noble conspiracy is bogged down in sordid practical details; and these lead in turn to the petty quarrels about who is the better soldier, who the nobler Roman. The brightness of former ideals has been irrevocably dimmed, and the report of Portia's death merely deepens the overriding sense of loss and diminishment.

Finally, the scene dwindles toward a chastened conclusion. The quarrel mended, messengers and Cassius gone, Brutus calls two fellow soldiers to sleep in his tent. Then, book in hand, he sits to listen to the soothing music of Lucius's harp. It is a moment of calm in which, I feel, we imagine that Brutus is striving to recapture something of a lost inner harmony, some momentary and homely respite from the cares that now weigh upon him. But then Lucius sleeps and the music ceases. Brutus is left terribly alone amid the sleeping figures that surround him. It is at this point that the ghost of Caesar enters, making clear that for this man there are to be no more quiet moments.

The whole dramatic movement between the mobbing of Cinna and the morning of Philippi is not important in terms of plot. But it is important for conveying to the audience the altered landscape after the crescendo of violence in the capitol and forum has subsided. The political tyranny Brutus sought to curb has reared its head in the persons of the dispassionate triumvirs. Brutus's ideals have been tainted by practical necessities, his domestic peace lost, his inner harmony disturbed. A weariness settles over the stage, a sense of passions ebbed. Shakespeare's plays are never concerned simply with action, but with the spiritual consequences and metaphysical implications of action. The sustained decrescendo movement following a play's crisis allows the audience to turn its attention to such consequences and provides the slowing of dramatic tempo that enables altered emotions to be felt.

One's total sense of Shakespeare's dramatic structure arises from a number of factors. Of course, some attention to the stages of an unfolding story enters into any consideration of dramatic structure, but Shakespeare's plays are too varied, too interwoven with mirror scenes and events redundant or unimportant for plot development for their structure to be fully comprehended by analysis of plot alone. On the other hand, thematic or didactic considerations do not by themselves adequately account for the arrangement of dramatic events, although adjoining scenes often reveal thematic correspondences or contrasts. As I have been arguing throughout this chapter, some attention must also be given to the theatrical shape of the plays, to the ways in which a succession of scenes is orchestrated to create sustained emotional and psychological effects that carry the audience to a fuller understanding of the contours of the dramatic experience in which it is immersed. Dramatic movements of the kind I have been exploring are unified by discernible rhetorical and affective strategies. They lead the audience to experience the plays, not as a succession of static thematic blocks, but as a series of dynamic movements, differing in tempo, tone, and atmosphere.

In the reaction against Granville-Barker's idea of the fluid, unbroken continuity of stage action, critics have perhaps focused attention too narrowly upon the individual scene as Shakespeare's basic unit of structure. Much is lost in taking too atomistic a view of the plays. We have lost some of Granville-Barker's concern for larger theatrical effects, for the way in which one scene may establish the emotional "set" with which we approach succeeding events or how scenes may be arranged to gather energy cumulatively from one another. Our awareness of overriding contrasts between darkness and light, public events and private, tumult and quiescence has been blurred.

In its fullest sense, orchestration refers to those techniques, such as counterpoint and repetition, crescendo and decrescendo, the alternation of sound and silence, darkness and light, crowd scenes and soliloquies, by which broader theatrical effects are achieved and by which the plays are shaped into dynamic theatrical movements. In attending to these orchestrational techniques the audience becomes receptive to the whole range of aural, visual, and kinetic effects produced by the sequential progress of stage events. These, in turn, lead to the fullest understanding of theme and idea. The dramatic art of the plays is inseparable from their meaning.

As a way of summarizing, extending, and applying this argument, I wish now to turn to the orchestration of a single play, *Twelfth Night,* written at the midpoint of Shakespeare's career, which will stand as my final example of the intimate relationship between Shakespeare's stage technique and the meaning, for the audience, of his plays.

NOTES

1. A perusal of the First Folio reveals that act and scene divisions were treated very casually and with great inconsistency in the printed texts. Some plays were divided into five acts and into scenes throughout. In others, such divisions gradually disappeared after several initial entries. Furthermore, none of the quarto texts published during Shakespeare's lifetime contains any sign of act divisions. See Wilfred T. Jewkes, *Act Division in Elizabethan and Jacobean Plays 1583–1616* (Hamden, Conn.: Shoestring Press, 1958), esp. 35–40. Therefore, the divisions that do appear in the First Folio may well be the additions of the editors, Heminges and Condell, or some other hand. Our present act and scene divisions of Shakespeare's plays, of course, are largely the work of eighteenth-century editors.

2. T. W. Baldwin, *Shakspere's Five-Act Structure: Shakspere's Early Plays on the Background of Renaissance Theories of Five-Act Structure from 1470* (Urbana: University of Illinois Press, 1947), esp. "Shakspere's Terence," 544–78.

3. It is now generally accepted that while Shakespeare knew of the

classical five-act structure and employed it in some plays, such as *Henry V*, he did not rigidly adhere to this plan in all his plays. For further discussion of act divisions in the public and private theaters of Shakespeare's time, see Jewkes, *Act Division in Elizabethan and Jacobean Plays*, 96–103.

4. A. C. Bradley, *Shakespearean Tragedy* (1904; reprint, New York: Fawcett World Library, 1967), 42.

5. Northrop Frye, *A Natural Perspective: The Development of Shakespearean Comedy and Romance* (New York: Harcourt, Brace & World, 1965), esp. 72–117. Barber, *Shakespeare's Festive Comedy*, esp. 3–15.

6. Granville-Barker's fullest statement of his objections to customary scene and act divisions is found in his study of *Hamlet* in *Prefaces to Shakespeare*, 1:32–38.

7. Granville-Barker and his contemporary, Sir William Poel, were, of course, reacting to nineteenth-century stage practice, in which elaborate sets and cumbersome spectacle had vastly slowed the action of Shakespeare's plays and broken their theatrical continuity. Granville-Barker advocated a return to Elizabethan stage practice, as far as that could be determined, in producing the plays. In this sense he was less radical than conservative, for he wanted to recover the method of staging that had obtained in Shakespeare's own time.

8. Hirsh, *Structure of Shakespearean Scenes*, esp. 1–31.

9. Jones, *Scenic Form in Shakespeare*, 98–102.

10. Ibid., esp. 3–40.

11. Ibid., 142–43.

12. Rose, *Shakespearean Design*, esp. 1–94.

13. There is no very good reason why II.i and II.ii should not form one scene, since Romeo remains on stage through both segments, though hidden from Mercutio's view in the first.

14. Rosalie Colie, in *Shakespeare's Living Art*, 135–46, discusses the various love rhetorics in tension throughout the play.

15. By a dramatic sleight of hand Shakespeare makes it appear that the storm scene occurs both on the night following the Lupercalian festival and on the night preceding the Ides of March. Thus, Cicero begins I.iii by asking if Casca has seen Caesar home, presumably from the celebration of the Lupercalia. Yet the scene ends with Cassius saying that before morning the conspirators will go to Brutus's house; and from there, of course, they proceed to Caesar's. This blurring of the actual time scheme, however, is seldom noticed in performance. The storm scene in I.iii effectively bridges an indefinite temporal gap while establishing very clearly a new psychological atmosphere on the stage. Attention now focuses, not on tensions between factions of the body politic, but upon the inner

turmoil, echoed in the heavens, of those who stand between the thinking and the acting of a great event.

16. Maynard Mack, "Teaching Drama: *Julius Caesar,*" in *Essays on the Teaching of English,* ed. Edward J. Gordon and Edward S. Noyes (New York: Appleton-Century-Crofts, 1960), 320–36, esp. 328.

17. J. L. Styan, in *Shakespeare's Stagecraft,* 161, reminds us that the kind of linguistic transformation we hear in the voice of Casca from I.ii to I.iii is one of the many instances in which Shakespeare is using his characters to serve the larger tonal needs of the work rather than their own development.

18. See Brents Stirling, "Or Else Were This a Savage Spectacle," in *Unity in Shakespearean Tragedy* (New York: Columbia University Press, 1956), 40–54; reprinted in *Shakespeare: Modern Essays in Criticism,* rev. ed., ed. Leonard Dean (New York: Oxford University Press, 1967), 206–17.

19. Mack, "The World of *Hamlet,*" esp. 502–7.

20. G. Wilson Knight, "The Embassy of Death: An Essay on *Hamlet,*" in *The Wheel of Fire,* 38–40, argues that all "normal" people shun Hamlet and that he poisons the robust atmosphere of the court world. Surely this is wrong. The significance of the episode with Horatio, Marcellus, and Bernardo is, as I see it, to suggest that though Hamlet *is* alienated from the court world, a band of loyal and normal figures on the edges of the court is sympathetic to the prince.

21. My thinking about the affective design of Act I of *Hamlet* has been influenced by Stephen Booth, "On the Value of *Hamlet,*" 137–76.

22. For a discussion of terminal heightening, see Johnson, *Form and Transformation in Music and Poetry of the English Renaissance,* esp. 65–68.

23. See Rose, *Shakespearean Design,* 49–59, for a good discussion of the thematic juxtapositions in the enormously long tavern scene of Act II of *Henry IV, Part I.*

24. The climactic structure of this scene is perceptively discussed by Emrys Jones in *Scenic Form in Shakespeare,* 8–13.

25. Rose, *Shakespearean Design,* 29.

26. The scene was very effectively done in just this way in a British production of *King Lear* staged at the Brooklyn Academy of Music by the Actors Company in February of 1974 under the direction of David William with Robert Eddison playing the part of Lear.

27. Michael Goldman, in *Shakespeare and the Energies of Drama,* 94–108, discusses the problem, for actor and audience alike, of enduring the horrors of this play. I am concerned with the techniques of stagecraft that make an escalation of tension possible.

28. Bernard Beckerman, in *Shakespeare at the Globe,* 40–45, argues that

Act III of *Lear* does not have a single climax, but rather a "climactic plateau" consisting of all three of Lear's scenes on the heath and in the farmhouse. I would argue that though Lear's own emotions do not necessarily become stronger as the act unfolds, the audience's do, largely because of the effect of the intervening castle scenes on our perception of Lear's plight.

29. G. K. Hunter first suggested to me that these two scenes are orchestrated to lead the audience by gradual steps toward the terrible intensity of Lear's passion as we move from distanced description to a "close-up" of the king on the heath.

30. Sigurd Burckhardt, in *Shakespearean Meanings* (Princeton: Princeton University Press, 1968), 237–59, discusses at length the differences between the errors and the punishments of Lear and Gloucester.

31. The performance in question was given by the Prospect Theater Company at the Aldwych Theater in London in the summer of 1972.

32. Bradley, *Shakespearean Tragedy*, 54.

CHAPTER 7

The Orchestration
of *Twelfth Night:* The Rhythm
# of Restraint and Release

A KEY THEATRICAL SEQUENCE in *Twelfth Night* occurs early in the play when the disguised Viola first comes as messenger to Olivia in I.v. Pressing past Olivia's kinsman and steward, Viola finds herself confronting a veiled figure. The visual irony is rich. A woman hiding her true nature behind a man's clothing faces a woman hiding her face behind a veil of mourning. In such circumstances, spontaneous and easy discourse is hardly to be expected. A further impediment to artless conversation results from Viola's role as Orsino's messenger. The speech she has "conned" so carefully reflects another's sentiments. Her uneasiness with her role and her script finds expression in a wonderfully compressed example of verbal counterpoint created by a single figure's speech. At one and the same time Viola attempts to deliver her prepared text and to make inquiries and deliver rebukes in a fashion not at all in keeping with the decorum of her assigned task:

> VIOLA Most radiant, exquisite, and unmatchable beauty—I
> pray you tell me if this be the lady of the house, for
> I never saw her. I would be loath to cast away my
> speech; for, besides that it is excellently well penned,
> I have taken great pains to con it. Good beauties, let
> me sustain no scorn. I am very comptible, even to the
> least sinister usage.

OLIVIA Whence came you, sir?

VIOLA I can say little more than I have studied, and that question's out of my part. Good gentle one, give me modest assurance if you be the lady of the house, that I may proceed in my speech.

(162–73)

Viola's uneasiness with her role as messenger, which leads her to interrupt her own speech, causes Olivia to inquire: "Are you a comedian?" (174).

Viola's spontaneous interjections, however, and not her clichéd rhetoric of adoration, are undoubtedly what pique Olivia's interest. Throughout the first ninety lines of her conversation with Olivia, Viola constantly repeats her initial interruption of her own script. In the midst of expounding the "text" of love that lies in Orsino's bosom, she suddenly demands to see Olivia's face. That wish granted and Olivia's pride rebuked, Viola returns to a clichéd description of how Orsino loves Olivia: "With adorations, with fertile tears, / With groans that thunder love, with sighs of fire" (241–42). When this rhetoric is met with a repulse, it is as if the restraints of her assigned role become too much, and she pours forth a description of how *she* would woo were she Orsino:

> Make me a willow cabin at your gate
> And call upon my soul within the house;
> Write loyal cantons of contemnèd love
> And sing them loud even in the dead of night;
> Hallo your name to the reverberate hills
> And make the babbling gossip of the air
> Cry out "Olivia!" O, you should not rest
> Between the elements of air and earth
> But you should pity me.
>
> (254–62)

This spontaneous and energetic speech at once rebukes Orsino's passive wooing and unwittingly reveals the forceful personality of Viola, a personality partially concealed by her disguise of dutiful servant. The pressure operating upon Viola to sustain a false and uncomfortable role is for a moment forgotten, and her exuberance in turn releases Olivia from the self-indulgent role of perpetual mourner in which she has hidden herself since her brother's death. The verbal fencing and the tired clichés of Petrarchan adoration give way before a fresher expression of feeling. By the end of the scene the proud lady recognizes that she has fallen in love; though, as always, those who scorn Cupid's power must pay a price. Olivia's punishment, like Phoebe's in *As You Like It,* is to fall in love with a woman; but at least there is no more talk of veils in her household for the rest of the play.

This encounter embodies many of the themes, motifs, and techniques of stagecraft that are developed in *Twelfth Night* as a whole. Here we see examples of disguise and concealment so central to the play and integrally connected to the questions it raises about identity, particularly sexual identity; here we hear the interplay of affected and spontaneous rhetorics so endlessly varied in subplot and main plot alike; here we feel the dialectic between constraint and release, passivity and action, that informs the psychological as well as the theatrical dynamics of the play. The movement from scripted to unscripted speech, from veiled to unveiled appearances, from repression to expression mimes in miniature the movement of the whole play and indicates what are to be some of the key elements in Shakespeare's orchestration of the theatrical event. Just how this entire play is crafted to create a meaningful theatrical experience for the audience and to cue its responses is my concern in what follows; and in this exploration I will have many occasions to return to Olivia's first meeting with Viola.

First let it be said that, like most of Shakespeare's plays, *Twelfth Night* conforms to definite generic prescriptions. The very title, *Twelfth Night; or, What You Will,* suggests the festive reversals of other romantic comedies, since *Twelfth Night* indicates the end of the Christmas revels, a time for games, celebrations, and the testing of authority through parody and mockery, while *What You Will* points to the inherent fantasy content of most of Shakespeare's earlier comedies in which what is lost is found, what is broken mended, and what is foolish redeemed from folly.[1] So in this play those severed by shipwreck find one another again; those who deny love's power succumb in time to its enchantments; and those who lack self-knowledge are given the chance, at least, to embrace it. However, there is much that is anomalous about *Twelfth Night* conceived of simply as a typical romantic comedy. It was written about 1601 and so is the last of the so-called "festive comedies"; but many readers and directors have found it somewhat less than festive in tone.[2] It is informed by a strain of melancholy that links it to *Hamlet,* the play probably closest to it in time of composition. It is not, of course, only the humiliation of Malvolio, which nineteenth-century critics such as Charles Lamb were fond of sentimentalizing, that lends somber overtones to the work, but also the presence of Feste, a clown decidedly less merry than Touchstone or Launcelot Gobbo, and the pathos of the heroine's situation: brotherless, disguised, and lovelorn in a strange country.

As I hope to show, while melancholy *is* one of the constituent moods of *Twelfth Night,* it is neither the dominant mood, nor the only unusual feature of the comedy. Unlike most of Shakespeare's other "festive" pieces, the action of *Twelfth Night* does not move between a green world and a city world, between Athens and the woods, Belmont and Venice, the Forest of Arden and the world of civilization beyond that forest. Instead, all the action occurs in the vaguely urban setting of Illyria, though something of a geographical dialectic is established between the count's palace and Olivia's house, with "the street" the neutral ground between these two locales and the setting for the play's dénouement. Equally striking is the absence in this play of an overtly dominant heroine of the sort one finds in Rosalind, Portia, or the witty ladies of *Love's Labor's Lost,* though I do not wish to call Viola passive, since it is only in promoting her own interests that she is reticent.

Also unusual is the play's minimal plot and its disparate foci. Certainly no one ever fell in love with *Twelfth Night* for its suspenseful action. While some of the tricks in the subplot depend for their immediate effectiveness upon audience anticipation, the main plot is remarkably lacking in real suspense, since we learn early on that Sebastian lives and is coming to Illyria. As C. L. Barber says: "It is amazing how little happens in *Twelfth Night,* how much of the time people are merely talking, especially in the first half, before the farcical complications are sprung. Shakespeare is so skillful by now in rendering attitudes by the gestures of easy conversation that when it suits him he can almost do without events."[3] For much of the play, any momentum the central plot might gain is retarded by the apparently random way in which Shakespeare constantly shifts the audience's attention from one stage group to another: from Orsino in his court to Olivia in her house, from Sebastian and his sea captain to Sir Toby and his pals, from the luckless Malvolio to the disguised Viola. The playwright is juggling many balls at once. The tricks against the steward, the misguided passions of Orsino and Olivia and Andrew, the relationship of Sebastian to Antonio, the predicament of the disguised Viola—each must be developed; and the danger is that the links between these disparate actions will not be apparent and the play will crumble into incoherence.

That audiences do not respond to *Twelfth Night* as a fragmented and static work is largely due to Shakespeare's subtle orchestration of stage events. The progressive experience of the work has a meaningful dynamic of its own that underlies and gradually clarifies the rich thematic unity of the work. Retrospectively, of course, which is how most critics approach *Twelfth Night,* its thematic patterns are relatively clear. The play, above all, is about the dangerous egotism that makes the self the center of the universe, leading to illusions, disguises, and posturing. Characters who indulge their egocentric fantasies are led through a maze of mistakes and embarrassing self-disclosures until, personal and social chaos at a peak, they are released into true and clarifying knowledge of the self.

In this basic movement, subplot and main plot run parallel, and the behavior of every character seems at times to comment on the behavior of every other character. Olivia, striving to live in an unnatural nunlike state of perpetual mourning, is at heart not so different from Andrew, her vain suitor, aspiring to be the gay blade and jolly wooer of a woman in every way his superior. Orsino, locked in the narcissistic pose of spurned lover, turns out to be not so very different from Malvolio, strutting about like a rare turkey cock in yellow hose and cross garters. Each holds a false vision of the self; each is, in essence, in disguise, though only Malvolio with his ridiculous get-up and broad smiles actually transforms his outer self. Olivia, however, for a time hides behind a veil, and Andrew in the orchard with a sword in hand is nearly as visually out of character as is Viola when she, too, is forced into a duel.

Viola, in fact, is the complicating factor in this tidy summation of the play's themes; for though more truly in disguise than anyone else, she is not the victim of overt self-delusions or egotism. Through her the playwright points to the most basic type of self-knowledge that the mature person must realize: the acceptance of one's sexual identity, not just one's social class or one's intellectual limitations.[4] Viola's androgynous disguise, though freely chosen, brings with it its own confinements, leaving her free neither to fight like a man nor to flirt like a woman, but left between in a debilitating state of indeterminancy before, with the arrival of Sebastian, sexual individuation can occur and the man and the woman in Viola find separate objectifications and separate modes of self-realization through love of what is opposite.[5] It is through Viola that the constraints and evils of disguise and the dangers of the unaccepted self find their most complex embodiment—and also their cure.

If the play examines the dangers of egocentricity and the disguised self, it explores these dangers by concentrating on the enervation and sterility that result from egocentric fantasies. The play has melancholy overtones because many of the characters flirt dangerously with a self-indulgence unto death. Orsino's languid passivity and Olivia's projected seven-year living entombment are but variants of the claustrophobic dark hole into which Malvolio is thrown for his deluded narcissism.[6] Even Viola, dwelling in imagination on the "sister" who pines away like patience on a monument in an excess of self-abnegation, flirts with thoughts of a living death. This extreme version of female passivity, which Viola escapes partly through her role as Cesario, partly through her veiled declarations of love for Orsino, is as life-denying and inimical to personal and social health as are Orsino's self-absorbed melancholy, Olivia's histrionic mourning, and Malvolio's self-absorbed rhetoric. It is a melancholy quite different from Feste's tempered understanding that "youth's a stuff will not endure" (II.iii.49).

A prime antidote to such self-indulgent sterility, of course, is the reckless abandon with which Toby and the "below-stairs" crew embrace life and community: eating, drinking, singing catches, and chasing away the night with an effusion of high spirits. They do not hide themselves from life through self-indulgent fantasies; they live it. But, of course, like Falstaff's life-enhancing energy, the vitality of Toby, Fabian, and Maria can exceed its bounds and in its turn become destructive and cruel. If Falstaff sees men as cannon fodder,

Toby sees friends as the source of income and good jests, and his cruelty to Andrew and to Malvolio points to the dangers of the unrestrained self. Toby is essential to the play's central dialectic between the inhibitions and constraints that isolate the self-absorbed in egotistical fantasies and the freedom of spontaneous, even reckless, action. In a Twelfth Night world of misrule, Toby is king for a day, but the free-wheeling excesses of his behavior are precisely what keep him from becoming a normative figure. That role, of course, belongs to Viola, who in her selfless service of Orsino finds the proper way to escape passivity and sterile egocentricity without embracing Toby's hedonistic recklessness. Selfless action in the service of others, the path of the true friend, the true servant, and finally the true lover, is Viola's way. Though her actions embroil her at times in comic difficulties, they are the actions of the mature and responsible self; and they find echoes in the equally selfless actions of Antonio and the nameless sea captain who rescue her and Sebastian from their watery graves.[7]

To say even this much about the thematic and psychological patterns in the play, of course, involves wandering back and forth, in retrospect, over its surface, imposing an abstract ordering paradigm upon events that, experienced sequentially, do not reveal a unifying meaning so readily. What this mode of criticism does, and it is a useful and necessary operation, is to spatialize a temporal phenomenon, to see it in one glance as a simultaneous whole. But in experiencing a play in the theater, the audience does not start here, with a summation of the play's overriding symbolic or psychological concerns, not even if we already know the play or know other romantic comedies of its type. In the theater we begin, not with abstract reflections on the sterility of egocentricity, but with the sound of a particular kind of music and a particular man's reaction to that music. What we subsequently experience is not a psychological treatise, but a particular succession of sights, sounds, and events that create a unique theatrical experience with its own tempo, rhythm, and pauses, its own moments of engagement and detachment, and its own natural points of emphasis.

What is remarkable about this and other Shakespeare plays is the extent to which the temporal experience of them — what the play *does* in its progressive mode — constitutes and controls what the play *means*. Retrospective and progressive modes of knowing a play are not mutually exclusive. The former has about it a satisfying finality and comprehensiveness, the latter always a dynamic tentativeness; but the former rests upon the latter and should be a more integral part of theater criticism than is usually the case. What I want to do now is to examine Shakespeare's orchestration of the implied temporal enactment of *Twelfth Night* to show how a satisfying and meaningful theater event takes shape for the beholder. In particular, I wish to highlight how the dramaturgy of the play repeatedly whets and frustrates the theatrical appetites of the viewer so that the sense of entrapment and stasis that overtakes so many of the play's characters becomes part of the audience's own theatrical experience and is used to focus attention on the *causes* of inaction both within the world of the play and within the theater event.

As I have already noted, *Twelfth Night* begins with music. It also concludes with a song and is informed by music throughout: Toby's catches, Feste's songs for Orsino, Sir Topas's gleeful songs for the imprisoned Malvolio. Music becomes a recurrent element in the play's unfolding—a means of creating particular local effects—but also a device for providing continuity or contrast between stage moments that may otherwise be widely separated.[8] It thus provides a way within the forward movement of the action for inviting momentary retrospection.

When the play begins, however, the audience knows nothing of the later songs: its whole concentration is focused upon Orsino and the strains he commands to sound, to stop, to sound again, and once more to cease. There could not be a more economical way of crystalizing for the audience the mood in Orsino's court or the outlines of his temperament. He is an aesthete, too overwhelmed by the emotional power of a single "dying fall" either to endure the piece's completion or even to find refreshment in the repetition of what he has just heard. The audience cannot lose itself in the music. It sounds too briefly and with too many interruptions from Orsino. In fact, we are probably impatient that he fails to allow the piece to end.

Quite clearly, it is not the music itself but Orsino's response to it to which the playwright is directing our attention. Music for the count is unmistakably a vehicle for emotional self-indulgence. He surfeits with sounds, and when they cease, he turns to language for a release of pent-up emotion. But when he talks, what becomes immediately apparent, again, is the preciosity of his sensibility. Music is food to be consumed in excess; sound, synesthetically, is like the wind carrying the smell of violets; love is like the capacious sea; he himself is like a hart pursued by the hounds of love. Metaphor and simile pile on top of one another, and Valentine's description of Olivia attempting to pickle her brother's memory in the brine of salt tears is but the capstone of the scene's metaphorical absurdities. It is with some relief that the audience leaves Orsino heading off to lie in a bed of flowers at the scene's end. More than forty-two lines of such heady stuff and the audience would probably recoil in disgust.

When Shakespeare so chooses, he can be wonderfully economical in creating striking openings for his plays. In *Twelfth Night* it is not gripping plot developments but an arresting stage mood that initially commands attention. Orsino's Illyria is an emotional hothouse. Music and language are used to reveal an overwrought, self-indulgent psyche and a court devoted solely to the care and feeding of its count's emotional excesses. There is much here to interest an audience, but not much to engage its sympathies deeply. The brevity of the scene, the artificiality of its rhetoric, even the breaking off of its music are all devices for keeping an audience at some distance from what it is watching and hearing, even as the stasis and enervation of this court are indelibly impressed upon us.

What Shakespeare then does is present two scenes in which, again, relatively little happens. They are not linked together narratively, but they afford further tonal contrasts with the play's opening segment. The orchestration of the play's first three scenes, in fact, depends heavily upon the principle of contrast for its effectiveness.[9] Successively the audience sees three groups of characters in three locales: Orsino and his followers in his court, Viola and the seamen on the coast, Toby and his friends at Olivia's house. Each succeeding scene is longer than the last (42 lines, 64 lines, 127 lines); and each is pitched in a different key, that is, each uses language in a strikingly different way to produce distinct tonal and kinetic effects. The differences are felt primarily because of the context the first segment establishes for the audience's perception of the next two. As Mark Rose has noted, if you reverse scenes i and ii, which was done in at least one production he had seen, Viola's conversation with the sailors loses much of its theatrical effectiveness.[10] It becomes functionally one-dimensional. It serves to set up the Viola plot, but it no longer provides a refreshing shift of pace and mood from what precedes it.

Viola, in her genuinely distressful situation, wastes little time in self-pity or self-display. She reaches out to know and establish a place for herself in her alien environment. Many of her speeches are questions: "What country, friends, is this?" (I.ii.1); "And what should I do in Illyria?" (3); "What think you, sailors?" (5); "Know'st thou this country?" (21); "Who governs here?" (24); "What is his name?" (26); "What's she?" (35). Her situation known as thoroughly as it can be, Viola decides on a course of action: "I'll serve this Duke" (55). The future, of course, is not all known. She says: "What else may hap, to time I will commit" (60). But she has done her best to place herself in a position of readiness: though the manly garb she will assume will confine her in unforeseen ways, it also cloaks her vulnerability.

The energy and stringency of the scene are primarily conveyed by the language employed as that language is heard against the aural ground provided by Orsino's lovesick mooning. The rhetoric of scene ii contains no conceits and hardly any metaphors, and it is swiftly propelled forward by Viola's logical questions. Language here is used as a means of finding out information and making decisions, not as a means of flaunting one's emotional sensitivity. After Orsino's speeches, it serves to heighten the audience's opinion of Viola. Vulnerable she may be, but she is not mired in an emotional bog.

When Toby, Maria, and then Andrew next come into view, the texture of what the audience hears undergoes another marked change. This is a scene of banter; in I.iii language is used for play, and the poetry of the two preceding scenes gives way to prose. The longest speech in this segment is Toby's nine-line exhortation to Andrew to demonstrate his talents in dancing; and for the most part the scene is devoted to quick-flying jests, though Maria's and Toby's fly somewhat faster, to be sure, than do Andrew's. Against the aural ground established by the businesslike dispatch of Viola's first appearance, the lighthearted expansiveness of this below-stairs world stands out sharply. Here, care is peremptorily banished as an enemy to life; and if a fat man is cast as Toby, as often occurs, his considerable girth becomes, like Falstaff's, a visual emblem of a life lived outside "the modest limits of order" (7–8). The scene itself sprawls; it is two or three times the length of the two that precede it, and what inner tension it has derives from wordplay and the exercise of nimble wits turning randomly to whatever topic lays to hand, not from Viola's purposeful march of questions.

What Shakespeare has done by stringing these three scenes together to form the opening movement of the play is to focus audience attention, not upon plot, but upon tonal and kinetic contrasts that illuminate some of the differing attitudes toward life and some of the different ways in which energy is expended in Illyria. Certainly the three scenes set the plot going and reveal much about the temperaments of Orsino, Viola, and Toby, respectively, just as they function to set off Viola as a norm between extremes; but they also suggest, through successive aural and kinetic shifts, the tonal and kinetic parameters of this fictive world: the attitudes and impulses that are repeatedly to be played off against one another. Stultifying self-indulgence, brisk assertiveness, playful and unfettered high spirits—these are some of the dominant moods of *Twelfth Night* lightly delineated for the audience as the play begins and then set up for more complex elaboration later.

In this regard, the opening movement of *Twelfth Night* is orchestrated somewhat like the opening of *Hamlet* in which the dissimilar "worlds" of battlements, court, and Polonius's family are successively juxtaposed before the partial closure effected by a return to the battlements. In both plays the initial scenes are crafted to help the audience hear, see, and feel important differences among discrete stage groups and to recognize the tension these differences can create. Of course, the opening movements of *Hamlet* and *Twelfth Night* are not identical. The aural, visual, and kinetic disjunctions between scenes are more pronounced and unsettling in the tragedy, the emotional stakes higher; nonetheless, Shakespeare's methods of orchestration and his theatrical strategies are similar. Economically delineating differences, his stagecraft also creates a field of tension resulting not from any one scene, but from the successive juxta-position of several. In *Hamlet* the protagonist at once feels and expresses the tension between his view of the world and that of Claudius. In *Twelfth Night* the direct articulation of tension comes later (recall, for example, the quandary of Viola in I.v, trapped between a desire to speak freely and openly and a desire to obey her lord and mouth his tired rhetoric); but in *Twelfth Night* the audience anticipates this tension during the play's first movement. If the three initial scenes heighten, by their centrality, the poise and purposefulness of Viola, they also hint at the vulnerability of such poise by foiling it against less balanced but equally powerful modes of expression and self-assertion.

The second theatrical movement of *Twelfth Night* stretches from I.iv, Viola's first appearance in Orsino's court, to II.v, Malvolio's discovery and reading of Maria's letter; and it is orchestrated quite differently from the opening movement. What primarily unifies this movement theatrically is an increasingly insistent dialectic, felt in the language and pacing of successive segments, between languor and action, constraint and release. Of course, on the level of plot, more "happens" in this segment than in the first three scenes, so there is a quickening of audience desire to see what will next take place. For example, Viola, disguised as Orsino's page, attracts the amorous passion of Olivia and is attracted to Orsino; Sebastian emerges unscathed from the sea and sets out for Orsino's court; and Malvolio offends both Feste and Toby in ways that cry out for retribution. Clearly, with Viola, the audience now begins to look ahead with some impatience to see how time and the dramatist will untangle these knots. Simultaneously, however, the audience lives in the "now" of a carefully orchestrated succession of stage events, and the rhythm of the second movement of the play creates a second kind of tension, largely unrelated to tension generated by the quickening narrative, through the repeated frustration of the-atrical energies of both a linguistic and kinetic type.

Let me explain using some specifics. In I.iv Viola appears in disguise. This is a crucial visual event, and good actresses usually are at pains to make it clear that a man's attire and a man's asser-tiveness are not entirely natural to Viola. The disguise, moreover, functions as the audience's first visual signal that Viola has done what she earlier promised she would do and that now a new phase of the action—Viola playing boy—is to begin. Further, the scene brings together what formerly had been separate: the melancholy count and the shipwrecked maiden. Most important, it becomes immediately apparent that the count and her costume inhibit the previously forthright heroine. As Orsino's page, Viola is not freely herself. Her refreshing energy is tamped down. She becomes entangled, willy-nilly, in the emotional enervation and the psychological self-indulgence of Orsino's court.[11] In I.iv she can neither deny Orsino's request that she woo Olivia, which she is loath to do, nor declare her own love, which she is all too eager to make plain. Orsino continues to churn out his lovesick rhetoric, but he *does* nothing in his own person to woo his lady. Instead, Viola becomes his unwilling go-between. Her exit must be an unhappy one, since now her true emotions can find no expression, and her energies must be directed to a task that gives her pain.

Act I, scene v, again highlights for the audience the pernicious consequences of disguise and false postures. Olivia's house is always an emotionally freer place than the count's palace; but in I.v the high spirits are more restrained, certainly, than when we first saw Toby rollicking with Sir Andrew and Maria. Feste is in momentary disgrace, Olivia is in mourning, and Malvolio is censorious. By wittily proving Olivia to be a fool, Feste temporarily holds in check the gravity hovering over the household, and he also wins Malvolio a reproof. But Feste cannot remove the real cloud hanging over the house: his lady's self-indulgent love of her mourner's role. When Feste proves her a fool, she bears him no ill will, but she also does not heed the real import of his words. Before Viola is admitted, Olivia calls for her veil, and her old posture is resumed. Only with Viola's entry does Olivia's true liberation from that posture become possible, and the heart of the scene is the encounter between veiled lady and disguised messenger that I briefly discussed in this chapter's opening pages.

The orchestration of this encounter makes the audience feel with great immediacy the constraining consequences of affected, false, or unnatural postures. False and evasive rhetoric permeates the scene and repeatedly stymies true communication.[12] The result, for the theater audience, is a sense of pent-up and thwarted energies. At first, the constraints of Viola's disguise and her assigned role force her to adopt a cloying speech and a stance that she quite obviously—from her own interruptions of the script—does not find congenial. In turn, her clichéd text of love invites Olivia to sink into the sterile posture of the proud lady cynically repelling a tedious and unwanted assault. When Viola finally drops the script to tell how she would woo were she Orsino, the audience hears a marked aural shift. Viola's language surges with life, and Olivia's pose crumbles. She is released into love; and in the last thirty lines of the scene, her former hauteur gone, she asks questions and speaks with new energy and purpose.

But the audience is denied a love duet. The barrier of disguise still stands between Olivia and Cesario and makes them speak at cross purposes. Olivia begins the ancient catechism of love: "What is your parentage?" (I.v.263); Viola answers with a riddle and a lie: "Above my fortunes, yet my state is well. / I am a gentleman" (264-65). Olivia offers the beloved money, Viola rejects it with horrified disdain: "keep your purse" (270). Olivia's released emotional energy is misdirected and finds no reciprocity. At the scene's end, Viola is still trapped in her disguise; Olivia has shed one false pose only to embrace another: no more a nun, she now loves a woman whom she mistakes for a man. The audience once more *sees*—in Olivia's outstretched hand and Viola's recoil from the purse—and *hears*—in Olivia's questions and Viola's evasions—the pernicious consequences of disguise and false postures. Action is stymied; free and uncorrupted discourse is impossible; and it is the aural and visual orchestration of the encounter that directs the audience's attention to this impasse.

This long scene is followed by two short ones: the first appearance of Antonio and Sebastian, and the brief encounter in which Malvolio gives Viola the ring Olivia has sent. As with most scenes involving Sebastian and Antonio, II.i comes like a breath of fresh air. Throughout the play, Antonio and Sebastian assume the straightforward attitudes characteristic of Viola in her unguarded or undisguised state. In a play in which disguises, actual or psychological, proliferate, these two go undisguised, though Antonio is the figure who could logically most profit from a false front when in Orsino's country. But his function is to embody honest and selfless service. He has neither time for affected postures of the sort that afflict Malvolio, nor a nature easy with disguise of any sort. Here, as elsewhere when he and the young Sebastian appear, they speak without either artifice or excessive wit. Theirs is the discourse of plaindealing and truth, in which language reveals intention and culminates in action. Great, therefore, is the contrast between Antonio's final selfless declaration in II.i that he will court danger to follow Sebastian to Orsino's court, and Malvolio's peevish and selfish complaint at the beginning of II.ii that Viola "might have saved me my pains, to have taken it [the ring] away yourself" (5–6). As many have noted, Malvolio is too self-absorbed to realize he is conveying a love token and too self-important to do his messenger's task with grace.

At the same time, the two adjoining short scenes underscore the contrasting plights of the twins. Sebastian in II.i casts off a false name and embraces a course of action; in II.ii his sister receives a ring that binds her more tightly in a net of duplicity and leaves her with few options but that of passive resignation. Her soliloquy in II.ii, one of the few in the play, begins with logical inquiry, "What means this lady?" (16), and ends in a tangle leading to an impasse:

> My master loves her dearly;
> And I (poor monster) fond as much on him;
> And she (mistaken) seems to dote on me.
> What will become of this? As I am man,
> My state is desperate for my master's love.
> As I am woman (now alas the day!),
> What thriftless sighs shall poor Olivia breathe?
> O Time, thou must untangle this, not I;
> It is too hard a knot for me t'untie.
>
> (32–40)

This is an agile soliloquy, still laced with questions, as were Viola's first speeches, but now the questions cannot be answered in ways that make a course of action easy. She is stymied, left with the antitheses and paradoxes of her androgynous state. Once again, stasis has replaced movement; Sebastian and Antonio's purposeful acts are overshadowed by Viola's perplexed questions and her shrug of resignation. Where is this trapped energy to go? While the audience, knowing Sebastian lives, does not fully share Viola's feelings of entrapment, her soliloquy creates a sense of stasis and complication that sets in high relief the wild outpouring of uncomplicated high spirits which follows.[13]

The dialectic between release and restraint that the whole second movement of the play embodies finds its final expression in the last three scenes of Act II: the midnight revels of Toby, the lovesick mooning of Orsino, and the boxtree scene. The orchestration of II.iii and II.iv is controlled by the various music that informs each. In II.iii, the below-stairs revelers jest, drink, and sing, in Malvolio's words, most uncivilly. They "squeak out" their "coziers' catches without any mitigation or remorse of voice" (83–84). Mitigation, in fact, is what the scene most wonderfully lacks. These are people in the mood for some excellent fooling, and so is the audience after observing Viola's becalmed and complicated situation. Sanctimonious Malvolio highlights, without really threatening, the exuberance of the revelers. They raid the wine cellar and sing carpe diem songs; he prates of manners and threatens to tattle to the lady of the house. When the scene ends with their plan to fool him with a false love letter, the audience is completely on their side and looks ahead with relish to the steward's mortification. But we are denied the immediate gratification of the plot's fulfillment, since the next scene plunks us down once again in the never changing, claustrophobic court of Orsino.

The Orsino scenes make clear that Shakespeare is effectively using both contrast and recurrence in the orchestration of this play. For the audience, the immediate impact of II.iv is felt in terms of its contrasts with II.iii. We move from a world of prose to a world of poetry, from jests to seriousness, from light airs to a melancholy dirge, from exuberance to an energy level so throttled down that utter immobilization threatens to set in. We are back in an emotional bog, and the impression of stasis is emphasized by the free-wheeling energies of the preceding scene and by the fact that the audience's expectation of the letter plot is cut off by the return to Orsino in his love melancholy. The tonal contrast between the two scenes is immense, highlighted by contrasts in music and language.

The sense we get of blocked or frustrated energy is further heightened by the fact that II.iv deliberately uses aural cues to send the audience's mind back to the beginning of the play. There Orsino entered with the line "If music be the food of love, play on" (I.i.1); here he enters saying, "Give me some music" (II.iv.1). In both cases he then goes on in highly complicated metaphors to expand upon his suffering and the immensity of his passion. The mood, the actions, the self-indulgent egotism are all unchanged, though here the clown's mocking invocation of the "melancholy god" and Viola's defense of women offer mild rebukes to Orsino's egocentric vision. Nonetheless, by recalling the beginning of the play, this scene heightens the audience's sense that in one central portion of the play's world nothing changes; no sunlight filters in; no veils are removed. If anything, the strong centripetal pull of Orsino's self-absorption seems to draw others into its orbit, and it is here that Viola tells her poignant tale of the "sister" who sat immobile and "pined in thought" (II.iv.3). Viola never becomes that immobile other self, for she ends the scene setting off once more to Olivia, but she comes dangerously close here to embracing the passivity that so engulfs Orsino.

This is the longest of the scenes involving Orsino up to this point. The others, I.i and I.iv, are each about 40 lines; II.iv is about 125 lines. It builds on those earlier scenes to give the audience its fullest sense of Orsino's monstrous self-love and self-indulgence. He does not hear the clown's mockery; he does not hear Viola's pain and her barely veiled declarations of love. All he hears is his own voice extolling the strength of his love, which is "as hungry as the sea / And can digest as much" (99–100). From this point in the play Orsino disappears until Act V; the play's exorcism of debilitating self-love focuses now on Malvolio, who in a sense undergoes *for* Orsino the humiliation that the count's self-absorption invites and that Olivia experiences in her own way in her misguided love for a woman. But before we leave Orsino, Shakespeare takes pains to develop fully his foolish self-absorption, while at the same time furthering the underlying theatrical dialectic of the play's second movement: its basic opposition of action and inaction, free speech and fettered speech, energy released and energy contained. When, in the specific theatrical context established by II.iii and the preceding scene, the audience is thrust once more into this world, frustration and uneasiness build up. We wait for release, and that need is partly satisfied and partly frustrated by II.v, the scene with

Malvolio's reading of the letter that culminates the second movement of the play.

The orchestration of the boxtree scene was extensively analyzed in chapter 3. My purpose here is, not to reexamine its basic contrapuntal structure, but to look at its place in the progressive orchestration of the whole play. Scene v of Act II culminates the second movement of the play by compressing its basic dialectic into a single scene of great humor and great tension. Up to this point the audience has been experiencing, in successive scenes, a basic rhythm of restraint and release, has been hearing successive contrasts between affected and free-wheeling speech. Through the contrapuntal orchestration of II.v we simultaneously hear the constipated pomposity of Malvolio, imagining himself a count and unintentionally parodying the high-flown rhetoric of the real count, Orsino, and the scabrous jests and unrestrained oaths of Toby and his companions. The scene thus aurally highlights a central opposition in the play by exaggerating the affectations of the steward and the coarse energy of the observers.

As Malvolio preens, the audience takes satisfaction with the conspirators in seeing self-love so grotesquely display itself. At the same time, a certain amount of energy simply remains unreleased because the conspirators cannot leap out and laugh Malvolio into the ground without ruining their own joke. They are reduced to sputtering in the bushes, and some of the audience's laughter is directed at them in their fuming impotence. The scene helps to impart a sense of closure to this movement of the play through the terminal heightening afforded by its economical compression of warring impulses held in such effective counterpoint. But it also points attention ahead, not only to the completion of the letter trick, but to the final fulfilling eruption of pent-up energy in the public and direct unmasking of affectation and self-love.

The first two movements of *Twelfth Night,* in which Barber is quite right to note that not much happens in the way of overt action, nonetheless create a complex theatrical experience through their careful juxtaposition of different moods, verbal styles, and kinetic impulses. Through the contrastive orchestration of speech, the audience *hears* the central tension of the play between affectation and honest speech and *feels* the quick movement of wit, inquiry, and plain dealing repeatedly tamped down by an antithetical languor and self-absorption. Thematically, of course, Shakespeare is developing the opposition between egotism and selflessness, claustrophobic self-absorption and self-forgetful action, as those trapped in literal disguises or unnatural poses are juxtaposed to the reckless Tobys and, less radically, to the plain-dealing Sebastians and Antonios of Illyria. But an audience first apprehends these thematic oppositions, not as neatly labeled abstractions, but as differences felt and heard in the contrastive rhythms and speech patterns of the theatrical continuum.

In effect, in the play's second movement, Shakespeare orchestrates the basic sensory components of performance to help the audience discriminate very precisely among the various characters and the attitudes toward experience they exemplify and, perhaps as important, to involve the audience experientially in the mounting frustration that eventuates in the plot from disguises and narcissism, and in the theater event from the repeated subversion of purposeful speech and the blocking of kinetic energy. In coming to the theater, audiences have a variety of appetites that crave satisfaction. Just as when we read a novel, we may want from our drama density of theme and complexity of characterization; but drama is a three-dimensional art form that also whets our sensory appetites for spectacle, for movement, for happenings of a very tangible sort.[14] We want not only the plot but also what we see and hear to have both complexity and momentum. In *Twelfth Night,* certain of our theatrical appetites are repeatedly thwarted but, I would argue, to good purpose. The stop and start orchestration of the play's second movement—in which free speech becomes fettered, action frustrated—creates impatience that focuses attention on the sources of that frustration, especially the affectation and deceit which trammel up honest speech and forthright action. This frustration also begins to bring to the level of consciousness the very issue of what I have called the audience's theatrical appetites and makes us regard them critically.

In fact, the third movement of the play—acts III and IV—seems designed in part to engender in the audience various kinds of self-consciousness about its desires and stance as theatergoers. The third movement of the play contains more action and consequently is orchestrated somewhat differently than what has gone before. The movement begins slowly, but by scene iv of Act III, the pace quickens, reaching a crescendo of madness and confusion that is sustained right through Act IV, when temporary closure is achieved by the brief and stabilizing scene in which Sebastian follows Olivia to the altar to be wed and mistaken beginnings start to find their true conclusions. Increasingly, the pent-up energies of the play's beginning find chaotic and purgative release in physical violence, visual malapropisms, and verbal excess. Twelfth Night madness overtakes the stage and catches up the audience in its confusion. As in the third act of *King Lear,* the sense of climax is sustained by the alternation of outbursts of confusion with quieter, more constrained actions, from which we are once more propelled into the thick of the fights and mistakes that now unravel with dizzying speed. This release of theatrical energy is exhilarating, particularly since so long dammed up; but it also eventually recoils on itself. With Toby and company, we are certainly in the mood for some excellent fooling; but in the end, the jokes pile on top of one another with unnerving rapidity and lead to violence and pain. Action and language seem to veer out of control.

Ultimately, the theatrical experience of the play builds in its own corrective to our Toby-like appetites for the simple release of energy in completely unguarded and unconsidered ways. John Hollander has argued that *Twelfth Night* kills the excessive appetites of the characters by indulging them utterly.[15] I argue that the same thing is true for certain of the spectator's theatrical appetites. We leave the third movement hungry for a theatrical and a moral norm: for action that is action, not chaos or stasis; for behavior that is neither self-regarding nor exploitative, but merely decent. After all, Twelfth Night is the *last* day of the Christmas revels, and the last day of any holiday season may leave us feeling oppressed by freedom and longing for a world of work and restraint.

Simultaneously the third movement of the play makes the audience self-regarding in yet another way. As critics of the play have shown, it is unusual in the degree to which it puts the audience in a position of superior awareness vis-à-vis the characters. We typically know more than they do in situation after situation.[16] One figure may know more than certain others; but we know more than any;

and often a trickster in the midst of his trick unwittingly and unnervingly becomes the butt of someone else's joke. In the third movement of the play, the events are repeatedly structured to put us in this position of superior vision. Yet so insistently is this the case, that in the end we become self-conscious about our own actual omniscience. If the characters on the stage are so wrapped in blindness, are we really more all-knowing? If they live in a world of illusions, is not the theater itself just such a world? If they rely on time and chance for illumination, do not we rely on the dramatist? If they are malleable, so are we. Within the plot, the play repeatedly gives the lie to fantasies of omnipotence and one's control of the universe. The same humbling awareness, I would argue, becomes part of the theatergoer's experience.

But let us now turn to acts III and IV. As I have suggested, the movement begins slowly with a sequence of short encounters between two or three characters leading up to III.iv, a scene of 300 lines in which at least twelve speaking characters appear. The events beginning this progression involve Viola and Feste, who are here alone together for the only time in the play; and their conversation has little to do with the action but much to do with the meaning of the play, since what they quibblingly discuss is the proper use of words and their easy corruption.[17] Their conversation forms a graceful dance, in which neither strives for effect, yet both answer jest to jest with an ease that masks art and even raises Feste's resentment, since he is used to being the undisputed master of such pregnant wordplay. Viola, however, is full of admiration for the fool's skill:

> This fellow is wise enough to play the fool,
> And to do that well craves a kind of wit.
> He must observe their mood on whom he jests,
> The quality of persons, and the time;
> And, like the haggard, check at every feather
> That comes before his eye. This is a practice
> As full of labor as a wise man's art;
> For folly that he wisely shows, is fit,
> But wise men, folly-fall'n, quite taint their wit.
>
> (III.i.58–66)

The clown and heroine not only articulate a major theme of the play, the corruption of language in the mouths of those who narcissistically note only themselves and not others, but their graceful and witty dialogue also provides an example of uncorrupted speech. It establishes a normative aural ground against which the audience can hear figured subsequent deformations of that norm by those too affected, too constrained, or too egotistical to use speech with ease or to mutual benefit. Andrew's subsequent self-conscious French, "Dieu vous garde, monsieur" (69), and Viola's subsequent self-conscious compliments, "Most excellent accomplished lady, the heavens rain odors on you" (82–83), are but variations on the theme of corrupted rhetoric, though the one springs from reaching for a courtier's elegance by a man not equipped to do so and the other from Viola's false position as Orsino's go-between. Viola and Olivia fence as they have done before, not even Olivia's curt request that Viola tell her "what thou think'st of me" (135) having the power to elicit an unguarded reply from the page. Viola continues, despite Olivia's misguided declaration of love, to speak in riddles: "I am not what I am" (138). There cannot be truly open speech between them while Viola wears a man's garb, making it impossible for Olivia to "note" her truly and for her to make her denials of love convincing.

Equally at odds verbally are Toby and Andrew in the next scene, in which Toby persuades his "friend" that Olivia really loves him and will be gratified if he challenges Cesario to a duel. This is patent nonsense, and even Andrew seems at first to sense so, "'Slight! will you make an ass o' me?" (III.ii.11). But Andrew hasn't enough perspicacity to note correctly the quality of Toby's friendship and too much self-love to continue long in an unflattering opinion of himself. So he allows himself to be bulldozed by Toby's coercive rhetoric. What the audience hears and sees is not plain dealing and honest interchange between friends, but a mismatch of wits and the exploitation of a foolish gull by the cruel high spirits of a master trickster. Only with the ensuing encounter between Antonio and Sebastian (III.iii) does the audience once more hear language used in an unguarded, unaffected, and nonexploitative manner, the original manner of Viola talking with the sea captain on the coast of

Illyria before the corruptions of disguise intervened to tangle her tongue with riddles, double meanings, and banal phrases.

The third movement of the play thus opens with a short series of aural variations, all figured against the initial ground of Viola's graceful exchanges with Feste and collectively revealing the corruption of her discourse in the mouths of those fettered by disguise, motivated by malice, or blinded by self-love, and its redemption by those who note themselves and others truly. But these three short scenes are simply the prologue to the real heart of the third movement, the frenzied scene of 375 lines that next erupts. I use the word *erupts* advisedly, because a certain tension—due to the repeated blockage of speech and action—has been building throughout the play that demands release.

On one level, of course, the story line has jockeyed a number of the characters into sterile or seemingly dead-end positions. Orsino is mooning endlessly in his palace; Malvolio is wrapped in his fantasies of being Count Malvolio; Viola is locked into man's apparel; Andrew is endlessly spending his fortune and his time in the vain pursuit of Olivia; and that lady is pining for Viola/Cesario. Clearly something has to happen to expose these false and unnatural postures and to kick these characters out of their dream world and release them into reality and self-knowledge. At the same time, the theater audience is ready for an emotional release. The play has been orchestrated up to this point to create a stop-and-go rhythm of stasis and partial release. Tension in the play's progressive form has largely been maintained by the aural and kinetic contrasts between adjoining scenes, but these same contrasts repeatedly suspend the movement toward climax and resolution. We are as becalmed as the characters. With III.iv a genuine sense of climax begins to build as action increasingly takes precedence over talk and as character after character begins to reap the fruit of his or her unnatural or affected posture. As each exposes his folly in its most extreme form, the audience is set free to laugh at a world gone utterly mad, until the laughter becomes strained by our growing awareness that things are spinning out of control.

The arrival of Malvolio, yellow-stockinged and cross-gartered, sets the tone for much of the rest of the play's third movement and shows how visual malapropisms—i.e., the creation of appearances that miss their intended effect—are increasingly used to create laughter and focus attention on inappropriate behavior. Any actor worth his salt can make Malvolio's appearance hilarious. The solemn and sage steward is suddenly trying to be a young blade, straining for an effect he cannot possibly create. Locked in his egocentric world, he has no idea how his behavior seems to those around him. While he prates of greatness, Olivia marvels.

MALVOLIO 'Be not afraid of greatness.' 'Twas well writ.
OLIVIA What mean'st thou by that, Malvolio?
MALVOLIO 'Some are born great.'
OLIVIA Ha?
MALVOLIO 'Some achieve greatness.'
OLIVIA What say'st thou?
MALVOLIO 'And some have greatness thrust upon them.'
OLIVIA Heaven restore thee!
MALVOLIO 'Remember who commended thy yellow stockings.'
OLIVIA Thy yellow stockings?
MALVOLIO 'And wished to see thee cross-gartered.'
OLIVIA Cross-gartered?
MALVOLIO 'Go to, thou art made, if thou desir'st to be so.'
OLIVIA Am I made?
MALVOLIO 'If not, let me see thee a servant still.'
OLIVIA Why, this is very midsummer madness.
(III.iv.35–51)

A striking feature of the aural orchestration of this play is how often face-to-face encounters turn into contrapuntal sequences of noncommunication. Here, of course, Malvolio utterly ignores what Olivia is saying; he hears only himself, the voice of his delusions. She has her mind on her love affair, not on her steward's plight, and packs him off to be cared for by her servants and kinsman. The sequence becomes a way of registering, on the ears of the theater audience, the utter breakdown of communication in Illyria. But Shakespeare is also now quickening the pace of the action, and Malvolio no sooner struts out of sight than Andrew enters with his bizarre "challenge" for Cesario, and another joke unfolds.

In the subsequent action, Shakespeare creates a strong and complicated crescendo effect by presenting in rapid succession a series of stage actions notable for their escalating visual humor and for their increasingly strong overtones of violence. After Malvolio has modeled his lover's attire and Andrew has had his challenge read by Toby, the scene's rising action receives a momentary check as Olivia and Viola have a brief duologue of sixteen lines in which Olivia gives Viola her picture. But the momentum of the scene again surges forward, as Toby and Fabian hustle back on stage to maneuver Viola and Andrew into a duel.

Once again, visual humor is intense. At no point is the inappropriateness of Viola's male dress more comically and concretely brought home than when she is set the task of wielding a sword. Neither is the flaxen-haired Andrew much more valiant. His foolish swaggering attempts to be a good fellow all end in his craven plea that if he can avoid a duel he will give his opponent his horse. "Disguise, I see thou art a wickedness / Wherein the pregnant enemy does much" (II.ii.26–27) might well be the motto for this as for surrounding scenes. On one side of the stage we see Toby pushing Andrew toward combat; on the other side Fabian doing the same for Viola.[18] The sight is hilarious, but also a little disconcerting. Swords are dangerous, even in comedy; and while Viola and Andrew do not seem much inclined to use them, it is hard to know where Toby's love of good sport will lead. He is not very considerate of other people's pates. Moreover, when Antonio enters and attempts to rescue Viola, we are confronted with a man who *will* use his sword and who is himself at danger in Illyria. He promptly finds himself seized by Orsino's officers and forced to reproach Viola with ingratitude for her failure to recognize him.

This interlude does not *much* distress the audience, for we now see how the plot must unravel, but it does check our laughter before the next farcical event, Sebastian's meeting with Feste, Andrew, and Toby, unfolds. The mistaking of identity is now proliferating wildly. In this new situation, both the clever Feste and the sly Toby lose their omniscience. Neither can note truly the person before him, and the pranksters nearly get roundly thrashed before Olivia's fortuitous entry calms the escalating violence. We have seen, in succession, Malvolio duped by a plot into behaving like an ass before Olivia; Olivia deceived by Viola's disguise into offering her picture as a love gift; Viola and Andrew manipulated by lies and their own false advertising of self into a duel neither wants; Antonio deceived by Viola's clothes into believing she is his friend; and Toby and company deceived by Sebastian's clothes into believing he is the duke's cowardly messenger. The consequences of these mistakes become increasingly dangerous. No one seems to know anything for certain; all confident assumptions prove illusions—a thought that cannot but bring pressure to bear upon the audience's own comfortable feelings of omniscience. When will we too be duped? What are the constraints upon our vision and power?

But even at this point, when the madness on the stage would seem to have been played out fully and when our appetite for action has been well satisfied, we find out that this frenzied movement of the play has not reached its conclusion. One more fillip remains, one more change to be rung on the theme of madness and disguise, and that is provided by the revelation of the imprisoned Malvolio and the sight of Feste capering about as Sir Topas. The steward, who never really would listen to anybody, now is desperate to have someone listen to him. He truly is in the dark hole created by his own ignorance and pomposity; and Feste, now as the fool, now as Sir Topas, gives him a dose of his own medicine: lets him see how it is to be snubbed and disregarded by those who for the moment have power. But this scene is delicately handled. It is both the culmination of the farcical madness that has overtaken the stage for several scenes and the clearest signal of its impending collapse.

Disguise has, by this point in the play, become a major visual motif; and events in the drama's third movement have increasingly linked disguise with violence and confusion. It is unsettling to the audience, then, when Feste gratuitously assumes the disguise of a curate—as Maria notes, Malvolio can't *see* Feste, so his robes are for our benefit, not the steward's. Attired thus, Feste assumes several voices in succession and breaks out in manic song as he harasses the hapless steward. This is funny, but it is also the capstone of the protean shape-changing and assumption of false roles that have already caused so much trouble in Illyria. One need not sentimentalize Malvolio's plight—he richly deserves a comeuppance—to feel that events are rolling out of control. Feste's final song, equating himself with Vice of the morality plays and Malvolio with the devil, suggests the extent to which the world has been turned on its head and order threatened.[19] It is thus with relief that the audience hears

Feste promise to bring Malvolio a pen and paper, and sees in the next scene Sebastian enter by himself and decide on an action that seems both natural and right. He is going to wed Olivia. In this topsy-turvy world, at least one Jack and Jill are going to make it to the altar.

By now the audience is quite ready for less madness. Action we have had in abundance and also emotional release through laughter. But the mistakes and the misperceptions have almost ceased to be funny. We are reeling from the pace of events and sensitive—because of the repeated undermining of each character's fix on reality and because wished-for events have snowballed almost beyond the point at which we can take pleasure in them—to our dependence upon the dramatist for the security of our perceptions and the control of our pleasure and pain.

What remains is the effecting of theatrical closure and the establishment of theatrical and moral equilibrium after the severe disturbance of both. The fourth movement of the play does just that. It brings illumination to the characters through release from disguises of every stripe, and it brings the theater event to a poised, if tenuous conclusion, as linguistic and kinetic energy find expression in a scene that is both energetic and highly patterned. In fact, V.i is probably the most schematically orchestrated scene of the entire play. And it must be. A great deal happens in it, but the happenings do not spin out of control. Watching the scene, we feel, what we so rarely feel in life, the perfect marriage of energy and restraint. The final movement of the play is four hundred lines long and falls into two distinct parts with the turn marked very precisely by Sebastian's final entry. Up to that point what is remarkable is the way in which Shakespeare orchestrates aural and visual events to create for a final time the sensation of impasse and frustration that results from mistakes of identity and the assumption of unnatural poses. One by one characters who have otherwise not shared a stage together assemble in one place, but their coming together at first does not result in the harmony one would expect.

The scene begins promisingly, however. The first striking event is the sight of Orsino walking the streets of Illyria and not holed up in his palace. We have come to expect that we will see him isolated from the world, listening to lugubrious music, and lamenting his unrequited love. It is a visual surprise, therefore, to observe him in the open air bantering with Feste and moving toward Olivia's.[20] This visual cue signals that his claustrophobic self-imprisonment may be over. There is, furthermore, relief in seeing Feste once more in his characteristic role of fool, begging for money, and no longer disguised as a curate.

But as more characters enter — the visual crescendo underscoring a rising sense of anticipation — language once more becomes hopelessly entangled. Characters have so long pretended to be what they are not that, even when they genuinely try to communicate, they still speak at cross purposes. Each successive entrance merely compounds the confusion of identities, and questions fly thick and fast with few satisfying answers given. Antonio is clearly revealed as Orsino's old enemy, but he *seems* to be lying about his rescue of Viola. Olivia makes clear her love for Cesario, but either she or Viola *seems* to be lying about the wedding that is supposed to have occurred. Toby and Andrew clearly have taken a drubbing in a duel, but either they or Viola *seems* to be lying about who gave them that drubbing.

Only when Sebastian enters can misunderstandings be resolved. His opening lines make plain that it was he who beat Toby and wed Olivia. "I am sorry, madam, I have hurt your kinsman" (V.i.201). A moment later he also redeems Antonio from the imputation of a lie by acknowledging him as his rescuer. Paradoxically, it is a visual image of doubleness, two identically dressed twins, that "natural perspective" of which Orsino speaks, that allows simple and single truth to emerge. Now there are more questions; but, like the satisfying ritualistic questions of the catechism, they have answers:

SEBASTIAN   Of charity, what kin are you to me?
              What countryman? What name? What parentage?
VIOLA   Of Messaline; Sebastian was my father;
              Such a Sebastian was my brother too.

                                       (222–25)

Students with a penchant for realism often object that it takes the twins an unconscionably long time to recognize one another. But, of course, realism is not the point. The point is that the tick-tock of question and answer, detail countered with confirming detail, is part of a ritual of recognition, a way of redeeming the self and language from the confusion into which both have fallen. And it is a theatrically necessary ritual, fulfilling a desire for direct, open, and reciprocated speech that has been frustrated for five acts. After the unanswered questions of the first half of the scene, the answered questions of Sebastian and Viola give special pleasure to characters and audience alike. Through them, characters find release from the prison of disguise and affectation in which they long have been locked. Orsino can now note Viola and her selfless service truly; Olivia, her "extracting frenzy" (273) past, can remember her servant Malvolio and note his letter truly. Only he, vowing revenge on the "lighter people" (329), cannot move from his dark and claustrophobic pride to accept what he is and the lessons the mad time of confusion has brought to light.

As the play ends, nearly all the characters stand before us released from their egocentricity and disguises. They possess knowledge only we, the audience, had previously possessed; and with that knowledge comes the humbling realization that many prior assumptions were wrong.[21] Orsino was wrong about his love for Olivia; Andrew was mistaken about Toby's friendship; Olivia was misled in her belief that Cesario was a man; and Antonio was mistaken about Sebastian's ingratitude. Now, in each instance, the truth stands revealed.

Of course, not everything in the Illyrian world is perfect; and the harmony achieved by play's end is notably tenuous. Malvolio, for example, is still angry; Antonio is never officially pardoned; Andrew does not find a love that is requited; and Orsino is insistent that Viola return to her maiden weeds before he embraces her and then promises she will be his "mistress and his fancy's queen" (377), a phrase that sounds rather too much like his earlier idealization of Olivia.[22] Nonetheless, though these details qualify the impression of harmony that marks the play's final moments, they cannot erase it. Most poses have been banished, and characters are given the opportunity to grow beyond their prior selves.

But the audience's experience is not over yet. It, too, must be released from the role of spectator and from the manipulations of the dramatist. For the spectator this release is effected by Feste's song. As the play began in music, so it ends in music. But the closing song is neither a mournful love lyric nor a high-spirited catch; it is simply a song sung by an aging clown about the frustrations and disappointments of living. This song is not self-pitying, but it *is* melancholy and resigned. It ushers the audience from the heightened world of Illyria, where many characters now seem poised to embrace a golden peace, back to a world in which "the rain it raineth every day," the world of our daily lives.

During the course of the play, we have become aware of our dependence on the dramatist; but his control has proved to be, after all, a benign control, an echo, perhaps of that providential power which wafted Sebastian to Illyria. The playwright has manipulated us and made us aware of that manipulation, but he has neither misled us (as he was later to do in *The Winter's Tale,* where for three acts we believe Hermione is dead when in truth she lives) nor cheated us of the happy ending we desire, though he has hedged that ending with qualifications that suggest how easily our desires could have been frustrated. More strikingly, by the way Shakespeare finally releases the audience from the play, he reminds us that, in the world beyond the theater, the forces which govern our experience are often less benign than the dramatist of *Twelfth Night* has been. Outside the theater, we are the pawns of time and chance, not the creatures of a generous playwright. And time and chance, while they sometimes bring ships safely to port, also bring pain, alienation, and frustration of desire. Feste's song, with its haunting refrain about the wind and the rain, is a chastening reminder of this truth and an important part of our experience of *Twelfth Night.*

The prior analysis has moved—progressively and, of course, too swiftly—through *Twelfth Night* to suggest in broad outlines how Shakespeare orchestrates the theatrical event to make the themes and the ideas of the play part of the audience's theatrical experience. My assumption here and throughout this book has been that the theatrical experience is both a cerebral and a sensory one, and that it is impossible to separate the two. My *emphasis* has been, however, on what is too often neglected in dramatic criticism: the orchestration of the sensory components of the implied performance as a means of guiding audience perceptions and shaping responses as the dramatic event unfolds in time.

In *Twelfth Night* Shakespeare constantly uses aural and visual cues to foreground particular events and to call attention to key motifs: disguise, corrupted language, affectation. And, as I have suggested, even the kinetic aspects of our experience of the play—our involvement in its rhythms of restraint and release—become integral to our understanding of what the play is about and to an understanding, finally, of its moral vision. We know the enervating consequences of false poses and self-indulgent egotism because we have felt their effects in the blocked actions, the contorted speeches, and the contrapuntal dialogues of noncommunication that repeatedly punctuate the play and make its theatrical course turn aside and lose the name of action.

The play is crafted to tamper with the satisfaction of some very basic theatrical appetites—a desire for movement, happening, clear speeches eventuating in insight and action. By stifling action and thwarting purposeful speech, the play creates an impatience based initially on theatrical frustration and then transmuted into moral anger; into impatience with the disguises, pomposity, and self-centeredness that create the stasis and sense of entrapment in the world of the play and that we feel in the theater as pent-up kinetic energy begging for release. As in *Hamlet*, another play of thwarted theatrical energies, impatience for a time may make us root for the brutal simplicities of a Toby (benign cousin of Claudius), fertile engineer of plots and actions of all sorts, before we come to recognize in the play's climactic third movement the insufficiencies of pure action undertaken without regard for its effects and human consequences. Moreover, the tension in the Illyrian world between human will as the shaper of human destiny and the power of time and chance resonates with the audience's own awareness of the dramatist's hand in establishing the parameters of its own perception and responses. In this most sophisticated of comedies, men are free and not free; the same thing may be said of the theatergoer.

In short, Shakespeare finds in *Twelfth Night*, as in all his plays, a very specific theatrical vocabulary by which the enacted script communicates with its audience. This is a vocabulary, not just of words, but also of gestures, sounds, images, and movements that are woven together to create theatrical events of great complexity. In orchestrating these sensory elements of the implied performance, Shakespeare always keeps one eye on the audience. The full dramatic meaning of his works is realized only in our responses to them. In this book I have examined some of the ways in which this interaction between play and audience is shaped: how Shakespeare's techniques of orchestration form a repertoire of performance strategies aimed at the full participation of the theatergoer in the dramatic event and his actualization of its meaning. That Shakespeare's art of orchestration is purposeful and complex I hope I have shown; that it is effective is proven daily in the theaters of the world.

NOTES

1. For a lively discussion of the importance of the play's double title and of the comic conventions informing the work, see Maurice Charney, "Comic Premises of *Twelfth Night*," *New York Literary Forum* 1 (1978): 151–65.

2. Many critics have noted the darker aspects of *Twelfth Night*. F. B. Tromly, in *"Twelfth Night*: Folly's Talents and the Ethics of Shakespearean Comedy," *Mosaic* 7, no. 3 (1974): 53–68, usefully summarizes the anti-festive overtones of the work (esp. 55–58). Ralph Berry, in surveying the last hundred years of the play's stage history, observes that late nineteenth- and early twentieth-century productions stressed the joyful, farcical elements of the play and cut whatever was at odds with a festive interpretation. Beginning with John Barton's 1969 RSC production, however, we have recently been given increasingly dark and bleak stagings of this work that downplay its celebratory dimensions. For Berry's interesting examination of how opposing aspects of the play have been emphasized in particular productions, see "The Season of *Twelfth Night*," *New York Literary Forum* 1 (1978): 139–49.

3. Barber, *Shakespeare's Festive Comedy*, 242.

4. For complementary and sophisticated analyses of the process by which mature sexual identity is attained by various characters in this play, I have found useful Helene Moglen, "Disguise and Development: The Self and Society in *Twelfth Night*," *Literature and Psychology* 23 (1973): 13–20; and J. Dennis Huston, " 'When I Came to Man's Estate': *Twelfth Night* and Problems of Identity," *Modern Language Quarterly* 33 (1972): 274–88.

5. For a provocative discussion of the function of androgyny in Shakespearean comedy, see Joel Fineman, "Fratricide and Cuckoldry: Shakespeare's Doubles," in *Representing Shakespeare: New Psychoanalytic Essays*, ed. Murray M. Schwartz and Coppélia Kahn (Baltimore: Johns Hopkins University Press, 1980), 70–109.

6. Many critics have explored the theme of narcissism in *Twelfth Night*, including, most recently, D. J. Palmer in *"Twelfth Night* and the Myth of Echo and Narcissus," *Shakespeare Survey* 32 (1979): 73–78. See also Anthony Brian Taylor, "Shakespeare and Golding: Viola's Interview with Olivia and Echo and Narcissus," *English Language Notes* 15 (1977): 103–6. Ralph Berry, in "The Season of *Twelfth Night,"* 145, describes an RSC production, directed by Peter Gill in 1974, in which the set included a golden Narcissus hanging over the stage.

7. As my discussion of the play will make increasingly clear, I regard Antonio as a positive figure of selfless friendship, who affords an important contrast to the selfishness of so many characters, especially Toby. This is a view held by John Russell Brown, in *Shakespeare and His Comedies,* 2d ed. (London: Methuen, 1962), 166–67; and by F. B. Tromly, in *"Twelfth Night,"* 65. A quite different perspective on Antonio is taken by Michael Taylor, in *"Twelfth Night* or *What You Will,"* *Critical Quarterly* 16 (1974): 71–80. Taylor sees Antonio as stubbornly willful and morbid in his pursuit of Sebastian, and a figure who parallels the lovesick Orsino in his sterile pursuit of Olivia. Since Orsino risks nothing for Olivia while Antonio risks all for Sebastian, and since Orsino eventually gives over his pursuit of Olivia because it is based on an illusion while Antonio remains faithful to his friend until the end, I question the force of Taylor's parallel. Moreover, not just Antonio's actions, but also his language, distinguish him from Orsino and others of the egocentric characters; and of that contrast I will speak more in the following pages.

8. For an excellent discussion of the thematic and philosophical significance of music in this play and its relationship to Renaissance thought about music, see John Hollander, "Music Mundana and *Twelfth Night,"* in *Sound and Poetry,* ed. Northrop Frye (New York: Columbia University Press, 1957), 55–82. See also P. T. Dircks, "Shakespeare's Use of the Catch as Dramatic Metaphor," *Shakespeare Quarterly* 24 (1973): 88–90.

9. Mark Rose also discusses the opening three scenes of *Twelfth Night* as a single unit in which the three segments comment upon one another, though his concern is primarily with thematic links, mine with sensory contrasts. See Rose *Shakespearean Design,* 75–76.

10. Ibid., 76. Kenneth Muir, *Shakespeare's Comic Sequence* (New York: Barnes & Noble, 1979), 91–92, also reports seeing a production in which a similar reversal of the first two scenes occurred, again with poor results.

11. Nancy Hayles, in a very illuminating essay, "Sexual Disguise in *As You Like It* and *Twelfth Night,"* *Shakespeare Survey* 32 (1979): 65–72, contrasts the function of disguise in these two comedies. In *As You Like*

It, its function is to give the heroine control of her situation, and in *Twelfth Night* its function is to withhold control from her (68).

12. Ralph Berry, in *Shakespeare's Comedies: Explorations in Form* (Princeton: Princeton University Press, 1972), 196–212, gives extensive attention to the way formal, written messages go astray or fail as instruments of communication in *Twelfth Night.* I think it is also important to note how often face-to-face communication breaks down in this play because of disguise or self-absorption.

13. J. Dennis Huston, in " 'When I Came to Man's Estate'," 287–88, comments upon entrapment as a key psychological motif of the play. Characters are locked in roles that inhibit them, even Feste, who *must* play the clown to live. I am exploring the way this psychological theme finds theatrical expression in a specific mode of orchestrating the play.

14. Michael Goldman, in *Shakespeare and the Energies of Drama,* is one critic especially sensitive to the way in which Shakespeare's dramas play with and put to good use the spectator's theatrical appetites and his desires for satisfying sensory, as well as thematic, resolutions to the theatrical experience. Similarly, Nigel Alexander, in *Poison, Play, and Duel,* offers a brilliant examination of the way in which, in that play, the thwarting of action becomes a test of the audience's theatrical patience and, ultimately, its morality. Generations of critics have castigated Hamlet for not acting, for being indecisive. But, Alexander asks, do we really want Hamlet simply to act, or do we want him to act in a way that is humanly decent and distinguishable from the way in which Claudius, Pyrrhus, Laertes, and Fortinbras act? I believe some of the same questions about action are raised in *Twelfth Night* and raised through the audience's immediate theatrical experience.

15. John Hollander, "*Twelfth Night* and the Morality of Indulgence," *Sewanee Review* 68 (1959): 220–38; reprinted in *Twentieth Century Interpretations of "Twelfth Night,"* ed. Walter N. King (Englewood Cliffs: Prentice-Hall, 1968), 75–89, esp. 86.

16. Bertrand Evans, *Shakespeare's Comedies* (1960; reprint, New York: Oxford University Press, 1967), 118–43.

17. For a discussion of language's corruption in *Twelfth Night* and of Feste as a critic and clever manipulator of language, see Charney, "Comic Premises of *Twelfth Night,*" esp. 160–64.

18. J. L. Styan, in *Shakespeare's Stagecraft,* 125–26, describes beautifully the way Shakespeare uses two stage groups to comic effect in this scene.

19. R. Chris Hassel, Jr., in *Faith and Folly in Shakespeare's Romantic Comedies* (Athens: University of Georgia Press, 1980), sees Feste's curate garb as an appropriate symbol of his healing, Pauline function in the play.

Hassel argues that, as Feste elsewhere brings humility and wisdom to egotistical characters, here he tries to do the same for Malvolio (169–75). I find much more ambiguity in this disguise than does Hassel, because disguise has been so consistently associated with the confusion and evil in Illyria.

20. F. B. Tromly, *"Twelfth Night,"* 64, views Orsino's journey into the street as a gesture that reveals his first real openness to life.

21. Hassel *(Faith and Folly in Shakespeare's Romantic Comedies,* 149–75), discusses humility as the prime end of the characters' moral education in *Twelfth Night.*

22. Huston, " 'When I Came to Man's Estate'," 288.

Index

Actors Company, The, 170n26
Adelman, Janet, 49n15
Alchemist, The, 59–60
Aldwych Theater, 171n31
Alexander, Nigel, 91, 100n13, 133nn9,12, 205n14
Antony and Cleopatra: aural contrasts in, 33–36, 36–39, 88–89; music in, 36–37; silence in, 88–89
Arnheim, Rudolph, 82, 99n6
asides: types of, 53; in *Hamlet*, 54; in *Cymbeline*, 54–55; in *King Lear*, 54, 120, 127
As You Like It: epilogue in, 6–7, visual contrasts in, 106; terminal heightening in, 152–53
audience, object of dramatist's control, 6–9
— distanced from action: in *Midsummer Night's Dream*, 7–8; in *Macbeth*, 10; in *Richard II*, 24–25; in *Othello*, 30–31
— aware of its status as audience: in *Richard III*, 57–59; in *Troilus and Cressida*, 116–17; in *Twelfth Night*, 190–92, 197, 198, 201, 202
audience expectations, manipulated, 40; in *King Lear*, 45–46, 158–59; in *Twelfth Night*, 59–62; in *Hamlet*, 112–14
— denied, 82–85
Auerbach, Erich, 23, 47n1
aural contrasts: in *Hamlet*, 14–18; in *Richard II*, 28–29; in *Antony and*

Cleopatra, 33–36, 36–39, 88–89; in *Twelfth Night*, 60–61, 184–85, 187; in *King Lear*, 121–24, 160–63, 164; in *Julius Caesar*, 144–45, 165

Baldwin, T. W., 137, 168n2
Barber, C. L., 23, 47n2, 133n13, 138, 169n5, 175, 203n3
Barton, John, 302n2
Beckerman, Bernard, 19n5, 53, 75n3, 76n7, 98n2, 123, 134n21, 170–71n28
Berry, Francis, 49n16
Berry, Ralph, 203n2, 204n6, 205n12
Booth, Stephen, 21n15, 170n21
Bradley, A. C., 137–38, 169n4, 171n32
bridges, aural: defined, 39–40; in *Romeo and Juliet*, 40–42; in *King Lear*, 42–46
Brooke, Nicholas, 76n8
Brooklyn Academy of Music, 170n26
Brown, Calvin, 52, 75n2
Brown, John Russell, 19n5, 20n13, 204n7
Burckhardt, Sigurd, 171n30

cacophony: in *King Lear*, 25, 126–28, 161–63; in *Othello*, 31–33, 49n14
change of key: 33, 164; in *Antony and Cleopatra*, 33–39; in *Hamlet*, 149–50; in *Twelfth Night*, 180–83
character: used rhetorically, 46–47; used to mirror another's psychic

207

A Note on the Author

JEAN E. HOWARD holds a bachelor's degree from Brown University (1970), a master's from the University of London (1972), and a doctorate from Yale University (1975). Her published articles in the scholarly journals deal mainly with the plays of Shakespeare, and she has presented papers before both national and international conferences of Shakespeare scholars. She is an associate professor of English at Syracuse University.